THE DUSTY
BOOKCASE

THE
DUSTY
BOOKCASE

A Journey Through Canada's Forgotten, Neglected and Suppressed Writing

BRIAN BUSBY

BIBLIOASIS

FIRST EDITION

Library and Archives Canada Cataloguing in Publication

Busby, Brian John, author
    The dusty bookcase : a journey through Canada's forgotten, neglected, and suppressed writing / Brian Busby.

Issued also in electronic format.
ISBN 978-1-77196-168-4 (softcover).--ISBN 978-1-77196-169-1 (ebook)

    1. Canadian literature--Miscellanea. 2. Literary curiosa. 3. Canadian literature--History and criticism. 4. Books and reading--Canada--History. 5. Canadian literature--Censorship. 6. Censorship--Canada--History. I. Title.

PS8219.B87 2017   C810.9   C2016-907970-8
                                         C2016-907971-6

Edited by Emily Donaldson
Copy-edited by Allana Amlin
Typeset by Chris Andrechek
Illustrated and designed by Seth

Published with the generous assistance of the Canada Council for the Arts, which last year invested $153 million to bring the arts to Canadians throughout the country, and the financial support of the Government of Canada. Biblioasis also acknowledges the support of the Ontario Arts Council (OAC), an agency of the Government of Ontario, which last year funded 1,709 individual artists and 1,078 organizations in 204 communities across Ontario, for a total of $52.1 million, and the contribution of the Government of Ontario through the Ontario Book Publishing Tax Credit and the Ontario Media Development Corporation.

PRINTED AND BOUND IN CANADA

For Stanley Whyte and Chris Kelly
As you know...

Contents

Introduction

We didn't read Canadian literature in Allancroft Elementary School. The books assigned at Beaconsfield High School were by John Steinbeck, Jack Schaefer, James Vance Marshall, William Golding, John Wyndham, Charles Dickens, George Orwell, Georges Simenon, and Fyodor Dostoyevsky. One class—not mine—got to read Edgar Rice Burroughs' *Tarzan of the Apes*.

My introduction to the country's literature came through scanning the racks at the local Kane's Super Drug Mart. They weren't at all difficult to spot. William C. Heine's *The Last Canadian* was obvious. The cover of Bruce Powe's *Killing Ground* promised a novel about "The Canadian Civil War." Others had maple leaves somewhere on their covers. This is how I came to read Richard Rohmer, whose *Ultimatum, Exxoneration, Exodus/UK*, and *Separation* were bought with money earned delivering our local newspaper. Somehow I discovered that Arthur Hailey was kind of a Canadian. I expect I'm one of a small number of people to have tackled all 440 pages of *Airport* as a pre-teen. Over time, I came to recognize that many of the books I was buying bore the Pocket, PaperJacks, and Seal logos. Using them as my guides, I added *Hit and Run* by Tom Alderman, Joy Carroll's *Satan's Bell*, and something called *Some Canadian Ghosts* to my collection.

In tenth grade, my Canadian book buying came to an abrupt stop. I'd like to say girls were the reason, but in truth it had more to do with the realization that nothing I read was much good. This confirmed the unspoken lesson learned in school: when it came to writing, Canadians weren't worthy of attention. The assigned reading for that year's English class included *Shane, The Pearl, Walkabout, The Chrysalids* and, predictably, *Lord of the Flies*. Of these, my favourite was *The Chrysalids*, in part because it takes place in post-apocalyptic Labrador, as opposed to, say, nineteenth-century Wyoming.

Make of that what you will.

Whatever remaining interest I had in my country's literature was kept alive through an American magazine, *National Lampoon*, which had just begun publishing something called the *Bombardier Guide to Canadian Authors*.

Bombardier Guide to Canadian Authors
"If these sketches should prove the means of deterring one family from sinking its property and shipwrecking all its hopes by going to reside in the backwoods of Canada, I shall consider myself amply repaid for revealing the secrets of the prison house, and feel that I have not toiled and suffered in the wilderness in vain."
—Susanna Moodie (1803-1885)

Written by Sean Kelly, Ted Mann, and Brian Shein, purportedly with financial assistance from Bombardier, its format was simple: brief entries followed by a rating on a scale of one to five skidoos.

The first to be so honoured was Margaret Atwood (one skidoo). This brief excerpt provides a fair example of the guide's style:

She is best known for advancing the theory that America and Canada are simply states of mind, the former comparable to that of a schnapps-crazed Wehrmacht foot soldier and the latter to that of an autistic child left behind in a deserted Muskoka summer cottage playing with Molson's Ale cans, spent shell casings, and dead birds hung from the light fixture, who will one day become aware of its situation, go to college, and write novels. She is better known, among Margaret-watchers, for taking gross offense at the suggestion (in a crudely dittoed literary periodical) that she may have sparked an erection in a considerably more talented Canadian author who shall here remain nameless (see Glassco, John).

That last sentence would've been my first encounter with Glassco's name. The incident described is one that demanded particular care when writing *A Gentleman of Pleasure*, my biography of the man. Rosalie Abella, the lawyer Ms Atwood hired to go after the "crudely dittoed literary periodical," now sits on the Supreme Court.

And here's Glassco again in the entry for "Callahan [sic] , Morely [sic]" (two skidoos):

Callahan, Morely *(1903–   )* Callahan's reputation rests largely upon his memoir of Paris in the twenties, *That Summer in Paris*, which can almost be put on par with a considerably more talented Canadian author's memories of the same period (see Glassco, John). The other foundation of Callahan's repute is a trio of endorsements from Edmund Wilson, Ernest Hemingway, and James Joyce. As for Wilson, who could trust a man known to Unity Mitford as "Bunny"? Hemingway thought Knut Hamsun was a genius, and with all respect to Joyce, who could take one Irishman's word about another?

The reference source appeared sporadically through 1978, then returned five years later. I was then at university, palling around with two of Sean Kelly's kids. It was a coincidence worthy of Isabel Ecclestone Mackay (not covered in the guide). Much more predictable was the presence of Frederick Philip Grove on my reading lists. The magazine's April 1983 issue, which marked its return, brought this well-timed entry:

Grove, Frederick Philip *(1879–1948)* As a young European aesthete, Grove (or Greve, to use his original German name) formulated an ingeniously decadent plan: to forsake stimulating companionship, rich culture, and the avant-garde of twentieth-century art in order to bury himself in a tedious and meaningless existence as a rural schoolteacher on the Canadian prairies, an existence he was to recount in a series of equally tedious books. His career as a novelist and essayist can thus be seen as a perversely protracted *jeu d'esprite* [sic], carried out with an unfortunate combination of Teutonic wit and Canadian flair for the dramatic. But not even Grove's dullness was equal to that of his public: when a scene in *Settlers in* [sic] *the*

Marsh (published in 1925, three years after *Ulysses*) vaguely hinted at nocturnal marital activities, denunciations of the novel as pornographic caused a mass of Canadian readers to virtuously refuse to buy, let alone read it, often smuggling themselves out of the country wearing false jackets in order not to be considered found-ins.

Grove's lone skidoo may have been an act of generosity. Sensitive Canadians all, Kelly, Mann, and Shein left no writer empty-handed. Farley Mowat rated two snowshoes; Mazo de la Roche received two bags of cash. There was also some playing around. Notably, George Jonas and Barbara Amiel, then "Canada's most formidable literary spouse-and-spouse team and toast of Toronto's propeller set" were awarded one skidoo humping another.

Every bit as relevant as *The Oxford Companion to Canadian Literature*, and at times just as funny, I've held onto the issues in which the *Bombardier Guide* features.

University was a bit of a wash. I entered as a directionless Canadian Studies student well versed in Rohmer, Heine, Hailey, Powe, Alderman, and Carroll. As I remember it, *Some Canadian Ghosts* was the only work of Canadian non-fiction I'd ever read.

I lie. I'd also made my way through the Amiel/Jonas collaboration *By Person's Unknown: The Strange Death of Christine Demeter*. It was a Seal paperback, you see.

A course titled "Introduction to Canadian Literature" introduced me to the New Canadian Library and the concept of a canon. The class took place on Wednesday evenings, which fit well with my job stocking seven-inch singles at Sam the Record Man. We studied four novels: James De Mille's *A Strange Manuscript Found in a Copper Cylinder* (1888), Thomas H. Raddall's *The Nymph and the Lamp* (1950), Hugh MacLennan's *The Watch that Ends the Night* (1958), and Brian Moore's *The Luck of Ginger Coffey* (1960). Each was better than the last, suggesting progression.

The Luck of Ginger Coffey was so good that much of the summer that followed—the summer of Prince's "When Doves Cry"—was spent reading Moore's other novels.

The following September, I began a Canadian literature course of which I remember nothing other than the fact that we students were required to keep a record of our "personal baggage"—biases that skewed our reading of the texts. Again, this was a course taught at a university… a university attended by adults who could vote and drink and drive. At this university—this Canadian university—one could graduate with a B.A. in English without taking so much as one course in the country's literature.

Canadian literature came to dominate my reading. I took other CanLit courses—studying Margaret Atwood, Morley Callaghan, Frederick Philip Grove, Margaret Laurence, and L.M. Montgomery, among others—but these only led me to question the canon. My extra-curricular reading was unguided, yet so much of what I read was superior. I learned there were other Brian Moore novels—early work that he'd kept hidden—and so sought them out. A course on American expatriate writers of the twenties led me to read Glassco. The discovery that he'd written a banned book of faux-Victorian erotica sent me on the hunt for that, too. I began scouring outdoor dollar bins—a habit that continues to this day—looking for the out-of-print and obscure.

The books covered in these pages in no way represent the best of the forgotten, ignored, and supressed in our literature.

We should read the forgotten because previous generations knew them well. My father read the works of Ralph Connor, as did his. Reading Connor myself has brought me a better understanding of the times these men experienced.

We should be curious about the ignored because recognition is so often a crapshoot; too much depends on publisher, press, and good fortune.

We should read the suppressed for the very reason that there are those who would deny us the right.

Looking over these reviews, I see my failings exposed:

I've spent perhaps too much time reading post-war pulp, in part because I'd hoped to find undiscovered novels by Mordecai Richler or Norman Levine, but also because they cover a reality that's all too absent in the polite Canadian hardcover fiction of their day.

I've focused too long on Basil King and Arthur Stringer in the hope of finding novels that were as intriguing as their very unusual lives; it's no coincidence that the titles I've chosen to review here are about as close as either man got to writing an autobiography.

Books by women are very much in the minority, and yet they rank amongst the most enjoyable. The same can be said about novels from French Canada. I honestly didn't recognize this until writing this book. I feel no shame at all for the focus on Grant Allen. The late Victorian's novels are amongst the most quirky I've ever read. And I do like quirk.

Consider this personal baggage.

This book is not meant as a criticism of CanLit profs three decades past, nor those who once taught at Beaconsfield High School or Allancroft Elementary School. It is a partial log of one reader's unguided journey. More than this, it is a plea to look beyond the canon, the latest award winners, and the grotesque gong show that is Canada Reads. Our literature is more interesting, more creative, more diverse, and much greater than the industry behind these things would have you believe.

ALLEN

Grant Allen's Wicked Novel

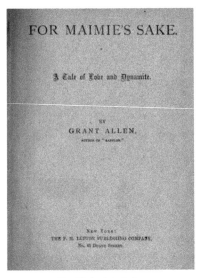

FOR MAIMIE'S SAKE.

A Tale of Love and Dynamite.

BY
GRANT ALLEN,
AUTHOR OF "BABYLON."

New York:
THE F. M. LUPTON PUBLISHING COMPANY,
No. 65 Duane Street.

For Maimie's Sake:
A Tale of Love and Dynamite
Grant Allen
New York: F.M. Lupton, [c. 1889]
232 pages

"For Maimie's Sake" is equally bad as art and as morals. "Maimie" is a young woman who has a penchant for falling dead in love with all the married men she comes across. This is called "innocence" by Mr Allen, but it would be very easy to call it something else. Our opinion of "For Maimie's Sake," briefly, is that it is a mischievous and nasty book, unrelieved either by mental insight or humour.
–*The American,*
February 13, 1886

It's said that Grant Allen forbade friends from speaking of his commercial fiction, with the exception of *For Maimie's Sake,* which he considered superior to the rest. True, the novel was written with an eye on filthy lucre, but it was just one eye. Allen, who knew the market better than anyone, recognized that it was too off-colour for serialization or lending libraries. Writing publisher Andrew Chatto, he described *For Maimie's Sake* as a "wicked novel," one that young women would find both shocking and appealing. I break with conventional criticism here to suggest that it was written tongue in cheek. 'Tis a farce, for goodness sake: *For Maimie's Sake? A Tale of Love and Dynamite?*

Maimie is Maimie Llewellyn, the bewitchingly beautiful, forever flighty product of an English seaside town. Despite her twenty years, the locals see her as an innocent child. That Maimie gives kisses so freely to Oxford tutor Adrian Pym and his visiting students only confirms their belief that she is naive and pure. In short, Maimie knows no better.

An unconventional upbringing is meant to account for her behaviour. Allen, the atheist son of a clergyman, tears a strip off his fellow non-believers through his portrayal of Maimie's father, a half-cracked sea captain who believes in Reason only and worships at the altar of Thomas Paine. In this early scene, the captain is reacting to his daughter's declaration that a visit to London would be "just heavenly."

"Just what?" the Captain cried, in a sharp tone of astonished exclamation.

"Just heavenly!" Maimie repeated, unconscious of her crime.

"There's no such thing," the Captain burst out, reddening in the face. "There's no such place. There's no such land at all on the Admiralty chart. There's no such world; there's no such existence anywhere as heaven. And even if there were, it wouldn't in the least resemble London."

Maimie does make her way to London, but only after her father drowns at sea. Now adrift, so to speak, she ends up living in lovely Regent Park with celebrated painter Jocelyn Capriani and his wife, Hetty. What the young women of two centuries past made of this arrangement I cannot guess, but these worldly, somewhat jaded eyes quickly recognized the Capriani marriage as "open," the term "kisses" used euphemistically. Eventually, Maimie and Jocelyn's smooching becomes a cause of concern for Mrs Capriani. For the first time in her marriage, she fears losing her painter husband to a paramour, and insists that he sever ties.

But who will care for innocent Maimie?

The Caprianis set their sights on Sydney Chevinix, the very same man Adrian Pym—*Remember him? The Oxford tutor?*—had suggested Maimie marry. Adrian himself can't marry Maimie because, as an undergraduate, he wed—*secretly*—a buxom barmaid named Bessie. Rendered "bloated and unwholesome from much drink," she dies before the novel's midpoint.

So, yes, Maimie and Sydney. And why not? What with his wealth, education, and breeding, Sydney is pretty much the most eligible bachelor in the country. There is, however... well, privileged Englishmen do have their eccentricities, don't they?

A former surgeon, since inheriting his uncle's vast estate Sydney has devoted time and fortune to the obsessive pursuit of a silent explosive. To this end, he's hired a Polish nihilist as his assistant. On the very day of their long-sought breakthrough, whilst walking on Primrose Hill, Maimie chances upon Adrian. Passion is rekindled: "'Adrian,' she said, 'dearest Adrian, I have loved a great many men in my time—almost every man I've ever met with: but I've never loved anybody yet as I love you, my darling.'"

Kissing ensues.

Maimie returns home, where Sydney shows off the product of his many years work: a silent pistol. She shoots once at a target, then accidentally on purpose at her husband: "'Sydney!' she cried, looking straight in his face, simple and truthful and direct as ever. 'You will never forgive me. You can't forgive me...'"

Of course he can. As life leaks out of Sydney, and Maimie tells him of her chance meeting with Adrian, he takes pen to paper and composes a suicide note, then turns to his wife:

"There's nothing to forgive, Maimie! It was the impulse of a moment. I know what you are, darling! A child, a dear little simple, innocent child, Maimie. If everyone else would only look at it as I look at it, they'd kiss you, so, and forgive you easily."

For Maimie's sake, for Maimie's sake... the phrase appears more than three dozen times in this 232-page novel. The title is apt. Sydney's faux suicide note is just one example of the lengths to which its characters will go. For Maimie's sake, a servant drives herself to an early grave, a hospital ward is set ablaze, a man kills himself in the Thames, and a nation is denied a discovery that would've secured its world dominance.

Allen was correct in describing his novel as wicked; it is also wickedly funny. Should further evidence be required, I point out that one character dies by exploding cigar.

Victorian Psycho

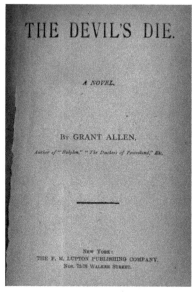

The Devil's Die
Grant Allen
New York: F.M. Lupton, [c. 1893]
271 pages

Mohammad Ali is the hero of this story; its greatest villain—there are several—is his friend Harry Chichele. Men of medicine, both were trained at London's Middlesex Hospital, at which the latter cultivated a keen interest in bacteriology.

As luck would have it, the pair find themselves in the Cornish town of Polperran (read: Polperro) at the very moment a yacht carrying two cholera victims comes into view. Ali and Chichele set out to rescue and minister to the infected, but it becomes quickly apparent that Chichele is not so much interested in saving lives as using them as case studies:

"Now, you couldn't possibly have two nicer or more typical cases than these; because the boy'll die and the man, I expect, will pull through somehow. So, if nothing untoward intervenes to prevent it, I shall have a splendid chance of seeing the course of the disease in both directions—death and recovery."

The fortunate survivor turns to out to be celebrated painter Ivan Royle. The two doctors care for their patient at the local manse, each—and here I include Royle—falling in love with Olwen Tregallas, the clergyman's pretty daughter.

Mohammad Ali considers himself out of the running. Though strikingly handsome, highly educated, and wealthy, he's aware that his skin is not of the right hue. And what would the townsfolk think of the reverend's daughter marrying a "Mussulman"? Such is Ali's devotion to Olwen that he encourages Royle to propose. His greatest fear is that the English rose will marry Chichele, who he has begun to believe is a bad seed.

But Chichele proposes first, and Olwen accepts. The clergyman's daughter looks forward to wedded bliss as her betrothed returns to his collection of bottled germs at Middlesex Hospital. He's hardly had a chance to sit down when a violent drunk of a woman is admitted with "lodging-house fever." Chichele leaps from his seat, aware that her post-mortem will provide the final piece of evidence required to complete his revolutionary theory on the advancement of the disease.

Oh, happy day!

However, Chichele's visions of wealth and glory—a knighthood for himself, a ladyship for his future wife—are quickly dashed as the wretched woman begins to rally.

"Confound her," Harry murmurs to himself. He tells Ali it's better that she die, considering:

"The valuable lives that would be saved for humanity! The wrenches that would be spared to parents and children? The hold we should gain over epidemic diseases! Why, our entire principles and practice of hygiene would be revolutionized offhand. Fever would be banished, cholera dispelled, diphtheria and scarlatina held at arm's length! Earth would become a really habitable planet, and the triumphant germ who now walks up and down this oblate spheroid of ours like a roaring lion, seeking whom he may devour, would have his fangs drawn and his claws pared by the calm, cool, dispassionate prevision of prophylactic science! All these good things would come to mankind—and I should be able to marry Olwen Tregellas! But no! That bloated, pasty-faced drunken old reprobate, lying in bed in her sins upstairs there, stops the way for all future progress!

So, Chichele kills her.

The doctor commits this ignoble act in an ingenious way, so is never under suspicion by anyone save his Mussulman colleague. Chichele will move to murder again; he is, as I've said, the greatest villain. He joins the others as the most interesting characters in the novel. My favourite is the child Lizbeth Wilcox, the waifish daughter of the "drunken old reprobate." Rescued from a life of poverty and misery, Lizbeth defies Dickens in proving herself truly evil. Her actions bring death, though the victim is not the one intended.

George Bernard Shaw thought *The Devil's Die* shocking. The impact was such that he drew upon Chichele in the creation of Dr Paramore in *The Philanderer*, his 1893 comedy. Shaw saw Allen's novel as flawed, but acknowledged the strength of its story.

Who am I to disagree with Shaw?

The plot is indeed riveting, though I will say that I found the last third a bit of a mixed bag. For reasons I won't describe—that would be spoiling things—Ali travels to the United States in search of Ivan Royle. There, he encounters prejudice unlike anything he has experienced in England. In New York, Ali endures the ignominy of segregated hotels and dining rooms: "If this was the treatment he received in New York itself, the enlightened and civilized metropolis of the Atlantic seaboard, what sort of reception might he expect to obtain from the wild westerners among whom Ivan Royle had pitched his tent on the rough and rugged slopes of the Rocky Mountains?"

What sort of reception? The sort offered by lawless men who believe in "Caucasian supremacy" and "Aryan culture." These men of the American west "don't mean to allow no more niggers, nor Chinamen or any sort." They'll kill both with keen enthusiasm.

I'm wrong. Harry Chichele isn't the novel's greatest villain.

Wings of Delusion

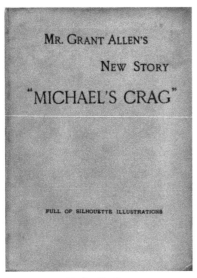

MR. GRANT ALLEN'S

NEW STORY

"MICHAEL'S CRAG"

FULL OF SILHOUETTE ILLUSTRATIONS

Michael's Crag
Grant Allen
London: Leadenhall, 1893
194 pages

There is only one fully realized character in *Michael's Crag*, but he is so interesting that the whole novel is carried on his non-existent wings. Michael Trevennack is an elderly English civil servant who spends his holidays on the Cornish coast staring out at a rock formation known as St Michael's Crag. Fifteen years earlier, a hundred or so feet below, he and his only son were struck by falling rocks. The boy was killed, while Trevennack was left with a blood clot in the brain that has him convinced he's the archangel Michael. Irascible and egotistical, the one thing that prevents the paper pusher from revealing his true identity is the love and counsel of a good wife.

As the only person aware of her husband's descent into madness, Mrs Trevennack works hard to keep all hidden until their daughter, Cleer, is wed. After all, no one in their right mind would marry a girl whose father is in the madhouse. The novel opens at about the point where Cleer meets and becomes betrothed to young engineer, Eustace Le Neve. Unfortunately, the fiancé just happens to be a good friend of Walter Tyrrel, the man responsible for the Trevennack boy's death. He confesses his guilt to Le Neve, describing what amounts to a boyhood act of misbehaviour. Though Le Neve breaks no confidence, the faux archangel figures it out and comes to see Tyrrel as a pawn of the Devil. Or could it be that Tyrrel *is* the Devil? Mad Michael is a bit confused.

In actuality, Tyrrel is just about the finest person one could hope to meet. Haunted by the death of young Trevennack, he does everything he can to advance Le Neve's career, thus enabling his friend to marry Cleer. He even goes so far as to bribe respected engineer Erasmus Walker into supporting his friend's plans for a railway viaduct. In doing so, Tyrrel fairly mortgages his future to a mysterious man who is known to scramble after every penny. "What can a man like that want to pile up filthy lucre for?" Tyrrel asks. The novel provides no answer; Allen teases, but he never delivers. After giving Walker the money, the now impoverished Tyrrel is plagued with uncertainty: "Would Walker play him false? Would he throw the weight of his influence into somebody else's scale? Would the directors submit as tamely as he thought to his direction or dictation?" But no, all turns out just fine; Le Neve is awarded the contract without so much as a hiccup.

This happy news comes none too soon for Mrs Trevennack, who recognizes that her husband is becoming increasingly unstable. However, her hopes that Le Neve, now financially secure, will quickly marry Cleer are dashed when the engineer becomes entangled in work. Months pass. Tension builds. Will her husband manage to conceal his strengthening delusions? Yes. What about at the wedding? No problem. Even when Trevennack spots Tyrrel hiding in the church? Don't give it a second thought. Okay, but how about when the delusional man spots his enemy on the street? Nope, still nothing.

All these roads leading nowhere and still I expected the climax to feature a confrontation between Trevennack and Tyrrel.

Never happens.

Instead, Trevennack, wandering the Cornish hills, encounters a ram he believes to be Satan. A long struggle ensues in which the old gent manages to kill the poor creature. Victorious, he throws himself off the cliff, trusting that his wanting wings will carry him home.

I didn't see that coming.

Romance Turns Russian Nihilist Reluctant

Under Sealed Orders
Grant Allen
New York: Grosset & Dunlap, [c. 1896]
321 pages

The beginning of *Under Sealed Orders*, a nineteenth-century novel of espionage and intrigue, reads like a work of Victorian erotica. It opens in the studio of painter Sacha Cazalet, where she is studying her model:

Sacha looked up at him in his becoming running suit; he'd been sitting, or rather posing, for her as joint winner at the tape in her spirited picture of "A Dead Heat—the Finish," and she thought to herself as she looked, though he *was* her own brother, that a handsomer or finer-built or stronger-looking young man wasn't to be found that day in the length and breadth of England. She drew a deep breath, and added a delicate touch to the stiffened muscle of the straining forearm.

Balancing the scene is Aunt Julia, "a distributor of tracts and good counsel gratis," fairly acting the role of chaperone. The threesome is joined the following day by the mysterious Mr Hayward, a bachelor who encourages athleticism in Sacha's brother—Owen—and delights in seeing him race other fit young men. A photographer by trade, Mr Hayward is Owen's "affectionate guardian." Two times a year, he sets business aside to take his ward off to some exotic locale or other.

This time, Morocco!

Mr Hayward informs the young man of their travel plans at the close of a chapter titled "Diplomatic Discipline." When next we see the pair they're standing together on the deck of a Cunard liner bound for Tangier.

The reader hoping for something akin to *The Romance of Lust* or *A Night in a Moorish Harem* will be frustrated. Mr Hayward's secret has naught to do with carnality; he is an exiled Russian prince who, having seen the suffering of the peasant, is ready for revolution. To this end, he has been grooming Owen—the son of a Russian aristocrat and English mother, both two decades dead—for a position in the British foreign service. Once accepted, his ward is to patiently wait for an opportunity to assassinate the Tsar.

Seems a real long shot, I know, but standing on the deck of the unnamed Cunard ship, Mr Hayward (né Prince Ruric Brassoff) has considerable confidence in his plan. Sadly, he hadn't anticipated his ward's urges.

During their travels, Owen is smitten by Ionê Dracopoli, an English-born Amazonian adventuress intent on making a solo expedition across Morocco on horseback. The guardian does his darndest to discourage a liaison, reminding his ward of his mission in life, but... well, Owen *is* twenty-one. He'd like to keep away, but sister Sacha just happens to count Ionê as a BFF.

Strange that brother and best friend hadn't met before.

Sacha sells a painting for a magnificent sum, which enables her to take a London apartment with Ionê and a very odd young woman they've nicknamed Blackbird. Try as he might, Owen can't resist a visit. It's not long before he declares his love for his sister's roommate (not the peculiar one).

Ah, youth.

In embracing Ionê, Owen rejects the mission laid out by Mr Hayward. Well, you can imagine the resulting turmoil.

From here Allen strikes out in directions that would spoil in the telling. Tempted as I am, I'll hold back.

In the context of author's œuvre, *Under Sealed Orders* is average, which is to say that it is much better than nearly every other Canadian novel of the day. Whether you deem it worth a read will have a whole lot to do with your interest in Russian history and politics. I don't much care for the topics myself, though I was very much interested in the household dynamics between "New Woman" adherents Sacha, Ionê, and Blackbird.

There's a part of me that is still twenty-one.

Amy Levy: Blackbird dying in the dead of night.

Anyone considering giving *Under Sealed Orders* a read are warned that spoilers follow. The image to the left may have already spoiled things, for which I apologize. In my defence, it spoils things in the Grosset & Dunlap edition, too—the plate coming one page before we learn that Blackbird has committed suicide.

The most interesting character in the novel, Blackbird, is modelled on English poet Amy Levy (1861–1889), herself a suicide. I wrote about this connection in my book *Character Parts*, so won't go on about it here, except to say that I perhaps over-simplified Allen's views on the New Woman. Blackbird is one of at least three of the movement's members to die in his novels; the most famous being Herminia Barton, heroine of *The Woman Who Did* (1895). All are depicted as victims of higher education, the female pursuit of which ran contrary to Allen's evolutionist beliefs. A frail slip of a thing, forever exhausted, Blackbird fairly struggles to stay upright, as this detail from another plate shows.

How vibrant Sacha and Ionê are! New Women both, what differentiates them from Blackbird is their level of education. It isn't that Sacha, a painter, and Ionê, an adventuress-turned-writer, aren't educated, rather they have received the proper amount of schooling. Only Blackbird, the most educated character in the entire novel, properly understands her misfortune, as she explains in a chapter titled "The Higher Education of Women":

> "It was my people who educated me. You see, they thought I was clever—perhaps I was to start with; and they crammed me with everything on earth a girl could learn. Latin, Greek, modern languages, mathematics, natural science, music, drawing, dancing, till I was stuffed to the throat with them. *Je suis jusque là*," and she put her hand to her chin with some dim attempt at feminine playfulness. "Like Strasbourg geese," she added slowly in a melancholy after-thought; "it may be good for the brain, but it's precious bad for the body."

Blackbird's single desire is for endless sleep undisturbed by dreams. To this end, she uses her chemistry skills to make poison distilled from laurel leaves provided by an innocent suitor. (Amy Levy killed herself by inhaling charcoal fumes.)

Allen knew Levy and exploited her life and death. In his essay "The Girl of the Future," published in *The Universal Review* eight months after the poet's suicide, he uses her death to argue against higher education for women: "A few hundred pallid little Amy Levys sacrificed on the way are as nothing before the face of our fashionable Juggernaut. Newnham has slain its thousands and Girton its tens of thousands."

His verse, "For Amy Levy's Urn," is as smug as it is sympathetic:

This bitter age that pits our maids with men
    Wore out our woman's heart before its time:
        Too wan and pale,
        She strove to scale

The icy peaks of unimagined rhyme.
There, worlds broke sunless on her frightened ken;
    The mountain air struck chill in her frail breath;
Fainting she fell all weary with her climb,
    And kissed the soft, sweet lips of pitying death.

Which is why I'd prefer to end with Amy Levy's own:

THE PROMISE OF SLEEP

Put the sweet thoughts from out thy mind,
    The dreams from out thy breast;
No joy for thee—but thou shalt find
                Thy rest.

All day I could not work for woe,
            I could not work nor rest;
The trouble drove me to and fro,
            Like a leaf on the storm's breast.

Night came and saw my sorrow cease;
            Sleep in the chamber stole;
Peace crept about my limbs, and peace
            Fell on my stormy soul.

And now I think of only this,—
            How I again may woo
The gentle sleep—who promises
            That death is gentle too.

The Busiest Man in England Lays Down His Pen

Hilda Wade: A Woman with Tenacity of Purpose
Grant Allen [and Arthur Conan Doyle]
New York: Putnam, 1900
383 pages

A novel written by a dying man, *Hilda Wade* ends in reconciliation, redemption, and a deathbed scene. Arthur Conan Doyle tells us that this is just as the author intended. I don't doubt it. A good friend, Doyle completed the novel Allen could not, following the story the stricken author sketched from his own deathbed. "He was much worried because there were two numbers of his serial, 'Hilda Wade,' which was running in 'The Strand' magazine, still uncompleted," Doyle writes in his own *Memories and Adventures*. "It was a pleasure for me to do them for him, and so relieve his mind, but it was difficult collar work, and I expect they were pretty bad."

Such modesty.

Doyle's chapters are every bit as good as the rest The best of *Hilda Wade* comes in its first half, in which narrator Doctor Hubert Cumberledge introduces our heroine. Hilda Wade is a nurse at London's St Nathaniel's Hospital. Not the finest of medical institutions, she leaves it for the more prestigious St George's, so that she might work with the world-famous Professor Sebastian, a man who has done more than any other to advance the science of medicine. Cumberledge understands fully—then he doesn't understand at all. Our narrator, who sees Sebastian as a godlike presence in a milieu in which death forever threatens, is bewildered that Hilda doesn't share his unquestioning admiration of the man.

There is mystery about Hilda. She reveals nothing of herself, yet knows much about others. Blessed with an eidetic memory and "the deepest feminine gift—intuition," she proves her character exemplary in several dramas that play out in St Nathaniel's and amongst Cumberledge's family and friends. Hilda's powers are boosted by her creator's theories about evolution and his high regard for Furneaux Jordan's 1896 *Character as Seen in Body and Parentage* (acknowledged, incorrectly, as "Character in Body and Parentage" in the novel's first edition). Nowhere is this more evident than in the third and fourth chapters—"The Wife Who Did Her Duty" and "The Man Who Would Not Commit Suicide"—in which Hilda correctly predicts that Cumberledge's gentle friend Hugo Le Geyt, QC, will kill his newlywed wife. The nurse goes on to forecast the murderer's suicide, which she is certain will be made to look like an accident. No clairvoyant, Hilda cites, by way of behavioural template, the actions of several of Le Geyt's ancestors and relatives:

> "Another, Marcus, was said to have shot himself by accident while cleaning his gun—after a quarrel with his wife. But you have heard all about it. 'The wrong was on my side,' he moaned, you know, when they picked him up, dying, in the gun-room. And one of the Faskally girls, his cousins, of whom his wife was jealous—that beautiful Linda—became a Catholic and went into a convent at once on Marcus's death: which, after all, in such cases, is merely a religious and moral way of committing suicide..."

It's my favourite passage in the book.

The doctor comes to play Watson to Hilda's Holmes. I like to think Doyle was amused. Midway through the novel, the secret of Hilda Wade—true name: Maisie Yorke-Bannerman—is revealed to both reader and villain. That villain is, of course, Sebastian. The professor tries to murder the nurse, but his ingenuity is no match for that of our heroine. He fails because hers is the greater mind; indeed, Hilda— Maisie, if you prefer—is the most intelligent Allen character I've ever encountered.

Given the circumstances of composition, it might be unseemly to complain about the novel's weaknesses. After Sebastian's botched attempt on her life, Maisie flees for Africa, seeking refuge there until it is safe to return to London. A besmitten Cumberledge employs detection methods learned from Maisie, managing to track her down in South Africa. Through the seven (of twelve) chapters that follow, narrator and heroine wander, as does the novel itself. Rhodesia, India, Tibet, and the Mediterranean figure as the narrative shifts, rather abruptly, from one of Victorian mystery and detection to a series of adventure stories set in the colonies. Each is interesting in its own way—one features an escape from a Matabele uprising by bicycle—but the reader recognizes that there was serialization to consider. Twelve numbers were contracted and, thanks to Doyle, twelve numbers were delivered.

Allen once described himself "the busiest man in England." I believe the claim to be true. He died at the age of fifty-two, leaving behind dozens and dozens of articles, poems, and short stories. The books he wrote numbered more than the years he lived; this would be meaningless if the quality of his output were poor, but Allen is easily the finest novelist born in Victoria's Canada.

He's a writer worth knowing. Doyle certainly thought so.

AWARD-WINNERS

Passion Over Reason in a Bland Bachelor's Lap

The Unreasoning Heart
Constance Beresford-Howe
New York: Dodd, Mead, 1946
236 pages

Mcgill student Constance Beresford-Howe had just received her B.A. when word came that she'd won the Intercollegiate Literary Fellowship Prize. The accomplishment was duly recognized in the May 12, 1945 edition of Montreal's *Gazette*: "Miss Beresford-Howe, who received her early education at Herbert Symonds School and West Hill High School, has been an honours student in McGill University's faculty of arts and science for the past three years and will graduate on May 30."

Beresford-Howe was back at McGill working on her M.A. when *The Unreasoning Heart* was published. That same academic year she wrote her second novel.

It was a remarkable beginning to what would become a long literary career. *The Unreasoning Heart* itself is not nearly so noteworthy, but it is unusual. Not even a handful of Montreal novels were published in the wake of the Second World War, and this is one of only two or three to attempt anything that might be considered literary. But what most intrigues is the behaviour of the female characters. Had *The Unreasoning Heart* been written by a man, I wouldn't hesitate to describe it as the work of a misogynist.

The story begins with Abbey, a sixteen-year-old orphan who is taken in—summoned really—by Fran Archer, a childhood friend of her recently deceased mother. The Archers live in a large house on Côte-St-Antoine in Notre-Dame-de-Grâce. Theirs is an unconventional household, supported largely through what I took to be investments made with inherited wealth. A handsome fifty-something widow, Fran is pretty much in charge. Brother Teddy is a divorced drunk who wanders

37

aimlessly, killing time, untroubled by his disrespectful daughter, Paule. Fran's children are more polite. Con, the eldest of the two, runs a printing company. When not at work he sometimes treats Isobel, the aggressive young widow next door, to a movie, though he much prefers the solitude of the upstairs library. David, the golden child, is married to Fay, a petite dynamo Fran found for him. He's always been his mother's favourite. Con was never nearly so good looking and was a problem as a baby.

The heart has its reasons.

Nothing much happens in *The Unreasoning Heart*. Dialogue dominates the novel as Fran, Paule, Isobel, Fay, and new arrival Abbey jockey for position with snide comments and outright insults. Meanwhile, the meek men do all they can to avoid drama and confrontation. For this reason, the only episode of any lasting significance in terms of plot comes as surprise. David disappears after Fay pushes him one time too many times. Though the girls are devastated, Fay herself couldn't care less and carries on with her life. Fran, meanwhile, moves toward complete mental collapse. Teddy takes another drink, Con phones the city hospitals. This in turn leads to the best bloomer I've ever read:

"Abbey—"

"What?"

"C'n I get into you bed?"

"Sure."

Paule transferred herself quickly and snuggled up to Abbey for warmth and comfort. She cried a little and dried her tears on the collar of Abbey's pyjamas.

"Everything's so queer now," she sniffled gratefully.

Read nothing into this encounter, Abbey has dedicated her life and body with newly budding beasts—at sixteen?—to Con, a man twice her age. Hers is the unreasoning heart.

On a sudden impulse she came over him and climbed onto his lap, her long legs dangling to the floor.

"You young hussy," protested Con, "are you trying to take away my good name? And me so careful all these years?"

"I just want to hug you some. You're always so remote and dignified. You ought to be hugged oftener."

"Go right ahead. I'd be a cad to refuse an offer like that."

She put her arms around his neck and rubbed her smooth cheek vigorously against his. Then she nuzzled her face lovingly into his neck and her fine, silky hair covered his shoulder. She lay there quietly, one hand resting against his breast. Con's long face wore a slightly foolish smile of enjoyment during the performance.

But, as she lay there so quietly, he gradually became aware of the beating of her young heart and the warmth of her small pointed breasts against him. A proudly uneasy pleasure swept through him. When she stirred a little, his arms closed around her. "Don't move," he said. She lay perfectly still, with closed eyes. He smoothed back the fair hair from her cheek and his fingers touched the warm flesh of her upper arm lingeringly. A heavy, using warmth pressed through his veins. He was afraid to move; afraid of her warmth, her sweetness, and her absolute trust. He sat there watching her face, feeling the fierce urge of desire in conflict with an inexplicable tenderness.

All at once he gave her a rough shake.

"Get off," he said abruptly. "You're too hard on my rheumatism."

Told you it was unusual.

What's Going on with *The Plouffe Family?*

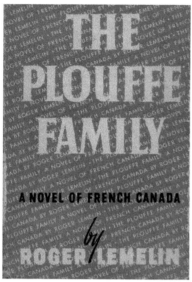

The Plouffe Family [Les Plouffe]
Roger Lemelin [trans. Mary Finch]
Toronto: McClelland & Stewart, 1950
373 pages

The Plouffe Family is out of print. How can that be?

Lemelin's original, *Les Plouffe*, is one of the cornerstones in our literature. A best-seller upon publication, it was quickly adapted to radio and, in 1953, inspired *La famille Plouffe*, Radio-Canada's very first television series. An English-language version featuring the very same actors began broadcasting the following year. There was also a miniseries and a feature film that cleaned up at the 1982 Genies.

My mother loved *La famille Plouffe*, and because she was drawn to wholesome, sentimental fare—*The Sound of Music* was her favourite film—I developed preconceived notions. These were cast aside when I finally read *The Town Below* (1948), the translation of Lemelin's first novel. Both dark and funny, what it said about party politics, sexual mores, and the influence of the Church in pre-Quiet Revolution Quebec surprised and delighted. *The Plouffe Family* didn't quite have the same effect, but only because I'd read the author's debut.

The Plouffe family—*les Plouffe*—live in St-Sauveur, the working-class quarter that lies in the shadow of Quebec City's upper town. Six in number, they fill a flat. Théophile, the father, rests on his laurels as champion of an otherwise forgotten cycling event. Mother Josephine cooks, bakes, cleans, and dreams of her heroine, Joan of Arc. The four Plouffe children—Cécile, Napoléon, Ovide, and Guillaume—live at home, despite the fact that most are well into adulthood.

Nineteen-year-old Guillaume was a late surprise.

Though not immediately apparent, *The Plouffe Family* is quite a dark novel. The first section—there are four, plus an epilogue—concerns itself largely with middle son Ovide's pursuit of Rita Toulouse, a co-worker in the local boot factory. On their first date they watch young Guillaume defeat the local rings champion. The second has Ovide trying to win her heart by performing selections from *Pagliacci* in the Plouffe's sitting room. Rita disappears during a scene change. She ends up being felt up by Guillaume in a secluded strawberry patch.

Ovide abandons the chase, but only temporarily. His is just one part of a family drama set during a time of rising turmoil. Théophile loses his job after he refuses to put out banners during the 1939 royal visit. A half-hearted strike is overshadowed by war, Guillaume signs with the Cincinnati Reds, Napoléon falls for a tubercular servant girl, and Cécile's love for her former boyfriend reaches a sudden, tragic conclusion. Riveting and just a bit titillating, it's easy to understand why *La famille Plouffe* worked so well on television.

In 1975, a quarter century after it was first published, Mary Finch's translation was added to the New Canadian Library. Is this not a bit curious? After all, *The Town Below* had been welcomed into the series fourteen years earlier. No one can deny that *The Plouffe Family* had much greater public recognition.

In 1985, McClelland & Stewart printed a new edition that used a still from the film on the cover.

I remember that second NCL cover, and blame it for reinforcing my preconceptions about the novel.

The Plouffe Family is no light-hearted romp. There is comedy, some verging on slapstick, but for the most part the humour is black. Darkness pervades and brightness falls.

The New Canadian Library never made up for that eighties cover; *The Plouffe Family* was dropped in the great purge that accompanied the launch of the series' ugly 1988 redesign.

The Plouffe Family is out of print. I had no idea until I started writing this piece.

Again, how can that be?

Mr Child's Simple Story of Dramatic Suspense

Mr. Ames Against Time
Philip Child
Toronto: Ryerson, 1949
244 pages

Mr. Ames Against Time earned Philip Child a Governor General's Award and the second of his two Ryerson Fiction Awards. It is, of course, standard reading for any student of Canadian literature.

I kid. I kid because I love.

It's true that Mr. Ames Against Time was so honoured, but I know no one who has read this novel. Even the very few contemporary critics and scholars who bother mentioning the work seem to have given it a pass. In his Canadian Literature in English, the usually reliable W.J. Keith errs in describing the novel as "a psychological spy thriller." It's not. Nor is it a "whodunit," as Irina Sobkowska-Ashcroft and Lorna Berman assert in Portrayal of Old Age in Twentieth Century Canadian Novels.

I will allow that Mr. Ames Against Time might be considered a crime novel. At its centre is the most tightly bound group of characters found outside a family drama. Mr Ames—he's nearly always referred to thusly—is a doorman at the Urania Burlesque Theatre, a seedy joint owned by crime kingpin Sol Mower. Mr Ames' son, Mike, gathers wads of bills as the crook's collector. Mike's sweetheart is Bernie Avery, a beautiful hoofer who performs daily at the Urania. Her father, a failed artist and boozehound, gets the occasional job painting signage and backdrops for the theatre. Bernie's best friend, hop-head Gipsy Beir— Mower got her hooked on the stuff—also performs at the Urania. Gipsy has something going with Mr Ames' former ward, Smoke, a rat-faced loser who does the worst of Mower's dirty work. All live in a building owned by the big boss. Mike loves Bernie, of course, but so does

Smoke. What Mower feels for the dancing girl is best described as lust.

When Mower is murdered, suspicion falls upon premier paramour Mike. Mr Ames is thrust into a terrible situation in which he must testify that the dying man accused his son of the misdeed. Never mind, the elderly doorman has unwavering faith that his example and gentle efforts will encourage the real murderer to reveal himself, thus saving Mike from the hangman's noose. Mr Ames' greater concern is that his weak heart will give way before he has achieved his goal. Ultimately, of course, Mr Ames wins the race *"Against Time."*

Now, before I'm accused of spoiling the plot, allow me to point to the dust jacket's front flap:

Mr. Ames
Against Time

By PHILIP CHILD

"The book is a story of dramatic suspense. The chief character, Mr. Ames, an old man, must struggle to save the life of one close to him whom he loves. Seemingly, everything is against him, including the creeping on of time toward a set and fatal date. On his side are only those resources of courage and strength which he can find in himself. Against desperate odds he wins his battle and saves the threatened life.

"The book has a dramatic plot with plenty of action in it. But what is (I believe) most important in the book is the character of the old man himself and those of the others who help or hinder him in his struggle. *Mr. Ames Against Time* tells of what happens in people's minds and spirits when they are faced with bitter odds. In fact it is really a book about courage—how and why it works in some people, in Mr. Ames for instance, and does not work in others."

—From the Author's Radio Interview

The very same words "From the Author's Radio Interview" are repeated on the novel's second page.

This is Morley Callaghan country, a harsh land through which sympathetic, simple people move, encountering moral dilemmas at every turn. Mr Ames is the exemplar:

He was one of those strange and simple people whose heart ached for other people. It was his secret belief that everyone in his world was in some way alone and afraid of something. This sympathy was with him a kind of disease of the soul, a kind of haemophilia of the heart: his heart bled for people and the heart's blood would not coagulate and form though scars over the simple emotion of love and pity.

Mr Ames might be strange and simple, but it's Smoke who steals the show. Whether wooing Bernie, fighting in the ring, or simply walking his limping dog, his are the most memorable and best-drawn scenes. There's a mystery about Smoke, whose origin is revealed after he's handed a book on his family by a helpful librarian:

"You'll have to sign this slip, please, and read it in the building."
    She handed him a slip of paper and pencil. Smoke looked at her with his pencil poised.
    "Got to sign this?"
    "Of course. It's a rule."... A strange young man, she thought.
    "Say, look. I only want to see it for a minute. Couldn't I look at it at the desk?"
    "Everyone has to sign."
    He hunched his left shoulder and arm so as to hide the slip and scrawled his name.
    She took the slip and glanced at it, casually at first; then she caught her breath and her eyes jerked up and met Smoke's.
    "Sure, that's my name," nodded Smoke with bravado.
    "Look here, I shouldn't read it if I were you. ... Better not."
    "Give it here!" Smoke snatched it from her, fled from the desk and round the corner of the hall out of sight.

And so Smoke learns that he was born into a family of rapists, murderers, and psychopaths. There's a decent amount of inbreeding, too, but nothing in his unhealthy genetic soup has caused haemophilia of the heart. Quite the opposite.
    Smoke checks out before the end of the novel, while Mr Ames survives *because* of his aching, bleeding heart. Others who are not similarly afflicted in the tightly bound group are doomed. One dies through poisoning, one overdoses, while a third succumbs to sheer terror while contemplating his own mortality, leaving...
    Ah, but that would be a spoiler—and this is a book worth reading. Besides, I've already told you about Smoke.

University Professor Writes
Roman À Clef Roman

Fasting Friar
Edward McCourt
Toronto: McClelland & Stewart, 1963
222 pages

Fasting Friar is a novel about the halls of academe and the politics therein, but I read it just the same. The premise intrigued: Paul Ettinger, a professor at a nondescript prairie university, publishes a racy *roman à clef* about a professor at a nondescript prairie university. Titled *The Proud and the Passionate*, it raises the ire of the president, the board, and fellow professor, Walter Ackroyd. Not one week after publication, rumours swirl that Ettinger is about to be sacked.

Ackroyd, not Ettinger, is the protagonist of the novel—by which I mean *Fasting Friar*, not *The Proud and the Passionate*. A solitary Milton scholar whose reputation far exceeds that of the university, Ackroyd takes pleasure in the thought that the budding novelist might be on the way out. He's long considered Ettinger a disgrace, dismissing the popular professor as a showman, a "sloop-minded snapper-up of unconsidered trifles... let loose in a classroom to wreak destruction upon the intellect." To Ackroyd, *The Proud and the Passionate* is irrefutable evidence that Ettinger simply lacks the intellect and good judgement expected of his position:

> He opened the book at random and began to read:
> Ackroyd threw the book across the room. From the back cover of the dust-jacket Paul Ettinger's face stared up at him.

The faculty begin to rally in defence of Ettinger, pressuring Ackroyd, their most esteemed member, to join the struggle. The asocial professor emerges from behind his office door, and is forced to recognize the assault on the very ideals that have been at the centre of his life's work. By degrees, Ackroyd becomes Ettinger's greatest champion, even as his dislike for the man grows.

McCourt himself was a professor, teaching at the University of Saskatchewan from 1944 until his death, in 1972. Very much a forgotten figure, before coming upon this novel I knew him only as the author of *Music at the Close* and *The Wooden Sword*, two of the New Canadian Library's many abandoned titles. The former won Ryerson's All-Canada Fiction Award, which means nothing. McCourt published six novels in total, *Fasting Friar* being the last. Three more followed, but failed to find publishers.

Given all this, I went into *Fasting Friar* expecting little. What I found was one of the most interesting and enjoyable reads since I began this exploration of the forgotten, neglected and suppressed. It's a complex, yet taut, novel written by a sure hand.

Apparently, it sold fewer than three hundred copies. It was no *The Proud and the Passionate*.

A Not-So-Nice Place to Visit

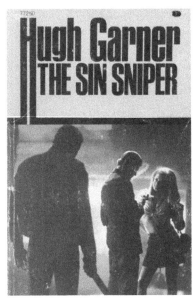

The Sin Sniper
Hugh Garner
Richmond Hill, ON: Pocket, 1970
277 pages

From the back cover:

HUGH GARNER
Won Canada's highest literary award, The Governor General's Award, for fiction in 1963. He has also been awarded three Canada Council Senior Arts Fellowships.

So what's he doing writing a cheap paperback original?
The answer is going full circle and then some—past *Storm Below* (1949), his debut, to *Waste No Tears* (1950), *Cabbagetown* (1950), and *Present Reckoning* (1951). Paperback originals all, the latter three brought more money than would've been garnered—sorry—through higher literary endeavours. It's true that *Storm Below* did well for the author, but not in an immediate sense. A man needs to eat and this man needed to drink.

Garner's seventh novel, *The Sin Sniper*, landed just months after his sixth, *A Nice Place to Visit* (1970). It enjoyed a higher print run, more editions, and as *Stone Cold Dead*, would eventually be adapted for the screen in a film starring Richard Crenna, Paul Williams, and Linda Sorensen.

Robert Fulford, who had a certain respect for Garner, was none too impressed. Writing in the *Ottawa Citizen* (November 5, 1971), he dismissed *The Sin Sniper* as "close to being dreadful," adding "one was left with nothing but baffling sense of being told to go left on Sumach, or right on Dundas, or left on Parliament."

I understand what he means. This is the novel's opening paragraph:

Detective Inspector Walter McDurmont of the Metropolitan Toronto Police homicide squad jockeyed his three-year-old Galaxie along Dundas Street East in the morning rush-hour traffic. He crossed the Don River over the Dundas Street bridge, swung left down River Street, made a right turn at Shuter, and stopped when confronted with the raised stop-sign of the school crossing guard at Sumach Street, near Park Public School.

Lest you get lost, the book features a map that looks to have been ripped from a city directory.

Garner's setting is Toronto's rough Moss Park neighbourhood. The premise is found in the title: a sniper is murdering prostitutes. First to die is Claudia Grissom, whose snow-covered body is found early one morning near the corner of Shuter and Jarvis. Bernice Carnival is shot the next day (Dundas Street, one block from the Dainty Dot, on the other side of Church Street).

Those looking for a good mystery will be disappointed. There's little detective work here; McDurmont banks pretty much everything on catching the sniper in the act. While he comes to focus the investigation on three suspects, one of whom indeed proves to be the sniper, nothing is provided that might justify his choice.

What saves *The Sin Sniper* is its characters Driving and walking through the streets of Toronto, turning left and veering right, these are real people moving between real places. I'm not suggesting this is a *roman à clef*, but I'm certain that Garner, a self-confessed alcoholic, drew heavily on the folks he met in drinking establishments, just as I'm certain that the drinking establishments in the novel would be recognizable to Torontonians of a certain age.

A Torontonian of a certain age himself, Robert Fulford would know much better than I just how true the novel is to the people and places of Moss Park. I enjoyed the tour as much as the encounters. Fulford concludes his dismissal of *The Sin Sniper* by writing that the book's only mystery is it's having been published. To me, the answer is obvious: Money. Pocket Books recognized this, as did PaperJacks with their reissue, as did the investors in *Stone Cold Dead*.

Meanwhile, we're still awaiting the screen adaptation of *Storm Below*. No money in it, I suppose.

Jalna's Dirty Little Secret Exposed!

The Secret of Jalna
Ronald Hambleton
Toronto: PaperJacks, 1972
175 pages

I remember Jalna... or rather, I remember *The Whiteoaks of Jalna*. The television adaptation of Mazo de la Roche's sixteen-book soapy saga ran on Sunday nights from January through April 1972. A nine-year-old aspiring architect, I'd lie on the floor, sketching the house by the glow of our colour Viking. My mother, more attentive than I, did her best to follow along with the aid of a Whiteoaks family tree she'd clipped from the pages of *Weekend Magazine*.

The Whiteoaks of Jalna was to have been our *Forsyte Saga*. CBC Television Drama poured nearly everything it had into the project, draining resources and, ultimately, crippling future productions. With a total budget of $2 million, it was such a big deal that even an elementary school student such as myself knew it was coming. *The Secret of Jalna*, thrown together in anticipation of the series debut, captures some of the excitement. Here, for example, is the book's poorly laid-out reproduction of an undated *Toronto Star* headline: "Jalna pilot bombs brickyard, makes TV history."

"Jalna pilot bombs" would have sufficed.

Polite company does not speak of the series. In *Turn Up the Contrast*, her history of CBC television drama, Mary Jane Miller devotes all of two paragraphs to this most of monumental of flops. Still, I think she sums things up nicely: "The problem was that *Jalna* readers, who wanted their old familiar story, were treated to an ill-conceived experiment in narrative structure complete with flashbacks, multiple plot strands, and intercut time frames, all edited in haste as the air date approached. Of course they were frustrated by this. Viewers unfamiliar with the novels were simply confused."

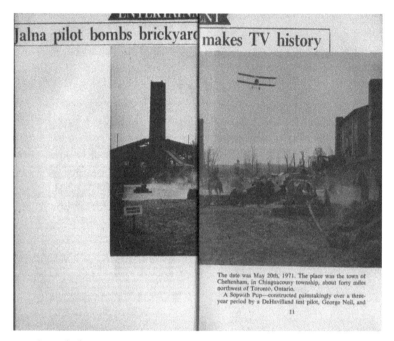

Jalna pilot bombs brickyard makes TV history

The date was May 20th, 1971. The place was the town of Cheltenham, in Chinguacousy township, about forty miles northwest of Toronto, Ontario.

A Sopwith Pup—constructed painstakingly over a three-year period by a DeHavilland test pilot, George Neil, and

11

Blame belongs, in part, to lead writer Timothy Findley.

The Whiteoaks of Jalna never made it to Beta, VHS, LaserDisc—you won't find it on DVD, Blu-ray, or Netflix. YouTube has no clips, and there aren't more than a couple of images online.

The series aired for a second and final time two years later. *Windsor Star* critic Ray Bennet speculated: "The great fiasco may have some camp appeal by now." He was wrong. But then camp appeal grows with time.

How soon is now?

Jalna's Dirtiest Little Secret Exposed!

A cautionary tale concerning literary executors:

"What is the secret of Jalna?" the cover copy asks before peppering the prospective purchaser with further questions: "Did a house called Jalna really exist? Who was Mazo de la Roche and why did she hide her origins? What kept the Jalna stories off television for ten years after her death?"

Anyone wondering about the existence of a house called Jalna would have found the answer in Hambleton's previous book, *Mazo de la Roche of Jalna* (1966). A polite biography, it went far in exploring de la Roche's life and why it was that she hid her origins, all the while skirting speculation that she and lifelong companion and cousin, Caroline Clement, were Sapphic sisters.

Ultimately, *The Secret of Jalna* is very much a reflection on the ill-conceived series. A rough gathering of short pieces about de la Roche's life, ancestry, and writings, it jumps around with no real purpose. Anyone familiar with *Mazo de la Roche of Jalna* will find nothing new other than the answer to that fourth question: "What kept the Jalna stories off television for ten years after her death?"

> In her lifetime, Mazo de la Roche stubbornly refused to permit any of her books to be broadcast on either radio or television in any sponsored broadcast; and though her will did not come right out and forbid commercial adaptations of her books, she left no doubt of her own opinion.

Hambleton goes on to add: "Today, the creator of the world of Jalna is dead, and the world is no longer self-renewing."

Cold.

Following de la Roche's 1961 death, repeated efforts were made to turn the Whiteoak Chronicles into a series. By 1970, two-thirds of her estate—represented by adopted children René and Esmée—were on board; the holdout was Caroline, whom Hambleton describes as "the only inheritor of the attitude of mind of her late cousin."

The paragraphs that follow are the most peculiar and revealing of the book. The reader is told: "Caroline Clement knew that Mazo, had she been living, would certainly not have agreed; but now, after ten years? For Caroline Clement is herself an old woman, subject to illness, easily tired yet plagued by insomnia, living on without Mazo."

Hambleton sketches a disturbing picture of a blind, frail, elderly woman being wooed over afternoon tea by Head of CBC Television Drama Fletcher Markle, George Desmond of the network's copyright department, and story consultant April Sinclair (who was present "because of her English accent; it would help to put Caroline at ease"):

> Caroline was sent flowers, talking books, and cassettes of her favourite music to hear during her solitary hours.

Then, after the agreement was signed, Mrs. Sinclair was given the task of telling Caroline Clement that other material was being added to up-date the Whiteoaks, since after all, Caroline had been invited to attend a private showing of the pilot episode together with the rest of the family. (She refused to attend, and gave it as her wish that no member of the family, nor her friends John Gray and Lovat Dickson, attend either that or any other arranged showing.)

Caroline heard her out, then said nothing for a long moment. At last she asked, in a quiet, numbed voice, "Can I do anything to stop it?"

April Sinclair said no.

Nothing more need be said, except for this: The series deserved to fail.

Langevin's Masterpiece;
Mcclelland's Disappointment

Orphan Street [*Une Chaîne dans le parc*]
André Langevin [trans. Alan Brown]
Toronto: McClelland & Stewart, 1976
287 pages

Jack McClelland believed *Orphan Street* the most important novel to come out of French Canada since *The Tin Flute*. I can't agree, but I will say that it's just about the greatest Canadian novel I've ever read.

Orphan Street didn't exactly set McClelland's house on fire; not only was it a commercial failure, the critics couldn't get it up. The publisher himself kept pushing it in the press long after sales had proven limp. Ever the optimist, five months after publication he wrote Langevin:

There are a lot of people around the country now who have read it, are talking about it and who are recommending it, and it would not entirely surprise me if it turned out to be a slow starter that will eventually gain momentum and do extremely well.

Unquestionably one of the difficulties with the book in English is that it starts more slowly than the English-reading public have come to expect. They found the opening chapter slow, somewhat baffling...

Orphan Street isn't such a difficult novel, but the first chapter is a real challenge, immersing the reader in the elaborate fantasies of its young protagonist, Pierrot. Nine years old, he has been removed—with a sudden jerk—from the uncomfortable confines of a Catholic orphanage by the bachelor brother and three spinster sisters of his deceased mother. Their motivation, such as it is, probably has something to do with familial duty. Their thinking is that maybe, just maybe, the boy is about to start down a path tread by his cheating drunk of a father. The truth is that they passed judgement before he arrived.

It sounds awful, I know, but you can't feel too bad about Pierrot. With his relatives' disinterest comes freedom.

Pierrot's new home with Uncle Nap and aunts lies in the shadow of the Jacques Cartier Bridge, at whose end the Molson brewery squats like a big brown brick. Consumptive Gaston, known to all as "the Rat," rummages through the refuse and deals in black-market goods. I spoil nothing in writing that he'll be dead before the novel's end. Before he goes, the Rat serves as a guide to the boy's little corner of war-time Montreal. Pierrot quickly makes friends with Jane, the very pretty red-haired *anglaise* in the adjacent apartment, with whom he spends a summer roaming city streets, parks, and wharves, sharing adventures the likes of which I daren't have dreamt at his age.

There is joy in life lived outside walls. Where the past was one of routine ruled by abusive older boys and grey nuns, now each day brings new experiences and people he had no idea existed. Pierrot's exuberance, his passion for the new and his interest in other people are all things his aunts cannot abide.

Orphan Street is not so difficult a novel, though later scenes will disturb. It's not so difficult until one remembers that the author spent much of his own childhood in a Quebec orphanage. Langevin's experience may not have precisely resembled that of Pierrot—the author would've been ten or so years older—but there is discomfort in the recognition. The best one can say is that we know Langevin was spared the unique horrors suffered by the Duplessis Orphans.

Did Pierrot?

Orphan Street came and went in less than a season; there was no second printing and no paperback edition. The novel was considered for the New Canadian Library—McClelland's recommendation, I expect—but this went nowhere.

The time is overdue for *Orphan Street* to be properly recognized. It's too much to expect the translation to do, as Jack McClelland hoped—"extremely well"—but it does deserve a return to print.

Sheila Fischman considers it a masterpiece.

BIGOTS &
BUSINESSMEN

Onward Brith'ish Business Men

The Destiny of The British Empire
and The U.S.A.
"The Roadbuilder" [pseud. W. G.
Mackendrick]
[Toronto]: Commonwealth, 1957
204 pages

The author makes it quite clear that this is not a book for everyone:

RESPECTFULLY DEDICATED

TO

THE SHORT-HAIRED BUSINESS MEN

OF THE BRITISH EMPIRE AND THE U.S.A.

MEN, CHUCK-FULL OF SENTI-MENT, ENTERPRISE AND GOOD-WILL who, given facts, can usually deliver an intelligent opinion and judgement quicker, it is alleged, than "hell can scorch a feather."

Having never been nearer hell than France and Belgium during war-time, I am unable to say if the above time limit is a reasonable one, but cheerfully and with confidence I submit the following facts, statements, and deductions, both Biblical and cheerful; to your mature business judgement, and knowing that they will be dealt with by a fifty-fifty mixture of grey matter and horse-sense, which is all one could ask.

THE ROADBUILDER
September, 1921

A short-haired business man himself, The Roadbuilder (né William Gordon MacKendrick) made a small fortune in the first half of the last century spreading concrete and asphalt over vast stretches of Canada and the United States. During the First World War he served as Director of Roads for the British Fifth Army in France and Belgium. These were wonderful years for MacKendrick, because he saw in each bloody battle a sign of the End Times. The Roadbuilder cheered the destruction and carnage. The 1917 capture of Jerusalem, at a cost of some 43,000 dead and wounded, was a happy event in which the British had at long last fulfilled God's will in taking the holy city from the Gentiles.

Yes, the Gentiles.

MacKendrick was a believer in Anglo-Israelism; his British weren't British but "Brith'ish." The "facts, statements and deductions" in this, his first book, are put forth as evidence that the people of Great Britain and their descendants are the true people of Israel. His king, George V, was the direct successor of the House of David. Lest a short-haired business man question his beliefs, The Roadbuilder is quick to point out:

> I may mention that my bank backs my word and judgement to the tune of between a quarter and half-million dollars overdraft each season, and they, as you know, have the habit of looking into the innermost recesses of one's make-up...

The Destiny of The British Empire and The U.S.A. is a directionless and nonsensical book that owes much to the two hundred and fifty or so Anglo-Israelist writings upon which it is based. It's a chore to read, despite some very simple, folksy language.

The opening sentences set the tone: "Say, reader, did you ever write a book? No! Well, neither have I, so we break even on that score."

Dealing with this chatty, chipper, rambling prose, I couldn't help but imagine The Roadbuilder as the very worst of dinner guests; and so I was tickled to find that he describes an evening in which he played that very role. MacKendrick's companions were fellows in the fight against the Hun. Officers all, a safe distance from the front, their time at the table was pleasant until MacKendrick "chucked out something about the Jews." He's soon interrupted by a dining companion, who whispers in his ear:

> "You know Major Blank is a Jew."
>
> Major Blank sat next to me on my left. Of course, I knew he was a Jew, as did everyone else, because he had the typical Jew nose and face, and the Jews' business capacity. I relied out loud: "He is a first cousin of mine! The Major belongs to the tribe of Judah, while I am from the Tribe of Benjamin, on my mother's side and from the tribe of Gad on my father's side."
>
> Turning to the Major I said, "By the way, Major, I suppose you remember that the Bible said of your people the Jews (Isaiah iii. 9):

'The shew of their countenance doth witness against them'? And so down through the ages, you can always tell a Jew as far away as you can see his face."

And then, in keeping with his beliefs, MacKendrick goes on to explain that the Jews are being persecuted "for having rejected and crucified our Lord." Later in the book, The Roadbuilder writes of the "synagogue of Satan," the "New York Jewish Bankers" supporting Lenin and Trotsky, and reports that "1,766,118 murders were perpetrated in Russia by the Jewish Reds."

As with The Roadbuilder's other works, a strong stench of anti-Semitism pervades. I should add here that MacKendrick was not a churchgoer; indeed, he spills a significant amount of ink ridiculing men of the cloth for failing to recognize the Brith'ish as the true children of Israel. "I have never joined a church," he writes with pride—a claim at odds with his Great War papers, where he recorded his religion as Church of England.

My copy of *The Destiny of The British Empire and The U.S.A.* is the "Fourteenth Revised Edition." I've not seen the previous thirteen, published over a period of thirty-six years, but wonder whether there have been any revisions at all. Published in April 1957, my version includes these predictions:

What does this mean to you? Since these material, earthy, and national promises dated for 1917 and all previous dates have been fulfilled, what about those for 1921, 1922, and 1923, and so on to 1936 when Armageddon is to be finished? You can depend on it that every divinely inspired prophecy from 1917 to 1936 will come true at the allotted time.

No less than three editions, thirteen thousand copies in all, were published after MacKendrick's Armageddon. Twenty-one years after the anticipated apocalypse, it seems that The Roadbuilder felt no need to revise his prophesy... at least not here. In 1942, during that other World War, MacKendrick published *This IS Armageddon! God Wins it for Britain and America*, a much slimmer volume in which he has the final battle taking place before the autumn of 1943, with Adolf Hitler literally pitching a tent in the shadow of Mount Carmel.

MacKendrick died a nonagenarian in 1959, by which time the Anglo-Israelism banner had been taken up by American Herbert W.

Armstrong, his son Garner Ted Armstrong, and their Worldwide Church of Christ (né Radio Church of God). Faded and torn, it's carried on by weak, stumbling folk today.

Now, of course, we have to contend with Rick Perry, his friends in the anti-Semitic American Family Association, and the hysterical New Apostolic Reformation Movement.

Carry on, Brith'ish Businessmen

Does it not make sense that The Roadbuilder and Henry Ford were friends? After all, the two captains of industry had much in common, not the least of which was a shared interest in the paving of America. Both were anti-union, pro-prohibition, and both believed that Jews were to blame for much of the world's ills. Though not a strong proponent of Anglo-Israelism like his pal, Ford furthered the movement through his newspaper, the notorious *Dearborn Independent*. The April 16, 1927 edition featured what is likely W.G. MacKendrick's most widely circulated piece of writing:

Does the Bible Predict Peace?

The answer is a definite No! There can be no world-wide peace for the next ten years. Students of Bible Prophecy may differ on some points, but I know of none who does not agree we are still in the Era of war.

The late war was referred to in the press as Armageddon, a name given in Scripture to the last struggle in which the forces of international evil are finally to be destroyed. The Bible indicates that Armageddon has yet to be fought and won and learned men look for it between the years 1928 and 1936.

The Bible describes this last war as the Great day of God Almighty in which Jehovah, in an unmistakable manner, shows the nations of the earth that He rules on Earth as in Heaven. The Chief Prince of Rish (Russia) will under Prussian guidance head the thirteen nations who start to wipe Anglo-Saxondom off the face of this earth. China will be with Russia, also Persia, Turkestan, parts of India, Abyssinia and most Mohammedan peoples of Asia and Africa will be brought into the Russian circle of things to fight against Anglo-Saxondom in Armageddon.

And that's just the synopsis.

Eight months later, felled by a libel lawsuit, the racist rag was no more. Its editor, long-time Ford employee William J. Cameron, took the bullet for his boss. It was a good gig while it lasted, one that carried a certain amount of weight. In 1923, for example, Cameron had been invited to speak in Toronto before the Empire Club of Canada. Sadly, he took ill, so members never got to hear "Mr. Henry Ford, the Man and his IDEAS and IDEALS." Enter MacKendrick, who instead provided rambling recollections of the automaker, concluding with a lengthy account of a conversation he and Ford had shared on Anglo-Israelism.

This was not the first the Empire Club had heard of the movement. Just seven months earlier, MacKendrick had spoken before the club on this very topic. His address, "Allenby's Campaign As Laid Down in the Bible," not only encapsulates much of the material found in *The Destiny of The British Empire and The U.S.A.*, but includes an alternate version of his dinner with "Major Blank" (here called "Major Leon"):

One night, in that little village of Clarques, to make a little conversation during dinner I said something about the Jews. Somebody sitting next me whispered that Major Leon (who was sitting on my right) was a Jew! I said, "Yes, Major Leon is a Jew, he is a first cousin of mine, because I am a Hebrew of the tribe of Benjamin. And by the way, Major, did you know that we are going to take Palestine, and that we are going to give it to you hook-nosed people for a national home?" [Laughter]

The members of the Empire Club, of which MacKendrick was one, don't exactly come off well here, so I was surprised to see that the text of the address, all 4,342 words of it, is on the Club's website.

"An amusing analogy of the Bible being a story of the British Empire," reads the description.

Not to these eyes.

The Canada Doctor: First Visit

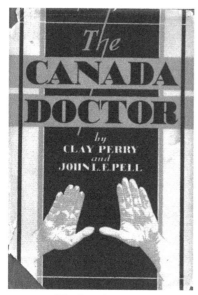

The Canada Doctor
Clay Perry and John L.E. Pell
Toronto: Thomas Allen, 1933
361 pages

This is not a Canadian book, but a book about a Canadian. Or is it? *The Canada Doctor* is an odd beast: a 361-page advertisement in the form of a novel infused with the stink of anti-Semitism.

Its authors were American. Perry and Pell penned one other book, *Hell's Acres* (1921), "a historical novel of the wild East in the '50s," but appear to have made more money when working apart. Of the two, Pell was probably the more prosperous. In 1922, he wrote the script for the silent film *Down to the Sea in Ships*, and two years later provided the "historical arrangement" to D.W. Griffith's *America*. The latter was a sweeping epic centred on the Revolutionary War, the former a crummy flick starring the stunning Clara Bow. I choose the former.

The Canada Doctor may be long, but it tells a very simple story. We start in a New York flower shop, Feidlestein's, where young Millie Waters pricks her lily-white hands preparing wreaths for the bereaved. Much younger sister Joan spends her days at Millie's feet until her dog, Crinkles, dashes out the door after the shop's cat. The little girl joins the chase and is immediately struck by a passing limousine. She's swept up by young Milt Feidlestein, who does damage to his face by inadvertently running into the back of a truck. It's all a bit comical, but we're not meant to laugh; this is serious stuff. Joan ends up unconscious in a Manhattan hospital, while her bumbling rescuer contemplates plastic surgery.

Nearly everyone in *The Canada Doctor* is dealing with a health issue of some sort. The widowed Mrs Waters, mother of Millie and Joan, is bedridden with inflammatory rheumatism; their landlady, Bridget Hogan, is a fellow sufferer; neighbour Mrs Rubinoff is slowly being crippled by ill-fitting footwear; and rich guy Hector Farrington, whose limo struck Joan, struggles with advanced arthritis and the lingering effects of a *femme fatale*.

The answer to all their problems just might be found in Dr Rocke, the Canada Doctor. First mentioned on page forty-nine, he immediately becomes the subject of considerable debate. Is Rocke a miracle man, as Bridget Hogan claims, or "a toe-twister who plays upon the imaginations of women and weak-minded persons," as Farrington contends? How is the reader to know? Roche remains up in Canada—off-camera, as D.W. would've said—practising medicine in a small Ontario town not far from Cornwall. After a great deal of humming and hawing and hand-wringing, Mrs Waters, Joan, Millie, Milt, Mrs Rubinoff, and her daughter Becky make their way north to see for themselves. Milt's physician, Dr Rettstein, joins in. Oh, and let's not forget Hector Farrington, along with his chauffeur and his housemaid.

It's not until page 310 that we get so much as a fleeting glimpse of the title character. The Canada Doctor returns six pages later, in a scene that seems designed to settle debate as to his talent. Surrounded by the afflicted, Rocke sits on a screw chair, which he uses to move from one to the next:

> He held a stockinged foot in his hands. He rested it on one of his bent knees and with both hands made a quick movement, bending the foot. Then he released it and reached for another. His hands passed from black sock to flesh colored stocking; from cotton to silk. The flexing operation was repeated.
>
> His movements were like those of some elaborate and precise machine, a machine which worked on gears, revolving and selecting in synchronized adjustment.

Rocke's healing hands have a particularly dramatic effect on Farrington. Resting his swollen right foot on the doctor's knee, the sceptical millionaire experiences a shock:

> Involuntarily he jerked back, but the pain was momentary. It was gone. It was followed by a creeping feeling of warmth, as if blood flowed again in a chilled and atrophied member.

And so, as blood appears to begin flowing again in his member, Farrington realizes his love for Millie. Is it necessary to report that this is the climax of the novel? The millionaire and the flower girl are soon in each other's arms. Here's the passage, presented exactly as it appears in the book:

He circled her waist and drew her up to him. She became breathless... as he bent his head and kissed her soft lips... and her tears became rainbows in the sun... and the petals and apple blossoms fell upon his head and shoulders... and he did not brush them off... for her lips were like petals and the sweet scent of these flowers of Canada which have perfume was as incense to his soul...

Hard to read... and I haven't even got to the anti-Semitic stuff.

The Canada Doctor: Second Visit

"A NOVEL OF TO-DAY" proclaims the title page. "A Romantic Novel" counters the dust jacket. A knee-jerk reaction favours the latter. Flip to the final pages and you'll find Milt Feidlestein falling for Rebecca Rubinoff as Hector Farrington's chauffeur and housemaid stroll hand in hand through an idyllic rural setting. Their employer follows with Millie Waters, "walking slowly beneath the arched torrent of petals which fluttered down at a breath of wind or a touch against branches or twigs."

It's no wonder that the closing scene belongs to Millie—this is her love story. An "exquisite young woman, fair of skin and hair, blue of eyes, budding like a flower, an uncanonized angel in disposition," from the beginning she arouses passion in very nearly every unattached male she encounters. Milt, for one, moons over her from across the floor of Feidelstein's Flower Shop. He's "worshipfully in love with this pretty *goy* girl," but cannot act. You see, though Milt works hard to transform himself into an "All-American," he cannot imagine this "earthly angel condescending to the low level of the 'kike kid.'" So, it's his father, Isaac, who makes the first move by wrapping an arm around Millie's waist and holding her tight with his "claw-like" hand: "*Nu, nu,* you shouldn't be foolish about old Isaac, my dear! It is no goot trying to... Dese leetle gold-diggers, dey vant to remember who is de real sugar-papa. Not any of my moneys vill you get for noddinks, remember."

Millie rejects the old man, as we knew she would, though her words come as a surprise: "I don't vant your money—or Milton's either, if that's what you think. I hate you! I hate you both, you cheap kike!" Undaunted, Isaac continues his pursuit:

"You say you don't vant Milt? You hate him? Vell, you don't hate his moneys. You couldn't haff *him,* anyvay. I guess so you don't vant him! You vant him bad enough. You *goy* girls is all alike, you. It vill giff anyt'ink for moneys. Yah, efen to such old fellers as me. Vy not? Get friendly vit de pocket-book. It is a sugar-papa dat you vant. I am it for you, eh?"

You'd think this sort of exchange between employer and employee would lead to termination. Maybe—but just moments later Crinkles runs into traffic, Joan is hit by the limo, and Milt has his unfortunate facial encounter with the truck.

You gotta wonder just what Milt hits. A handle? A taillight? Whatever it is, the thing alters his appearance, leaving a wound that makes him look "entirely the Jew." When Millie visits his hospital room, she finds it hard to hide her revulsion. Milt understands: "Oh, I know I look the kike I am, just now... I've seen myself in a mirror. You now see Milton Feidlestein as he really is—and as he will be, when he is old. A Jew, a cheap kike..."

So much self-loathing, and yet Milt is such a good guy. He not only covers Joan's stay in the hospital, but brings her ailing mother to see saintly Dr Rocke. "Begorry, 'tis a big-hearted kike," remarks cabby Red Hogan. "There's a lad with a soul, even though he is a Jew," observes his sister-in-law Hattie.

Authors Perry and Pell torture poor Milt, but there's purpose behind the pain, a message that is none too subtle: stick with your own kind. Just look to the example set by the Hogans, Irish immigrants whose marriage, the only one depicted in the novel, is happy. (Though Bridget does sometimes worry about her mate's weight: "That man of mine is like to get hungry any toime. I've knowed him to eat two breakfasts and three lunches and a dinner in wan day, fergitful loike, such an appetite he has.")

So it is that, in the end, long-suffering Milt comes to realize that he belongs with a Jewess who had "always thought him wonderful," and Farrington's loyal chauffeur shows that he knows his place by hooking up with fellow servant Hattie. Meanwhile, Farrington himself declares his love for Millie, but only after learning that she comes from a wealthy family that went into decline because her heroic father was crippled in the Great War.

All three couples move toward matrimony, but not before encountering the novel's last sentence: "It is love."

So, yes, "A Novel of Romance"—but in 1933, the year Adolf Hitler came to power, *The Canada Doctor* was also very much "A NOVEL OF TO-DAY."

The Canada Doctor: Final Visit

In their foreword to *The Canada Doctor*, Clay Perry and John L.E. Pell ward off lawsuits:

> ...characters are fictional but in them will be found a composite of the hundreds of thousands who have not only sought soundness of body but have fought for faith and so have learned, as the great healer says in the story, that...

Well, you get the idea.

The novel's dust jacket is much more forthcoming. We learn, for example, that Perry "found in the northlands of Ontario a character in whom there was more romance than any he ever created, and, in collaboration with John L.E. Pell, re-created in 'Dr. Rocke of Johnsburg' a fictional counterpart of this man whose real name is on many lips."

This romantic figure of whom so many lips speak is Dr M.W. Locke of Williamsburg, Ontario. Forgotten today, in his time Locke was both very famous and very controversial. A medical man, a miracle man, or a charlatan, the country doctor was celebrated the world over as one who could cure arthritis, rheumatism, and related ailments by simply manipulating a patient's foot. Locke was visited by people from every continent save Antarctica, and is said to have treated as many as 2,500 souls a day. An exaggeration to be sure—no one was really keeping count—but there's no doubt that the number was very high.

Once and future prime minister Mackenzie King was treated in this manner, as was the novelist Rex Beach. The latter wrote an enthusiastic piece for *Cosmopolitan* describing a treatment that lasted no more than twenty seconds.

Locke lived a modest life—his death in 1942 came while cranking up his old Ford—yet he made a great deal of money. These earnings came not only from his practice, but from sales of the shoes that bore his name.

Of his own design, they were sold exclusively through Simpson's in Halifax, Montreal, Hamilton, and Regina. George H. Wilkinson sold them in Windsor. Americans had a handy advertisement that appeared on the back jacket of *The Canada Doctor*. Clear evidence, I think, that after publication authors Perry and Pell remained welcome at Dr Locke's table.

A Quiet Revolution and
Still Cowards Complain

The Squeaking Wheel;
Or, How I Learned to Stop Worrying
About the French and Love the Bomb
John Mercer [pseud.]
n.p.: Rubicon, 1966
103 pages

Let's get rid of this so as to not track it into tomorrow.

I came upon *The Squeaking Wheel* in an Ontario thrift shop; its bold, if inept declaration—"4TH. [sic] PRINTING OF THE BEST-SELLING BOOK ALL CANADA'S TALKING ABOUT!"—did attract.

I don't remember talk of this book; but then I was only just learning to speak when *The Squeaking Wheel* was first published. Sure looks like it was popular. The copyright page records four printings in three months! Two in February 1966 alone! In the foreword, author John Mercer tells us that the first two printings amounted to "many thousands" of copies. So why is this the only one I've ever seen? And why was there no fifth printing?

I'd ask John Mercer, but he's a fabrication, a pseudonym for two men to hide behind. "English-speaking Montrealers who have a curious desire not to be blown sky-high to a Protestant Heaven by a few well-placed sticks of dynamite," they reveal nothing more about themselves than that they work in the fields of advertising and medicine. Even today their identities are a mystery.

More furious than funny, those familiar with Rebel Media comment pages will recognize the John Mercer style. Irrational anger and uncontrolled ranting accompany fantastical statistics presented without citation. Quotations, even those pitching the book, lack attribution. It's all here, including that old saw about Quebecers being horrible drivers: "It has often been said by opponents of French-Canada that one way to solve the problem of Quebec is to give every inhabitant a car and turn all the traffic lights green for one day."

Take care now. Those words come not from the authors, but the "opponents of French-Canada." Or so the John Mercer men would have you believe. The reader will soon recognize that they too are opponents.

The Quiet Revolution is five years old, the Bi and Bi Commission is just beginning, and already the authors, who "have lived all their adult lives in Quebec," are fed up. Their message is clear: "Quebec is a conquered country and its people are a conquered people"... and somewhat inferior:

> We are a little tired of hearing about biculturalism and French-Canadian culture. We don't quite agree with a noted politician who recently said the only thing French-Canadian culture has produced is strip-teaser Lily St. Cyr and hockey-player "Rocket" Richard.

Again, don't you be pinning this on John Mercer. That stuff about the stripper and the hockey player comes from some politician. Who? Who knows. The men behind the pseudonym are only repeating what they've heard, and they don't quite agree.

Not quite.

The Squeaking Wheel was never talked about by "everyone in Canada"; not even Montreal's English- and French-language presses gave it much attention. Serious discussion of the book is limited to a few sentences in journalist Solange Chaput-Rolland's *Reflections* (1968):

> The pens of these English-speaking compatriots are certainly not very brave. Of course it is true that, when one describes unpleasant reality, one receives in return unpleasant insult. But liberty of speech demands the dignity and courage of that speech. And those who hurl invective at their compatriots, while keeping themselves well hidden, are not really respectable citizens.

Though I can't top that, I'll add that I don't think the cowards hiding behind the pseudonym were Montrealers. Real Montrealers know it's Lili, not "Lily"; and they know she was not French-Canadian, but American.

I'll add that we Canadians know not to hyphenate "hockey player." There, sweet Virginia, I've scraped the shit right off my shoe.

The Hairdresser as Straight Man

The Happy Hairdresser
Nicholas Loupos
Richmond Hill, ON: Pocket, 1973
175 pages

The first thing the author wants you to know is that he's no queer. Sure, there are plenty of "bloody faggots" polluting the industry, but he's not one of the "fairy nice boys." A red-blooded son of Sparta, for Nicholas Loupos it's all about "pussie." He wants you to know that, too.

Messy, unfocused, and something of an ego trip, *The Happy Hairdresser* is nevertheless remarkable in that its author not only chose to publish this memoir under his own name, but display it in his London, Ontario beauty salon. No entrepreneur myself, both decisions raise all sorts of questions, most concerning the wisdom in boasting about bedding customers and their daughters—one of whom is sixteen. Frankly, I cannot fathom how publishing this wouldn't be bad for business:

In this permissive promiscuous society, while the mother is chasing her lover and the father is chasing his secretary, naturally their able-bodied daughter is trying to get in her kicks as well. And since she holds true to that old adage "Like mother, like daughter," the best place to get the ball rolling is at the beauty salon.

A copy of the *Sensual Woman* [sic] in one hand, and a fresh joint of marijuana in the other, she parks herself in your chair, jiggles her unfettered boobs, and eyes you shamelessly while you try to avoid chopping off an innocent ear. No wonder the majority of hairdressers suffer from such occupational ailments as ulcers, bad nerves, strained eye muscles, and swallowed glands.

Since more often than not these hot-ass Lolitas are high on booze, sex, or drugs—occasionally all three—and because they are easier to make than females in any other age group, and for more obvious reasons, they are the hairdressers' pets.

Times change and so do people—hell, Burton Cummings did in just one season. Still, I was surprised that Pocket, a division of Simon & Schuster, soon to be acquired by Gulf+Western, would've published so crummy and hate-filled a book. At first I blamed editor Jock Carroll—photographer, really—the man responsible for much of the crap sold at United Cigar Stores during the Trudeau years. Then I learned that Pocket's New York parent published its own edition the very same month. I've not seen it myself, but understand that all mention of things Canadian were removed, even from the cover.

Critic William French expresses his appreciation in the February 5, 1974 *Globe and Mail*:

If they want to claim it, they're welcome to it, and let's just hope that American readers don't find out where it came from. It's a badly written piece of junk, and to identify it as Canadian would deal our cultural heritage a severe blow.

Seems pretty harsh, though French does allow that *The Happy Hairdresser* might, *just might*, have some sort of sociological value.

What did this reader learn? I learned that the vast majority of women's hairdressers are straight, and that most women own two or three wigs.

Or have times changed?

The Bigots of Yesteryear

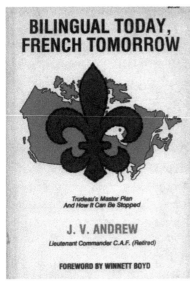

BILINGUAL TODAY, FRENCH TOMORROW

*Trudeau's Master Plan
And How It Can Be Stopped*

J. V. ANDREW
Lieutenant Commander C.A.F. (Retired)

FOREWORD BY WINNETT BOYD

*Bilingual Today, French Tomorrow:
Trudeau's Master Plan and
How It Can Be Stopped*
J.V. Andrew
Richmond Hill, ON: BMG, 1977
137 pages

Author Jock Andrew once claimed that *Bilingual Today, French Tomorrow* sold over one hundred thousand copies. While I don't doubt it, the laziest of investigations reveals that pretty well every figure in the book is false.

Bilingual Today, French Tomorrow is the work of a bigot who, expecting to be labelled as such, attempts a pre-emptive strike. "We are not really sure of what a bigot does," he tells the reader, "and therefore anyone can readily be called a bigot without having anything proved."

I know what a bigot does, and will add that there's proof enough here. Let's begin with Andrew's description of French Canadians as a race. Quebec, which they control, is "an impregnable bastion, breeding-pen, and marshalling-yard for the colonization of the rest of Canada with both French-Canadians and with imported, made-in-France, Frenchmen."

When Andrew wrote these words, made-in-France Frenchmen comprised two percent of all immigrants to Canada. But never mind that. What lingers is the image of the breeding-pen, a fixture decried as part of "Quebec's breeding-project," in which French Canadian families are "little more than breeding units. Work, to many family-heads in this category, becomes pretty much a take-it-or-leave-it affair." Andrew will also have you know that in Quebec cars are used primarily to ferry fathers between home and the local tavern.

Andrew's contention—he dares call it conspiracy—is that Pierre Trudeau, Gérard Pelletier, and shadow-player Marc Lalonde were seeking "the takeover of Canada for the French-Canadian race." The goal would be achieved within a matter of mere years under cover of programs promoting bilingualism. English-speaking Canadians would find "their country" colonized, and watch helplessly as "the relative population ratios of English-to-French swing from 75:25 to 50:50 to 30:70 to 10:90 to 0:100."

Quel désastre!

"There is nothing that has come out of Quebec or French-Canada that I can think of that is either particularly distinctive or particularly desirable," writes Andrew. Lest my French-Canadian wife take this to heart I rush to add that the author also thinks little of Canadians as a whole, writing that we would all trade living in Canada for Florida.

Andrew's opinion of the country he swore to defend is dimmer still: "The marriage of Quebec with English-speaking Canada was at best a shotgun affair. It was brought about for the sole purpose of putting up a united front against the United States in 1867." Should Trudeau's nefarious plans be thwarted, he believes that it's just a matter of time before English-speaking Canada opts for union with the republic to the south. "Hollywood has made Americans and English-speaking Canadians one and the same people"—or didn't you know that?

Anyone wondering why the English-speaking Canadians of 1977 couldn't see "the French racial takeover of Canada" must recognize that the media was both suppressed and in the pay of the Trudeau government; *Reader's Digest* is given special mention. Andrew contends that Gérard Pelletier "imposed just as an effective censorship on Canada as was exercised on Nazi Germany." Doubters will find evidence in the 1974 Dominion Day celebrations on Parliament Hill:

> The program definitely put Mr. Pelletier at least on a plane with Dr. Goebbels. I can recall a movie-cut of Hitler slapping one of his cronies on the back and doing a little jig on the occasion of the French surrender during World War II. I can just imagine Mr. Trudeau in the same role, during that performance on Parliament Hill, slapping Gerard [sic] Pelletier on the back, and saying, "Hey old buddy, you sure gave it to them that time."

Yes, Andrew can imagine. He imagines that he lives in a country in which he might be imprisoned for his words. He imagines that he lives in a Canada in which those accused of bigotry are beaten, stoned, and shot. He imagines unseating Pierre Trudeau through a Progressive

Conservative/Parti Québécois alliance—all the while lamenting: "in many other countries, the actions of Mr. Trudeau and Mr. Pelletier would have long since resulted in a revolt by the military and a hasty execution of those two politicians."

Most of all, he imagines "racial chaos" that has, in his mind, brought the country to the brink of civil war. Andrew tells of witnessing an Ottawa bus driver hurl an insult at a Quebec motorist:

> If some French-Canadian passenger on the bus, or another driver, or a pedestrian, had taken issue with that bus driver, there would have been a fight. And what is important is that there wouldn't have been just two people involved, because I would have been in it too. And I would have been on the side of the bus driver. And I would have been in that fight dressed in the uniform of a Lieutenant Commander in Canada's Armed Forces.
>
> My point is this. Canada is just one hot afternoon and one small incident away from open hostility.

Let us imagine a uniformed member of Armed Forces working not to diffuse, but to inflame such a situation. Let us imagine him doing so in the belief that his actions might be the spark that leads to great bloodshed. Let us give thanks that Lieutenant Commander Andrew is no longer an active member of our Armed Forces.

Richard Rohmer's *Retaliation:*
The Chairmen Rave

Retaliation
Richard Rohmer
Toronto: PaperJacks
298 pages

I wonder when Eaton's closed down its book department. Well before the end, wasn't it? I know it was still going on June 26, 1986, because that day I visited the downtown Montreal store where Jacques Hébert was signing copies of his most recent book. I bought a copy for my mum.

No one else showed up. A publicist tried to slow my departure by taking photos. Somewhere out there are shots of me with the senator (I'm wearing a Batman T-shirt). The only other book I can remember ever buying at Eaton's was a copy of Robert Harlow's *Scann* that had been marked down to twenty-five cents (on the cover, in the tradition of yard sales).

No one really went to Eaton's for books. Yet the lone paperback edition of Richard Rohmer's *Retaliation* provides strong evidence that the store's president, chairman, and CEO was also a reader and a critic in providing the cover blurb: "This romp has appropriate amounts of financial ledger-demain, unscrupulous political acts, violence and romance. Lots of action and lots of fun."

Romp isn't the right word, nor is "ledger-demain" (he means legerdemain), but unscrupulous political acts, violence, and romance do figure. Whether their amounts are appropriate depend, I think, on individual taste. Romance barely registers, levels of violence and political activity are a touch lower than one might expect in a thriller. Legerdemain is simply not in evidence.

The story is really quite simple: Paul James, former executive of the "Canadian International Bank of Canada," comes up with a plan that would see the bank team up with the "Toronto Depository Bank" and

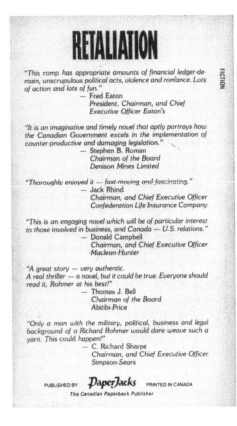

Saudi Arabia to purchase "BankAmerica." Such is his confidence in the scheme that he commits $100 million of his own money—made in "the oil patch in Calgary"—to the effort. CIBC chairman Ross Harris encourages his old colleague to team up with the "Royal Canadian Bank," the "Bank of Montreal-Quebec," and Kuwait to also buy "Citicorp." There's no competition between banks, it seems.

Paul moves fast. Within two weeks, he has rented a Swiss castle, loaded it with computers, and begun buying stock in both American banks. Disaster threatens when the Mafia abduct the computer supplier and his ugly daughter. This proves a momentary glitch. The ransom is paid, the kidnappers are killed, and the money is returned. The Mafia seek revenge, but fail. This being fiction, they throw in the towel.

By the end of the fourth trading day Paul has succeeded in getting a controlling interest in the two banks, thereby earning $1.86 million on his investment. Washington is pissed and imposes strict sanctions and the Canadian economy collapses, resulting in "a depression worse than that of the 1930s." Paul suns himself at his Barbados getaway.

FIN

"This could happen!" C. Richard Sharpe, Chairman and CEO of Simpson-Sears, exclaims. Frankly, I thought the whole thing so patently absurd that any criticism would be stating the obvious. Allow me this small observation: Paul's risky investment brings a return of 1.86

percent. Though inflation is in the double digits, this is portrayed as considerable. As a result of American sanctions, the value of the Canadian dollar falls to sixty cents U.S. The downturn appears to have no effect on Paul's fortune. At the end of the novel, the Canadian banks are on the brink of collapse. Ross Harris regrets nothing.

What do I know? I'm no business executive.

Thomas J. Bell, chairman of the board at Abitibi-Price, echoes C. Richard Sharpe with "very authentic… it could be true."

Who else do we have?

Well, there's Stephen B. Roman, who once tried to sue Pierre Trudeau for coming out against the sale of an Ontario uranium mine to the Americans. Seems he still held a grudge.

There's also Donald Campbell, Chairman and CEO of Maclean-Hunter, publisher of Rohmer's *The Green North*. Bit of a book connection there, as there is with Jack Rhind, who, apart from being Chairman and CEO of Confederation Life, was a director with Cannon Book Distribution.

Not a banker among them, I note.

Bilingual Today, French Tomorrow Redux

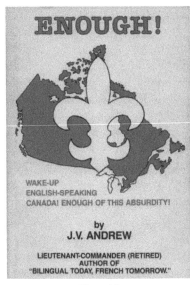

ENOUGH!

WAKE-UP
ENGLISH-SPEAKING
CANADA! ENOUGH OF THIS ABSURDITY!

by
J.V. ANDREW

LIEUTENANT-COMMANDER (RETIRED)
AUTHOR OF
"BILINGUAL TODAY, FRENCH TOMORROW."

Enough!
J.V. Andrew
Kitchener, ON: Andrew Books, 1988
153 pages

How very far away yesterday's tomorrow seems. In 1977, the year Jock Andrew's *Bilingual Today, French Tomorrow* made a splash, the Blue Jays played their first game, Jimmy Carter pardoned Vietnam draft dodgers, and plucky Sid Vicious turned twenty. I myself turned fifteen. Iggy Pop's *Lust for Life* was released on my birthday. The song "Sixteen" comes from that album. In 1977, I thought of sixteen-year-old girls as elusive older women.

Iggy is still with us; so too is Jock Andrew. The last I saw him was in a choppy video from 2013 that someone uploaded to YouTube. I don't expect you to watch it—it's not worth it, really—so I will go ahead and tell you that it ends with a map of Canada being flushed down a toilet.

Jock Andrew doesn't much care for this country and is pretty sure you don't either. He himself prefers Spain, and assures the reader he'll be gone in two years if things don't change.

Bilingual Today, French Tomorrow was all about Pierre Trudeau's secret plan to make Canada a unilingual country ruled by French-speaking overlords. As evidence, Andrew pulled facts and figures from his ass.

Eleven years later, *Enough!* finds Andrew in a bitter mood tinged with regret. Our lieutenant-commander (ret'd) ended *Bilingual Today, French Tomorrow* with dreams of glory: a military coup, a civil war, or, at the very least, a scuffle on an OC Transpo bus. Andrew had pledged to stand up to "the French racial-takeover of Canada," and was willing to risk jail time for his bold stance. Instead, he crumbled at the first confrontation—a television interview with Toronto physician Morton Shulman, in which he was called out for pulling stuff out of his ass.

Why did Andrew pull stuff out of his ass? "Because hard facts were impossible to obtain when I was writing the book," the author sniffs in defence.

Andrew writes in *Enough!* that the exchange with Shulman left him traumatized. I write that Andrew learned nothing from the experience. *Enough!* presents still more pieces of his shit. For example, Andrew would have me believe that my wife, like all French Canadians, "is sworn by secret oath to the extermination of English Canada and the English language." He claims that her church is "dedicated to the single goal of avenging the French defeat of 1759." He'll tell you that Catholic Pierre Trudeau issued thousands of secret Cabinet Directives:

Are you aware that through these secret Cabinet Directives there are units of Canada's Armed Forces that are organized and trained for the sole purpose of subduing any signs of civil or political unrest in English-speaking Canada?

Are you aware that through these secret Cabinet directives [sic], provision exists for emptying Canada's jails to accommodate dissident English-speaking Canadians in case English-speaking Canada wakes up?

Do you wonder why such an effort has been made to convert the RCMP to French-speaking control when the Province of Quebec doesn't even use the RCMP?

Are you aware that French-Canadian Mounted Policemen have been planted in every city and town in English-speaking Canada to spy and report on English-speaking Canadians who may not agree with the total Frenchification of this country?

Are you aware that Trudeau created a secret service for the express purpose of spying on people such as myself who have chosen to think for themselves?

Jock Andrew's vivid imagination is matched by those of his readers'. Dozens of pages are devoted to letters he received in response to the earlier book, the first coming from a fellow who had dared express "something similar" about French Canadians. "I was regarded as a racist," he gripes, before proclaiming his support of apartheid in South Africa and Ian Smith's Rhodesia. Likeminded *volks*, Andrew's correspondents consider gun control a means of keeping English-Canadians in line, believe the Canadian International Development Agency funnels money to the

IRA, and see Hitler "as a 'nice man' when compared with the likes of Trudeau." Canadian peacekeepers are alleged to be collaborating with Cuban mercenaries in Africa.

In *Bilingual Today, French Tomorrow*, Andrew urged Joe Clark and René Lévesque to work together to take Quebec out of Confederation. But that was *so* 1977. *Enough!* sees him advising Saskatchewan, Alberta, British Columbia, and the Northwest Territories to separate, while at the same time issuing English-speaking Canadians a call to action:

> If every last one of us doesn't get off our rear-ends right now, we and our children and our grandchildren will have lost this country before we've had time to figure out what has happened. I'm not talking in terms of years now. I'm talking about months.

Over four hundred and eighty months have passed since *Enough!* was published. Canada remains a united, bilingual country. French continues to be taught in our schools and our cereal boxes are still printed in both official languages.

So, what is Jock Andrew doing here? He promised us he'd be moving to Spain.

CATHOLICS &
CLERGYMEN

Maria Monk's Immortal Book

Awful Disclosures of Maria Monk; or, The Hidden Secrets of a Nun's Life Exposed!
Manchester: Milner & Co., n.d.
192 pages

Born, raised, and educated in Montreal, I knew nothing of poor Maria Monk and her trials and tribulations until my university years, when I happened upon a brief mention of her while researching a paper. A casual, entirely unscientific survey of acquaintances and friends suggests that my experience is unique only in that I learned of her at a relatively early age. Most had never encountered Miss Monk's name—and yet, since its initial publication her *Awful Disclosures* has sold hundreds of thousands of copies under dozens of imprints. Forget *Bonheur d'occasion*, never mind *The Apprenticeship of Duddy Kravitz*, this is the best-selling work of fiction ever set in Montreal.

When first published in January 1836, this Gothic tale of horror, with its secret doors, underground tunnels, and subterranean prisons, was presented as fact. Maria Monk, once a nun at the Hôtel-Dieu convent, had bravely stepped forward to expose the true nature of the Roman Catholic Church.

Her story, as presented, is a simple one. The daughter of uncaring, non-observant Protestants, she chooses the Catholic faith and, after a failed marriage, takes the veil. That very afternoon, her horrors begin:

> Father Dufresne called me out, saying he wished to speak with me. I feared what was his intention; but dared not disobey. In a private apartment, he treated me in a brutal manner; and from two other priests, I afterward received similar usage that evening. Father

Dufresne afterward appeared again, and I was compelled to remain in company with him until morning.

It is, as Maria soon learns, the will of Pope Gregory XVI that the nuns perform "some peculiar deeds." What exactly does the *pontiff* have in mind? She cannot say—these are acts "of which no decent or moral person could ever endure to speak." The Pope's will ends up as just one in a series of shocking revelations. The reader learns of diseased priests who take "Holy Retreat" in secret rooms, where they are tended by the sisters. Infants born of priests and nuns are baptized, smothered, and thrown into lime pits in the convent's cellar. Uncooperative nuns are beaten and murdered. In her fifth year as a novice, pregnant with a baby fathered by Abbé Patrick Phelan (1795–1857), Maria escapes the nunnery, and with surprising ease makes her way south to the sanctuary of a New York City almshouse.

The *Dictionary of Canadian Biography* describes Maria Monk as an author. I'm not so sure. Indeed, I wonder whether her use of writing instruments progressed much beyond childhood, when she stuck a pencil in her ear (causing brain damage). The Catholic institution in which she was housed was not a nunnery, but an asylum dedicated to the reformation of prostitutes. To what extent the awful disclosures stemmed from Maria Monk's messed-up mind is lost to history. The book was, at the very least, set down by other hands: American Presbyterian ministers J.J. Slocum and George Bourne, Reverend William K. Hoyt of the Canadian Benevolent Society, and New Yorker Theodore Dwight (author of the anti-papist novel *The Roman Republic of 1849*). We know this because of numerous court proceedings—most concerning squabbles over the enormous amounts of money Maria's story generated.

Like any successful franchise, there were illustrated editions, sequels, and spin-offs. The most noteworthy was *Further Disclosures of Maria Monk Concerning the Hotel Dieu Nunnery of Montreal*, published in 1837, the very same year that she fled her Presbyterian minders. As might be expected, tracts were released by people on both sides attempting to get in on the game. Among the first were *Decisive Confirmation of the Awful Disclosures of Maria Monk, Proving Her Residence in the Hotel Dieu Nunnery, and the Existence of the Subterranean Passages* and *Awful Exposure of the Atrocious Plot Formed by Certain Individuals Against the Clergy and Nuns of Lower Canada, Through the Intervention of Maria Monk*. It was claimed that another book, *The Escape of Saint Francis Patrick, Another Nun of the Hotel Dieu*, was written by a nun Maria had known. The last in this sorry parade, *Maria Monk's Daughter*, purportedly the autobiography of her second child, was published in 1875, twenty-six years after Maria's death in a New York City prison. She'd been arrested in a brothel after robbing a john.

Maria Monk's image has undergone a number of makeovers—as has her book. One 1970 edition replaces the title with *Terror Behind Locked Doors* and pitches itself as "A BOOK THAT WILL NOT DIE." Nearly four decades later, the bold claim has held true—in fact, *Awful Disclosures of Maria Monk* has never been out of print, and lives on at several internet sites run by anti-Catholic kooks and conspiracy theorists.

Of War and Methodism
(But Mostly Methodism)

Neville Trueman, the Pioneer Preacher:
A Tale of the War of 1812
W.H. Withrow
Toronto: William Briggs, 1900
252 pages

"Towards the close of a sultry day in July, in the year 1812, might have been seen a young man riding along the beautiful west bank of the Niagara River," begins *Neville Trueman, the Pioneer Preacher.* The key word here is "might." A young man *might* have been seen riding. That young man *might* have been a Methodist preacher. That Methodist preacher *might* have done the things attributed to him in this novel. One thing is for certain, Neville Trueman was not his real name.

The author owns up to this fabrication in early editions, going so far as to append a footnote to the novel's very title. In this fourth and final edition, however, Withrow drops the bit about "slightly assumed names," along with the opening verse about "the dreadful clouds of war." Everything else is otherwise as it was in 1879, when *Neville Trueman, the Pioneer Preacher* made its debut in the pages of *The Canadian Methodist Magazine,* a periodical edited by the author, Rev. William Henry Withrow, DD, FRSC.

His Tale of the War of 1812 opens on the very first day of the conflict. Rev. Neville Trueman, "a prominent figure in the history of early Methodism," is riding along the Niagara bluffs toward the home of Squire Drayton, son Zenas, and chaste daughter Katherine. Though a Vermonter, Neville Trueman cannot support his country's war of aggression. "I believe the colonists were right in resisting oppression in '76," he tells his hosts, "but I believe they are wrong in invading Canada now, and I wash my hands of their crime." There are, he prophesies, horrors to come in this ruinous and unjust war.

Were it not for the reverend's next words, I might've clasped this man of the cloth to my bosom. "What I dread most is the effect on religion," says Neville Trueman, revealing that what troubles him most is not the coming violence, the destruction and the slaughter, but the obstacle the war poses to the project of converting Canadians to Methodism.

Such a trooper, that Neville Trueman! In the years that follow, he moves from battlefield to battlefield administering to the spiritual health of the wounded and the dying. He's here, he's there... but he's not everywhere. Despite being the title character, Neville Trueman disappears for dozens of pages at a time. We make the reverend's acquaintance in chapter one, but don't see him again until we're well into chapter five. For non-Methodists, Neville Trueman's greatest moment of glory comes in chapter nine, "A Brave Woman's Exploit," in which he happens upon Laura Secord. So weak is the Heroine of Upper Canada, that it falls upon Neville to deliver information of an American invasion to James FitzGibbon.

Rev. Withrow makes much of his research in this historical novel, claiming "pains" taken in "the careful study of the most authentic memoirs, documents, and histories referring to the period; by personal examination of the physical aspect of the scene of the story; and by frequent conversations with some of the principal actors in the stirring drama of the time." To be sure, there are footnotes, but the laziest of eyes will take in the sorry fact that by far the most cited reference is Withrow's own *History of Canada*.

One day in the future someone might attempt to separate fact from fiction.

Might that person be me?

Not on your life.

Love and Unhappiness

The Master Motive [À l'œuvre et à l'épreuve]
Laure Conan
[pseud. Marie-Louise-Félicité Angers;
Theresa A. Gethin, trans.]
St Louis: B. Herder, 1909
254 pages

Our first female French language novelist, Angers hasn't been accorded much attention outside Quebec; it wasn't until 1974 that *Angéline de Montbrun* (1884), the work for which she is best remembered, appeared in English. So, what to make of this earlier translation of a lesser work? Its existence, I think, can be explained by looking to the publisher. Herder was a house devoted to pastoral publications, and was so successful that it was recognized with an entry in *The Catholic Encyclopedia*. The house continues today as Herder & Herder, which offers titles like *The Local Church: Tillard and the Future of Catholic Ecclesiology* and *A Celebration of Priestly Ministry: Challenge, Renewal, and Joy in the Catholic Priesthood*. As a romance-infused historical novel, *The Master Motive* wouldn't really fit the publisher's current list; but a hundred years ago it vied for attention with Herder's fine edition of *The Necromancers*, a gothic horror novel by celebrated convert Father Robert Hugh Benson (son of the Archbishop of Canterbury).

I haven't read Benson—not *The Necromancers*, not *Come Rack! Come Rope!*, or *Oddsfish!*, or any of his other novels—and so can say nothing of his talents. Of Angers, I can only comment on this book, which was a great challenge. Looking at *The Master Motive* beside the original French, I see that the problem isn't the translation, but an uncomfortable marriage of plot and pulpit.

Set in seventeenth-century France and New France, *The Master*

Motive is a work promoting piety, sacrifice, and, ultimately, martyrdom. At its centre is Gisella Meliand—Gisèle Méliard in the original French—a beautiful orphan girl who leaves her studies at the Cistercian convent of Port-Royal-des-Champs to live with distant relatives, the Garniers. On her final day, she is cautioned by the Abbess that "happiness is like those intoxicating liquors which can only be taken in safety in small quantities, and then, well diluted."

The happiness contained in this vessel is very watered down. What starts out as a romance between sixteen-year-old Gisella and her fiancé, Charles, son of Monsieur and Madame Garnier, is quickly swamped by talk of trial, tribulation, and duty. Samuel de Champlain makes an appearance, as does Father Brébeuf, joyless men who appear fairly beaten by their tasks.

Gisella Meliand did not exist, but her betrothed, Charles Garnier, was very real. *The Dictionary of Canadian Biography* covers his life in just nine sentences, the relaying of which spoils *The Master Motive*—not that this will stop me. A Parisian, Garnier was born in either 1604 or 1605 and arrived in New France during the summer of 1636. Garnier never married; rather, he was ordained as a priest roughly three centuries before being canonized by Pope Pius XI. His end, during an Iroquois attack on the Georgian Bay village of Saint-Jean, was not pleasant. Angers' novel closes with news of Garnier's final moments, spent running "hither and thither, to comfort the dying and prepare them for heaven." The reader is told that he "fought his way into the burning huts and baptized the children and catechumens amid the flames," before being felled by a gunshot to the abdomen.

This sad spectacle of a priest desperately trying to baptize those who had rejected his Faith has some claim to accuracy, and reminds the reader of the words Charles had written to our heroine:

Oh, Gisella, what happiness there is in baptizing him and seeing him die! Have you ever thought of the astonishment, the overwhelming joy, of a poor savage who passes from the depths of misery to the splendors of heaven?

And, so, a happy ending.

Reverend Kerby Treads Carefully

The Broken Tail
George W. Kerby
Toronto: Briggs, 1909
189 pages

The cover promises Mounties, but this is really a collection of a prairie pastor's tales. George W. Kerby was a Methodist minister from Ontario. He came West in 1903 to shepherd the good souls of Calgary's Central Methodist Church, and seven years later became the first principal of the newly established Mount Royal College.

Reverend Kerby's stories would've come early in his prairie ministry. As such, they provide some idea of a pastor's place during the opening of the West. At the time of his arrival, Calgary, a city of six thousand or so, was one of the most populous in the North-West Territories, and the province of Alberta was naught but a twinkle in Wilfrid Laurier's eye. Though the three stories in *The Broken Trail* are tinged with tragedy, the reverend is quick to defend this, writing in his preface that he intends not "to convey the impression that the West is in any way worse than the East." Rev. Kerby would also like the reader to know that the facts of the stories have been in no way altered, though some liberty has been taken in adding "coloring and shading to give them a better literary value."

For the most part, I think he succeeded. The first, "A Son of Holland," begins much like a gothic novel, but with a switch in gender: in place of a heroine, the pastor presents crying Dutchman Wilbur Wolfendon. A fine specimen of a man, "tall and broad-shouldered, neatly groomed and garbed," our hero appears unexpectedly at the parsonage one Christmas Eve, desiring to unload his tale of woe.

And what woe!

Orphaned as an adolescent somewhere in the Netherlands, Wilbur is made the ward of a conniving uncle who sends him to a monastery in France. There, he falls under the influence of a young Russian monk, Father Cyril, who shows him "many personal favors," and with whom he walks "arm in arm in the secluded haunts of the abbey." Wilbur seems ready to accept "no other home than the home of Father Cyril, and no other friend than the young Russian Benedictine," when he is visited by a playmate from childhood. Their time together brings some suspicion of uncle's motives *vis-à-vis* his parents' estate, and awakens a strong desire in Wilbur to return home. Father Cyril's kisses and pleads, but his "many endearing terms" cannot dissuade Wilbur. As Rev. Kerby writes, "even that, strong and true as the love of a man for a man could be, could not silence the home stirrings in his soul."

A month or two later, Wilbur flees the monastery: "My only regret," he said, "then and now is Father Cyril. He had a great love for me, and I know I had for him."

"Just like Jonathan and David," Rev. Kerby observes, "or Cicero and Laelius and other immortals. That could have happened only in the classic circles of Europe. It is almost impossible in the modern life of a new country."

Whatever is the author getting at?

Wilbur hasn't entirely soured on monastic life. Indeed, according to Rev. Kerby, the fugitive novice believed that "only through such discipline and sacrifice that men of certain proclivities—which he did not specify—could find the joy of living." Wilbur tells the clergyman that monasticism is "the only thing for men with temperaments like Father Cyril," adding that "it did not suit [Wilbur's] temperament—he was much too masculine for that."

Wilbur returns to his uncle's home in Delftshaven, but the stay is brief. After a few weeks, under cover of night, he's drugged and abducted by evil henchmen. Poor Wilbur awakens the next morning to find that he has been committed to an insane asylum. There he stays for fifteen months, until a change of staff brings new people not involved in the conspiracy.

Finally free, Wilbur succeeds in making something of himself in the civil service. He falls in love with the beautiful Isabel, sister of the very same childhood friend who visited the French monastery all those years ago. Though she loves him too, her father does not approve—everybody knows that young Wilbur was in a lunatic asylum; besides, the man has no money, no property and no title, having been cheated of it all by his dastardly uncle.

Unable to marry the woman he loves, Wilbur does what any man would in following the trail of the heartbroken to western Canada. It's a mistake. The farther he gets from Isabel, the more his love grows. Sure, Wilbur has some adventures—for a time he serves in the North-West Mounted Police (that's meant to be him on the cover)—but try as he may, he just can't stop thinking about Isabel.

Sitting in the Central Methodist parsonage that magical Christmas Eve, he suddenly gets the sense that Isabel's obstructive father is no more: "'Dead—I feel he is dead!' The answer was given with the authority of one who had psychical insight into the hidden things."

Wilbur then announces that he will walk across Canada to Isabel. The triviality that is the Atlantic Ocean makes no never mind.

"You are aware," remarks Rev. Kerby, "that you are just as liable to be frozen to death in the attempt, even to reach Winnipeg, as if you were making a dash for the North Pole!"

It was at this point that I began to feel like I'd once read something of Wilbur Wolfendon's sad story elsewhere. A few pages later, seeing this A.M. Wickson illustration, everything clicked.

It turns out that I'd first learned of Wilbur through George Johnston's *It Happened in Canada* (1973), a book my mother bought me when I was ten.

Eight hundred miles across a continent to win a bride.
Page 72.

If Rev. Kerby's claim is correct, that the facts in *The Broken Trail* have been in no way altered, then Johnston is wrong; Isabel did not travel to Winnipeg, rather Wilbur walked to the city—a distance of roughly thirteen hundred kilometres—on his way to her Amsterdam home.

Or has the pastor been caught out?

The story of the young Hollander who was walking across a continent to meet his love appeared in the press, although the details differed somewhat from those related in my study. It enlisted the sympathy and interest of the citizens of that city, and money was immediately subscribed to enable him to finish his journey to Holland.

Differed in what way, I wonder. Is Johnston correct? Did Isabel make an Atlantic crossing?

Never mind. The biggest question I have is whether Wilbur Wolfendon really existed. Rev. Kerby tells us that his trek was covered in the press, so how is it that searching his name on the web brings just two hits: *The Broken Trail* and a lone sentence in *Insight 2*, a textbook published in 1980? Further investigation is in order.

Call in the Mounties.

Reverend Kerby Warns Against the Dime Novel

Because he was a man of the cloth, I'm inclined to give Rev. Kerby the benefit of the doubt. I believe he was told that crazy stuff about an orphaned lad and his evil uncle, just as I believe that the teller walked from Calgary to Winnipeg in the dead of winter. What I doubt is that the man's name was Wilbur Wolfendon. Rev. Kerby tells us that the trek received a good deal of attention, so how else can we explain why his name does not feature in the dozens of contemporary newspapers found online?

A greater mystery is why Rev. Kerby chooses to hide the identity of the man at the centre of "The Desperado," his second tale. The sorry soul the pastor refers to as "Ernest ———" is Ernest Cashel, an American outlaw who made headlines throughout Canada and the United States in the years before *The Broken Trail* was published.

BROKE OUT OF PRISON

MAN UNDER SENTENCE OF DEATH MAKES DARING ESCAPE.

At Point of Revolver He Forces Guards Into His Cell and Then Decamps.

The Californian, December 11, 1903

But, as we all know, the Mounties always get their man.

ERNEST CASHEL HANGED.

CONFESSION OF THE MURDER OF RUFUS BELT.

He Replied to Rev. Mr. Kirby's Question That he Was Guilty— The Execution of the Death Sentence at Calgary Without Unusual Incident.

The Yukon Sun, January 24, 1904

Rev. Kerby isn't so much concerned with the sin as the sinner. We're told nothing of the murder that brought Cashel's death sentence. There is a loose account of the prison break and subsequent recapture, but most of "The Desperado" has to do with the pastor's work to secure the condemned man's salvation.

FOUND YESTERDAY WILL HANG TODAY

Ernest Cashel, Condemned Murderer of the Northwest, Captured Near Calgary.

The Globe, February 3, 1904

Not everyone accepted the story, but I again find myself giving Rev. Kerby the benefit of the doubt. I believe him when he writes that Cashel confessed, repented, and received communion in the last minute or so before his execution.

Cashel blamed novels for his fate. Such was his conviction (no pun intended) that he left behind a warning, which Rev. Kerby shared in the pages of this book and at a special post-execution event held at Hull's Opera House:

Young men of Calgary: —

Remember, boys, I am not in a position to make any exaggeration. Here is my experience in regard to books, such as Diamond Dick's, Nick Carter's, Buffalo Bill's and James Boys.' I think by my own experience they are the starting of a romantic life. I know I used to read those books before I left home, and think how nice it would be if I could belong to a gang of brigands. Well, boys, I did have lots of fun as long as it lasted. But when my days were numbered I thought of my romantic life, boys. Oh, boys, take my advice and stay away from saloons, gambling-houses, and shun bad company, especially the house of ill-fame, for you know one bad woman is worse than ten bad men. She can lead you into the clutches of the devil before you are aware of the fact, and I tell you with a true heart, stay away from those bad women.

Here is the story of my life, boys. I used to read novels when I was home, and that started me to going into bad company, drinking, gambling, and the first thing I knew I was looking out from behind the bars. I met some bad men in jail, and we planned, and I got out, but they caught me again, and I got out again, and so on for five years, till I landed in a condemned cell. Escaped again, but Providence proved against me, and I was fetched back to meet my fatal doom on the scaffold. I had to leave my dear ones at home and go among strangers, lay out nights, go without anything to eat for two days at a time, be wet and cold, and I have sat down many a time and thought of my dear old mother at home, breaking her heart, longing for her boy.

Oh, boys! Don't go away from home. Just think of Ernest—me in my doomed cell. I would die a dozen times to take the disgrace off my family. But, boys, it is too late now. Oh, what is my dear old mother doing to-day? Maybe she is dead. I wish I could see her, but she is far, far away from here, and I am going to be hanged in about twenty-four hours. Take my advice, dear boys, and stay at home, shun novels, bad company, drink and cigarettes. Don't do anything you are afraid to let your mother know.

Ernest ———

One hundred and nine years later, the dime novel is long gone and the Twinkie looks to be in trouble.

I blame video games.

Reverend Kerby Comes Upon a Blazing Bosom

I think I've been more than fair in accepting Rev. Kerby's stories. I won't be so gentle here.

Rev. Kerby's last tale, "The Outcast," is the shortest because there's not much to tell. Solly, "a well-built, clean-shaven Hebrew" tells the pastor of a cabin on the outskirts of town in which a young woman named Esther lies dying. And then she does.

Never mind. The important thing is that Rev. Kerby was there to comfort and guide during Esther's final hours. "Her soul was struggling in the vortex of incredible sorrow," he writes. "The fires of hell were ablaze in her bosom."

The inferno's origin is explained in this exchange with able-bodied Solly:

"She is your wife, I suppose?"

"Nay, sir," he replied, raising his heavy eyebrows, and with a look of surprise. "She is my luve."

"Your love?" I repeated. "You mean—"

"My luve," he again interjected, and there was a slight agitation in his manner. "I've luved her for four years."

"Four years—not so bad, sir, for a Hebrew..."

Yep, not so bad. But the pastor believes he's found further fuel feeding the raging breast fire in another visitor, "a woman of prepossessing appearance":

She bowed gracefully and shook hands with both of us. "This is her friend," he continued. "She don't talk much English," and forthwith they began an animated conversation in French.

I observed her very closely. She was elaborately made up with paint and powder, and was heavily perfumed with parme violets. Almost immediately the awful conviction dawned on me that the bundle of humanity in the comer was a unit in the vast army of degraded and blighted womanhood.

One of two things we learn of Rev. Kerby's character through this book is that he was quick to judge. His consideration of Solly serves as an example of the second: "There was pity in my heart for him. He was born in the ghetto of Chicago, a child of dirt and darkness. But ignorance in this day and age cannot be innocence, not even for a Hebrew."

Yes, not even for a Hebrew.

Hollander, whose "physical prowess was the primal glory of the race," and Solly, forever "gesticulating wildly after the manner of his race," are the two ends of a thread of racism that runs through Rev. Kerby's book. Lest I be judged too quick to judge, consider this passage in which the author sets down his thoughts on immigration:

These men and women coming to us, so different in language, customs and ideals, constitute one of the most serious of our national problems. But the initial, experimental stage has already passed, and the immigrants from the northern countries of Europe have so readily adapted themselves to our conditions, and so easily assimilated our ideas, that we have nowhere in the empire a more contented, thrifty and patriotic people, and none more worthy of the privileges of citizenship.

On the other hand, we have to reckon with a very grave peril in receiving the ignorant and inefficient—the lazzaroni from the slums of Southern Europe, born to be seekers for a soft job, preferring to extort money rather than to work for it, and forever sowing the seeds of anarchy and moral degeneracy, and who breed crime, disease and death wherever they go.

I don't see that *The Broken Trail* features any anarchist immigrants. Moral degenerates? I suppose in Rev. Kerby's eyes that would be Solly, Esther and Ernest Cashel (the sweet-smelling, prepossessing prostitute might count, but I'm betting she's from Quebec and not an immigrant). Crime? Well, that would be Ernest and Esther (providing the pastor is correct in assuming her to be a fallen woman). Disease? What's Esther dying from anyway? We're never told. Death? Easy—Ernest killed a man.

The thing is that Ernest, Esther and Solly weren't from Southern Europe, but the United States.

In the end, *The Broken Trail* proves itself a degraded book, a blighted book... but it is prepossessing.

Spirits

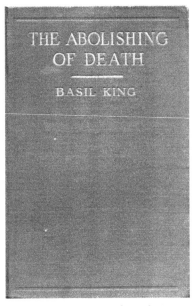

The Abolishing of Death
Basil King
New York: Cosmopolitan, 1919
197 pages

An anonymous work, in 1909 *The Inner Shrine* topped American lists, besting books by Rex Beach, Mary Roberts Rinehart, and George Barr McCutcheon to become the year's biggest-selling novel. There was considerable speculation and argument as to who might be behind this work. William Dean Howells was considered, as was his less formidable daughter Mildred. Some were certain that the novel had come from the pen of Edith Wharton. It was reported that a man in New England had revealed himself as the author on his deathbed. And then there was Henry James; might *The Inner Shrine* be his work?

Harper and Brothers watered this seed by repeatedly boasting in advertisements that the novel possessed "that certainty of touch which marks the master." Theirs was not a consistent campaign, however; that which marks the master in one advertisement is the sign of a fresh voice in the next. "Once in a lifetime," begins one advert, "a brilliant star may flash across the sky and it is interesting to note how quickly comes wide acclaim." This same notice presents the testimony of "reader" Lilian Whitting: "Many of us are lying awake nights trying to conjure up the author of 'The Inner Shrine.' Which takes hold of one as no work of fiction has for unremembered years."

The delicate Miss Whitting would suffer three years of sleepless nights before a relatively unknown Canadian named Basil King stepped forward to confirm that the novel was his.

Contrary to that advertising copy, acclaim had not come quickly to the writer; *The Inner Shrine* was preceded by no less than five King novels. All published under his own name, they had enjoyed little more than complimentary notice and respectable sales.

With *The Inner Shrine*, however, King's fortune took flight. Further flashes across the sky included *The Wild Olive*—from "the anonymous author of 'The Inner Shrine'"—which became the third best-selling novel of 1910.

Newfound fans saw much to admire in King's own story. Born to a couple of modest means in 1859 Charlottetown, from the moment of his first breath the author had struggled with ill health. And yet, despite all adversity, he'd graduated from the University of King's College to become an ordained minister in the Anglican Church. In 1900, King was serving as rector of Cambridge, Massachusetts' Christ Church when he began losing his sight. Forced into retirement and facing blindness, the reverend made the rather curious decision to pursue a life in letters. Now, with riches earned from *The Inner Shrine*, *The Wild Olive*, and his many other novels, this unfortunate soul had been afforded comfort in a grand Cambridge house that he shared with his wife.

The charitable will understand why some believed *The Inner Shrine* to be the work of Henry James; it was a well-constructed novel, fairly typifying literary realism. True, King's characters were a touch wooden, and he was given to sentimentality, but the man's plots could be quite clever. The reverend's greatest flaw was a disposition toward didacticism; he was prone to preach. King's second novel, *Let No Man Put Asunder* (1901), reads much like a lengthy sermon against divorce, while *The Contract of the Letter* (1914) hammers the head of the reader hard with the very same message.

Dour stuff, yet there is a quirkiness in King that can make for some very entertaining reading. I imagine this was the case even a century ago. *The Contract of the Letter*, for example, features a divorced man's detailed fantasy in which he drinks himself to death; this, so that he might finally prove the great love he has for his ex-wife.

King is never more interesting and enjoyable than when he deals with the otherworldly. Religion does come into play, but it's not quite in keeping with Anglican doctrine. We see this in *The Inner Shrine*, which begins with a mother's "presentiment of disaster"—one that proves correct with the news that her son has been killed in a duel. King's 1918 novella of the Great War, *Going West*, tells a tale of two soldiers—one American, one German—who quite literally die in each other's arms. In death, the American, atheistic Lester, watches the pious German comfort his family from beyond the grave. The doughboy isn't able to do the same until he recognizes that he lives on in "one great intelligence that understands all our needs."

Published mere months after the armistice, *The Abolishing of Death* is also influenced by the First World War. It began as a series of articles on "Life and Death" commissioned by *Cosmopolitan*, then the magazine of Sinclair Lewis, Upton Sinclair, and George Bernard Shaw. King submitted two pieces, but these were withdrawn after, as he puts it, "certain things began to happen."

What had happened was this:

The retired reverend had been enjoying a quiet afternoon in the company of a young woman he identifies only as "Jennifer," when suddenly, unexpectedly, this "average American girl" decided to try her hand at "spirit writing." King assures us that Jennifer possessed "nothing of the mystic, the mediumisticy the spiritualistic, or the morbid," and yet within minutes she was transcribing communication from the dead.

Though taken aback, the reverend tells us that he witnessed nothing that contradicted his beliefs. Spirit writing was, to his mind, "the logical extension of the Christian revelation." A good number of the departed vied for King's attention, but one man, identified as the British chemist and photographer Henry Talbot (1800–1877), soon became his "chief correspondent." Watching Jennifer's slender hands, the reverend writes: "It was as if the words: 'Talbot—Chemist' had been written, and one knew of a famous chemist of that name."

It was as if…

A curious aspect of this most curious of books is King's fleeting mention that his dearest friend from another plane isn't Talbot at all. The reverend later explains: "to avoid the use of a name well known throughout America and Europe, and of which I do not feel authorized to avail myself, I call Henry Talbot. As the interest of these papers is entirely in the nature of the message, the exact name of the speaker is of less importance."

And so, the writer substitutes the name of one famous dead man with another.

The Abolishing of Death was one of the better books in a cortège that included such works as *Raymond; or, Life After Death* (1916) by Sir Oliver Lodge, FRS. Plaintive, yet positive, they carried the conviction that one could communicate with deceased loved ones. Like his good friend Sir Arthur Conan Doyle, Sir Oliver believed he'd been in contact with a son who had been killed in the Great War. That the accounts of the afterlife experienced by his son Raymond Lodge and the "Henry Talbot" of Basil King didn't mesh was not cause for skepticism. The former's account of factories, tobacco, and cricket matches on the next plane were, according to Talbot, naught but, "different aspects of the same truth," much like "the different reports of travelers who come to us, say from London or Paris."

For those who had lost young men in the war, considerable comfort could be drawn from these books. Talbot assures King's readers that on the next plane lost limbs grow back, disfigurement disappears and all "assume the aspect he bore at his most beautiful."

"You can *never* destroy life," Talbot reassures. "Life is the absolute power which overrules all else. There can be no cessation. It is impossible."

This next plane, which King inexplicably identifies as "the new Heaven," is much like our world, but "enhanced, magnified, beautified, purified." It's a sort of nebulous psychedelic wonderland that would have found favour during the Summer of Love:

> We are the prismatic colors of His glory. As goodness is reflected in us—and goodness is God—we give forth God again. Note the difference in colors; we do not all reflect all of Him, nor do we do it in the same way. *Les nuances se détachent nettement, mais se confondent dans une harmonie infinie.*

This new Heaven is a place in which no wish is left ungratified. "I am a mother now," writes one of King's other correspondents—"a woman who had never been married, and in whom we supposed the earthly springs of maternity to have dried up."

Reading the words Jennifer transcribes, one can only envy the dead. That said, we must remember that we are all put on earth with a purpose:

> The Canadians have a mission for which they have been specially selected. They are to represent the Anglo-Saxon God-Idea. Their task will be one of production. It is not yet clear to me just how, but they will represent God. They understand the mission of sex better than any people, and this will be the kernel of their greatness. They are greatly honored here, and much loved.

As the articles that make up *The Abolishing of Death* were appearing in *Cosmopolitan*, readers were quick to accuse King of pulling a fast one—this was, after all, the very same man who had for years hidden his authorship of *The Inner Shrine*. However, the reverend remained unshaken. In the book's foreword, King writes that he understands the sceptics, and allows that he would be one of their number had he not witnessed Jennifer's gift.

Indeed, the reverend was unyielding in his belief that those on the other plane could not only provide solace, but guidance to those possessed of this mortal coil. Nowhere is this better expressed than in the story he provided for the 1920 silent film *Earthbound*. King's unlikely hero is Richard Desborough, a married man having an affair with his best friend's wife. Friend Jim discovers the betrayal, kills Richard, and the murdered man finds himself *earthbound*. Throughout most of this eight-reeler, he moves as a repentant ghost, seeking to right the wrongs he has caused not only Jim and his wife, but his own widowed bride and fatherless child. It's only through doing this good work that Richard is able to grow spiritually and rise to the next plane.

Coming nearly two decades after his literary debut, *The Abolishing of Death* was sold as King's first book of non-fiction. A few more novels followed, but these were interspersed with other spiritual works like *The Conquest of Fear* (1921) and *The Discovery of God* (1923). In 1924, shortly after the publication of *The Bible and Common Sense*, it was reported on the front page of Toronto's *Globe* that the reverend had finally lost his battle against blindness. Four years later, on June 22, 1928, King died at his beautiful Cambridge home.

He has not been heard from since.

A Penthouse Killing in Montreal

The Pyx
John Buell
New York: Farrar, Straus & Cudahy, 1959
174 pages

In 1965, as the centennial approached and Expo 67 was beginning to take shape, Edmund Wilson published *O Canada*, his "notes on Canadian culture." A slight book worth no more than a quick thumb through, it's remembered today only for the critic's oft-repeated pronouncement about Morley Callaghan: "...perhaps the most unjustly neglected novelist in the English-speaking world."

Wilson really didn't know much about Canada; in the book's first sentence the septuagenarian writes that his introduction to the country's "cultural life" took place only nine years earlier. The critic then goes on to thank Robert Weaver, "an official of CBS"—he means a CBC employee—through whom he met all sorts of Canadian writers and academics.

Only three English Canadian novelists are discussed in *O Canada*. As one might expect in someone new to the literature, MacLennan follows Callaghan, but the third, John Buell, is a true surprise. Studying at Concordia, CanLit canon comrades Callaghan and MacLennan peppered my reading lists; Buell, professor emeritus at the very same institution, was never mentioned. My copy of *The Pyx*, the first of his five novels, was bought in 1984 for fifty cents at a garage sale not two blocks from the Loyola campus. A signed first edition, for twenty-seven years it moved back and forth across the country without being read.

Why did I wait so long?

I'll blame the spoiler of a film, which I caught as a kid on CBMT, our local CBC—not CBS—station.

Here's a coincidence: like *The Penthouse Killings*, *The Pyx* begins with a woman falling from a penthouse. In this instance, the deceased is not addicted to cocaine, but heroin. She is Elizabeth Lucy, a high-class call girl who—and I don't mean to be clever here—is very much the heroine of the novel. Police Sergeant Jim Henderson investigates the death, but this is less a detective story than a woman's struggle with herself and her situation.

Wilson makes much of Buell's background—a French-Canadian mother, an English-Canadian father—and describes *The Pyx* as a French novel. I was reminded more of Graham Greene than Georges Simenon (yes, Belgian, I know), but most of all, I thought of Brian Moore, with whom Buell shares considerable talent in creating convincing female characters. Elizabeth is one, but there are others, including friend Sandra and Meg the madam.

It's difficult to write much about *The Pyx* without ruining things for the potential reader—and this novel is highly recommended. I'll add only that Wilson all but dismisses *The Pyx* as "a horror story," writing: "It is not really a serious book, but it creates an ever-tightening apprehension that may hold even a reader not particularly susceptible to the coils of this kind of fiction."

Nonsense—you will be held. Consider that a personal guarantee.

Small Town Boy Makes Good, Founds Small Town

Jean Rivard
Antoine Gérin-Lajoie [trans. Vida Bruce]
Toronto: McClelland & Stewart, 1977
280 pages

"The classic novel whose themes have influenced French-Canadian literature for more than a hundred years."

So why is the translation out of print?

Jean Rivard is everything that was good and bad about our moribund, once-important New Canadian Library. The thing is just about as ugly as can be, complete with clumsy cover pitch. NCL's *Jean Rivard* is no "classic novel," but a translation of two novels: *Jean Rivard, le défricheur* and *Jean Rivard, économiste*. Both have been bowdlerized.

A "great man," Jean Rivard is a student of nineteen when his father's death calls him back to the family home in Grandpré. He is at a loss as to what to do next. Jean Rivard's education had set him on the path to becoming a lawyer or doctor, but those professions are so overcrowded that its members scramble to feed themselves. Fearful of being a burden to his widowed mother—*of twelve*—Jean Rivard turns to the *curé* of Grandpré, M *l'abbé* Leblanc, who advises the young man to take up farming. Pursuing a professional career will only lead to debt and hardship, he is warned. "Even supposing that you are one of the privileged few in your profession," sayeth the *curé*, "you will be thirty, perhaps older, before you can marry."

Thirty! Before lying with a woman!

The way to the marital bed is clear. Jean Rivard takes the modest inheritance his father left him and leaves fictional Grandpré "in the valley of Lake St. Pierre on the north shore of the St. Lawrence" for the very real Eastern Townships. There, he buys one hundred acres of land, which he begins to clear with the aid of his jovial hired man Pierre Gagnon. All proceeds extremely well "thanks to a Providence that seemed to take our hero under its special care." Sadness comes only in the form of letters from Gustave Charmenil. Jean Rivard's old schoolmate, poor Gustave, has followed the very path M *l'abbé* Leblanc had advised against and is wasting money in pursuit of a career as a lawyer. What's worse, the young man is also caught up in city life, which involves significant expenditures on dress and things cultural.

Meanwhile, Jean Rivard stays the course. Three years after arriving in the Townships, and one year ahead of schedule, he marries pious Grandpré girl Louise Routier, bringing *Jean Rivard, le défricheur—Jean Rivard, Settler* in this translation—to a close.

I lie.

In fact, the novel does not end with a wedding, but with a prolonged discourse delivered the following day by M *l'abbé* Leblanc. His message:

- of all professions, farming is most suited to bring happiness;
- recognize and appreciate your heritage;
- live modestly;
- don't get too big for your britches.

The sequel, *Jean Rivard, économiste*, goes along at a good clip. We all know that time passes more rapidly with age. Other farmers follow Jean Rivard in clearing neighbouring woodland and become successful in turn. The great man is held in such esteem that the settlers name the new community Rivardville. The community grows. Jean Rivard becomes head of the militia, justice of the peace, is elected mayor, and founds a *lysée. Jean Rivard, économiste—Jean Rivard, Economist*—ends with a tour of Rivardville, an idyllic community in which the air is clean and the people pious and pure.

I can see I've been a bit unfair in criticizing the NCL bowdlerization. In her introduction, translator Vida Bruce writes that she removed much of the repetition; she also spared me from spending time on pages that look to have been lifted from an accountant's general ledger.

In the bulk maintained, we find passages such as this:

Canada owes part of its prosperity to the manufacture of these alkalis [potash and pearlash]. In the course of these last three years alone our country exported more than fifteen million francs worth of potash and pearlash. In European markets potash from America is held in the highest esteem as long as our forests remain, this product will continue to be one of our principle sources of wealth.

What follows relates directly to Jean's ability to generate wealth:

> On his return to Louisville Jean Rivard had to stop for a day or two at Lacasseville. There, while looking after various affairs he made the acquaintance of an American merchant named Arnold who had been established for some years in the same village. He knew that Jean Rivard was clearing land and asked him if he didn't intend to get some profit from the ashes produced by the wood he would be obliged to burn in the course of his operation. Jean Rivard replied that his intention had at first been to convert the ash into potash or pearlash but that the lack of roads and hence the difficulties of transportation obliged him to abandon the project.
>
> After a lengthy conversation, in the course of which the perspicacious American was convinced of the strict honesty, intelligence, and industry of our young settler, he proposed entering into a mutual agreement. He, Arnold, would undertake to procure on credit the kettle, basins, and the rest of the things necessary for the manufacture of potash and transport them at his own expense to Jean Rivard's cabin, on the condition that Jean Rivard would commit himself to deliver to the said Arnold, in the course of the next three years at least twenty-five bushels of potash at twenty shillings a hundredweight. The ordinary price for potash was thirty to forty shillings, but Arnold in this case, paid the costs of transportation, a consideration of prime importance to Jean Rivard.

Nothing is lost in the translation.

These arid passages speak to purpose. Gérin-Lajoie's Jean Rivard novels aren't meant to entertain or enlighten, but to inspire readers to follow the non-existent great man's path—a course the author regretted not having chosen himself. Facts and figures are there to validate the author's overly romantic depiction of rural life.

If anything, the Jean Rivard novels proved even more influential than Patrice Lacombe's *La terre paternelle* (1846) in establishing the *roman de la terre*. It is truly remarkable that they weren't translated earlier. The New Canadian Library cover pitch may be clumsy, but its claim is true: these two novels had an influence on French-Canadian literature lasting more than a hundred years.

I'm not so sure that was a good thing.

Come, Come, Come—Nuclear Bomb

Arming for Armageddon
John Wesley White
Milford, MI: Mott Media, 1983
218 pages

As someone who came of age during the Reagan presidency, I admit to having held some pretty bleak views about the future. But never was I so pessimistic as Torontonian John Wesley White, whose *Arming for Armageddon* I happened upon while killing time in a local Salvation Army Thrift Store.

White was an Associate Evangelist with the Billy Graham Evangelistic Crusade and a recipient of "the Ph.D. from Oxford University," but not much of a writer; indeed, the bulk of his book consists of quotes from others, whether those people be real or imagined. Johnny Carson, Charlie Brown and "Mark MacGuian [sic], our Canadian Minister of External Affairs [sic]," are among the hundreds he cites in support of his contention that the reader will soon witness the "final tragic triumph of 'Evil' over 'Good!'" We are, he assures us, at the "edge of the end of times." The Antichrist will soon make his presence known. "He'll emerge as a nice guy... not unlike the burglar who was caught in a break-in, wearing a President Reagan mask." Just who is this swell, yet truly evil being? White speculates repeatedly that the Antichrist is Spain's King Juan Carlos. Why? Well, for one, he rejected the path of righteousness laid down by Franco.

Of other world leaders, White wonders: "Are they, like the maniac of Gadara, actually demon-possessed?" Nice guy Ronald Reagan gets a pass (no thought that he, too, might be wearing a President Reagan mask), as does genocidal Guatemalan General José Efraín Ríos Montt, whom White describes as having come to power through "spiritual miracle steps" (known in the secular world as a *coup d'état*). Margaret

Thatcher is another leader who, it appears, is demon-free. The Iron Lady's words—"We are reaping what was sown in the sixties: The fashionable theories and permissive claptrap!"—are used to support his condemnation of our then-prime minister's estranged wife:

> Margaret Trudeau is a pathetic figure, a morose example of flower power gone sour. Is Margaret Trudeau's hedonism relevant to the bursting dyke that will unleash Armageddon? Yes!

Signs of the coming final conflict spread far beyond the dance floor of Studio 54, they are found in the pages of *"MacLean's* [sic]*"*, *"The Toronto Globe and Mail* [sic]*,"* the writings of Margaret Atwood... everywhere, really:

> The Antichrist is referred to frequently in both Daniel and Revelations as "The Beast" and certainly Hollywood is on to this with *The Raging Bull* [sic], *The Elephant Man*, and, yes, believe it or not, *The Beast* and *The Little Beast*.

(Hollywood has produced three films titled *The Beast*; all silent, they were released between 1914 and 1916. IMDb has no listing for anything called *The Little Beast*.)

White's is a strange world in which his hometown has a team called the Mapleleafs, "troups" do the fighting, music mag *Sounds* is a "Nazi-Fascist organ," astronauts are the world's leading creationists and Laurie Anderson's "O Superman" tops the charts on both sides of the Atlantic. Anderson's song, he informs us, concerns the character Christopher Reeve was "acting for." Avert your eyes, children, Superman is but one in a series of creations "preparing the human psyche for an Antichrist who can solve the problems that have stumped man on his own." "We've seen them come and go," White writes, "the Purple Monster from Mars in *The Purple Monster Strikes*; Motha the Martian in *The Flying Disc Man from Mars*." He then points to unnamed characters featured in *The Phantom from Space*, *Devil Girl from Mars*, *I Married a Monster from Outer Space*, and, curiously, *The Man Who Fell to Earth*.

And on he goes: Jimi Hendrix and John Belushi committed suicide, Sid Vicious is by turns a person and a band (his/its theme song is titled "Anarchy"), "most of us have had a micro-electronic impression imposed on our hand," John Diefenbaker expresses his opinion from beyond the grave, the Ayatollah Khomeini is a communist plant, Anwar Sadat was assassinated by Muammar al-Gadhafi, the Dead Sea covers one of the largest untapped sources of oil, and Harry Truman's 1948 victory over Thomas Dewey was "inarguably a vindication of God's ancient promise to Abraham."

It's tempting to dismiss White as a clumsy loon; and yet, after spending an afternoon with his book, I find myself wondering when the "bursting dyke" will reveal herself.

DICKS & DRUGS

Ontario, Opium, and Cocaine

Up the Hill and Over
Isabel Ecclestone Mackay
Toronto: McClelland, Goodchild &
Stewart, 1917
363 pages

The plot of *Up the Hill and Over* features perhaps the most remarkable and improbable coincidence in all of Canadian literature. I put this out there as a warning: a spoiler follows.

Isabel Ecclestone Mackay wrote this, her second novel, while living in Vancouver, but its setting is the small-town Ontario she left behind. Coombe is the sort of place where Sunday travel is frowned upon, unmarrieds daren't picnic together, and ladies are advised to take care lest their belt pins become unclasped. Into this darkly Presbyterian community strolls handsome Henry Callandar. A celebrated doctor, his cheerful-yet-reasoned persona hides heartache, heartbreak, and anguish. Years earlier, upon learning of his beloved wife Molly's death, Callandar suffered a breakdown, collapsing on his mother-in-law's poorly scrubbed doorstep. The doctor's retreat from his home in the messy, busy metropolis of Montreal to the seemingly simple, sleepy town of Coombe is to be the final step in his rehabilitation.

The first person he meets is Esther Coombe, granddaughter of the man for whom Callandar's adopted home was named. An angelic schoolteacher, she supports a household that includes a sister, a kooky aunt, and a widowed, thieving, opium-addicted stepmother. That's right, opium. Cocaine, too.

Callandar and Esther's few trivial adventures and minor meetings lead to love. Within weeks, the doctor can no longer suppress his desire to reveal his true feelings and proposes marriage. Told that Esther is gathering flowers in a local meadow, Callandar sprints towards a figure he believes to be her. But that's not Esther's blue dress, only one that resembles it. Nor is that her white hat, the circumference is off by an inch or two. And, of course, the figure is not Esther, but her step-mother... who, Callandar is shocked to discover, is the wife he's been mourning all these years.

The reader will not fall off his or her chair; preceding pages provide plenty of foreshadowing, preparing us for what's to come. There's the discovery of a mysterious letter, talk of inescapable fate, and this paragraph:

What are they, anyway, these curious combinations of unforeseen incidents which under a name of "coincidence" startle us out of our dull acceptance of things? Can it be that, after all, space and circumstance are but pieces in a puzzle to which the key is lost, so that, playing blindly, we are startled by the *click* which announces the falling of some corner into place? Or is it merely that we are all more closely linked than we know, and is "coincidence" but the flashing of one of numberless invisible links into the light of common day? Some day we shall know all about it; in the meantime a little wonder will do us good.

Yes, a little wonder will do us good... so, don't you go criticizing my clever plot twist.

"YOU!" HE SAID. IT WAS ONLY A WHISPER BUT IT SEEMED TO FILL THE UNIVERSE. "YOU—MOLLY!" *See page 264*

This pivotal scene is captured in a plate that precedes the title page—the ultimate spoiler, I suppose.

It seems Callandar's scheming mother-in-law lied about the death and convinced Molly that she'd been abandoned. And the good doctor had changed his name, so his wife never suspected he might be her first husband. Adding to this unfortunate set of circumstances, Molly, too, has changed her name, becoming Mary—Mary Coombs. And, conveniently, she'd never been home when Callandar had come to call on Esther.

Any threat of *scandale* is prevented by the doctor's decision to do the honourable thing and quickly remarry Mary (née Molly). But what of Esther? Does Mary's resurrection destroy his love for her? It does not. In fact, such are Callandar's feelings for the schoolteacher that he tortures the poor girl by expressing his love, adding, with deep regret, that he must wed her stepmother. Chin up, Esther copes with the situation as best she can, but before long the town gossips are remarking on her weight loss. It seems love's labour is lost until—*happy day!*—Mary dies of an opium overdose.

I'm being a bit flippant here. In fact, most of the characters are sad, some blaming themselves for Mary's dramatic demise. Poor Dr Callandar is hit hardest of all, experiences a relapse, and is "taken away to Toronto for special treatment." Not to worry, he's soon cured, and returns to Coombe eight pages later, very much in love with Esther, and then the novel ends.

Q: From where exactly does a lady living in early twentieth-century small-town Ontario procure opium and cocaine?
A: Detroit. According to the author, both are available through the post from druggists, who are "not called druggists exactly."

Of Magic Mushrooms and Bad, Bad Boys

Bannertail: The Story of a Graysquirrel
Ernest Thompson Seton
London: Hodder & Stoughton, 1922
230 pages

Three confessions:

- I was forty-six when I decided to finally read Ernest Thompson Seton;
- I chose *Bannertail* because it was the shorter of the two Seton titles I owned;
- I didn't think I would enjoy it.

I enjoyed this book. Should I have been surprised? In his day, Seton was the master of the "realistic animal story," which he helped create. We may quibble over the term today—*just how realistic?*—but at its best the genre could be both entertaining and educational.

In *Bannertail* we learn an awful lot about the habits of the grey squirrel—or "graysquirrel"—yet Seton never allows the facts to get in the way of a good story. The book begins with great drama: Bannertail is orphaned when a farm boy clubs his mother to death. A sibling is also clubbed, while another has the life crushed out of him. The actions of a future serial killer? Not at all. The young lad "had yielded only to the wild ancestral instinct to kill, when came chance to kill." You know how boys are: they collect horse-chestnuts to throw at cats, destroy any nest they come across, and take great joy in killing small animals. One victim is Bannertail's future son Cray, who is not much more than a kit himself when he's shot for sport.

Witnessing her son's death, Bannertail's mate, Carey, is resigned: "'It had to be.' For this is the fulfilling of the law; this is the upbuilding of the race; this is the lopping of the wayward branch." You see, Cray had not yielded to *his* instinct; he'd been too inquisitive and wouldn't stay out of sight. So, Carey dismisses her son, and nearly does the same with her mate when Bannertail, too, fails to heed the internal "warning whisper" that tells him to stay away from toadstools:

The lust for that strong foody taste was over-dominating. He seized and crunched and revelled in the flowing juices and the rank nut taste, the pepper tang, the toothsome mouthiness, and gobbled with growing unreined greed, not one, but two or three—he gorged on them; and though stuffed and full, still filled with lust that is to hunger what wounding is to soft caress. He rushed from one madcap toadstool to another, driving in his teeth, revelling in their flowing juices, like the blood of earthy gnomes, and rushed for joy up one tall tree after another. Then, sensing the Redsquirrels, pursuing them in a sort of Berserker [sic] rage, eager for fight, desperate fight, any fight, fight without hate, that would outlet his dangerous, boiling power, his overflow of energy.

Carey recognizes that Bannertail had taken "into his body and brain a madness that would surely end his life." Though she resolves to give him a chance to mend his ways, Bannertail's return home is anything but happy. His mate sniffs his whiskers: "She liked not his breath."

It's worth noting, I think, that this story of a squirrel's experience with the "flowing juices" was published during America's Prohibition Era.

A Comic Book Artist's
Absurd Murder Mystery

Artists, Models and Murder
Tedd Steele
Toronto: News Stand Library, 1948
141 pages

Mothers, don't let your sons grow up to be private dicks; the hours are awful and so few require their services. Consider this novel a cautionary tale.

It's been two months since Steve Black left New York to set up shop in Metropolis and he's still awaiting his first client. What this particular dick thought was a smart move—"there's [sic] only three other detective agencies here"—has brought only bitterness: "There's not enough crime in this burg." This goes some way in explaining why it is that Steve allows himself to be hired by broken-hearted Webster Reynolds.

A successful artist—he smokes gold monogrammed cigarettes—Reynolds' story is fascinating. For nearly four years he's been involved with model Marcia Hunter. They became engaged around the end of year three, but decided to put off marriage until they'd saved up a nice nest egg. All went according to plan until Marcia suddenly, inexplicably spent three thousand dollars on an oil painting. "I called the thing a bloody daub," says Reynolds, "and told her she has [sic] been taken in for spending so much money."

The purchase was uncharacteristic of a woman who'd never paid more than two hundred dollars for a painting. More mysterious still is the unexpected appearance of the artist, Pierre Robinette. Newly arrived from Paris, he offers ten thousand dollars to buy back his work. After Marcia refuses, Robinette starts in on winning her heart and Reynolds pops the Parisian paramour in the snout.

An artist himself, Steele's intriguing premise is made fun through his wishful alternate reality. Artists are invariably handsome, sophisticated, and well-paid, attributes they share with the writers in fellow Torontonian pulpist Keith Edgar's *I Hate You to Death* (1944). I was reminded also of *The Penthouse Killings* by Horace Brown (1950) in that both its private detective and Steve Black are dimwits.

If the case covered in *Artists, Models and Murder* is typical, Steve's lack of thought and his inability to put two and two together would be understandable. He suffers numerous beatings in his first twelve hours on the case, losing consciousness no less than seven times. I counted. (Steve, poor Steve, thinks it was only five times.)

The cover copy errs in mentioning a Manhattan murder before going on to claim: "Artists, models and gunfire are bound up in a swift-moving train of events that thrust Steve into a multitude of situations both hair raising [sic] and hilarious."

Hilarious? No, but that train of events moves so rapidly that one wonders whether *Artists, Models and Murder* is a parody. In one scene, Steve comes upon a murdered model, is knocked out, revived, surrounded by policemen, encounters an old acquaintance, is cleared of the crime, and, at the end of it all, told by the coroner that the murder occurred within the last thirty minutes. In another, newspapers report that a thorough investigation involving forensics has proven that Steve is responsible for a murder that took place less than two hours earlier.

No, not a parody, just sloppy writing. Hilarity is intended in the private dick's quick quips and head-scratching descriptions. "I felt as giddy as the Empire State Building's spire," a drunken Steve tells us. "My stomach kept leaping over the middle rail of an escalator and my one good eye was showing me the damnedest display of pyro-technics I had ever witnessed."

Artistic licence, I suppose.

Everything is explained at the end by the villain. He's going to kill Steve, so what the hell. "Take a seat there on the chair and I'll outline the beginning of the whole affair," he tells the private dick. Seven pages later, I found it was all beginning to make sense, more or less, though by that point I'd become obsessed with two unrelated questions:

Did Tedd Steele do the cover illustration?

Why does that cover not feature his name?

From Penthouse to Pavement

The Penthouse Killings
Horace Brown
Toronto: News Stand Library, 1950
157 pages

Characters come fast and furious in *The Penthouse Killings*; I counted eight by the end of page two. This avalanche of names and faces is a transparent trick, thrusting the reader into the whirlwind that is the life of Private Detective Squire Adams. You see, our improbably named hero has been given under fifteen hours—cover copy claims forty-eight—to help police solve the murder of a woman whose body was tossed from the top floor of Manhattan's Hotel Glamora. Failure means that Squire can kiss his dick license goodbye.

It's not hard to see that the NYPD needs help, but is it really so smart to put Squire in charge? As the private dick and several dozen boys in blue move about the sixty-five-storey hotel, two more murders take place and the dead woman's body goes missing. A few people try to take their lives before Squire's eyes—though, to be fair, only one is successful. We're at hour ten before anyone—in this case, Ace Milliken of the Homicide Bureau—thinks to secure the scene of the first murder.

> "Excuse me, Mr. Adams, it's none of my business mebbe, but don't you think we oughta turn that mob out of here? They may be messing up clues."
> The private eye was thoughtful for a moment.
> "I've been wondering the same thing, Ace. But I'd say not. Somehow I feel it's better to have them all where we want them for the time being. If we've missed any clues, we're liable not to find them now, anyway. Okay?"

Um… okay.

With so very many Manhattanites packed into the hotel, owned by playboy Handsome Harry Hanover, it's to be expected that Squire would know one or two. There's the first victim, coked up, blonde-haired beauty Fritzi Hahn, "the dame with the —." I add that she was also known for her "—." Squire was "the one real love of her life." The second, Lydia Krakochenko, another old flame, is one of Handsome Harry's seven ex-wives. Lydia might be "the world's greatest ballerina," but she's not particularly memorable; certainly, she won't rank amongst what the cover copy promises as "the most fantastic characters you've ever encountered." Speaking for myself, I spotted just one candidate: Handsome Harry's hulking sibling Edith, a hermaphrodite who practises obstetrics at nearby Mercy Hospital.

We don't see much of Edith, "the half-man, half-woman sister," but Squire is present on every page. The reader will see him as a bumbler, but not so his fellow fantastic characters. "Young man, you must have a fine mesh in that mind of yours," says Edith, who is impressed by Squire's memory. This about a man who, as the conclusion draws near, suddenly remembers an old secret pertinent to the case. "Lydia told me once," Squire explains, "and I had forgotten it, for she told me in bitter self-mockery..."

Um... okay.

It spoils nothing to reveal that Squire solves Fritzi's murder—that is, if one accepts his shaky account of what transpired—and he has his license renewed.

"I hope we get together again some time," says one cop as he walks out the door.

But it never happens. There was no second Squire Adams mystery. Who, after all, would hire him?

Dope Rings in Canada? Oh, My!

Die with Me, Lady
Ronald Cocking
Toronto: Harlequin, 1953
224 pages

If you are having dinner with a group of Montrealers and suddenly bring up the subject of Toronto, chances are that someone will remark, "Toronto? Please. Not while I'm eating."

—Al Palmer, *Montreal Confidential*, 1950

There was no *Toronto Confidential* for the same reason that there's no Toronto equivalent to William Weintraub's *City Unique: Montreal Days and Nights in the 1940s and '50s* (1996): post-war Montreal was sin city; post-war Toronto was dullsville.

Montreal's noir writers—Brian Moore, Ted Allan, David Montrose, Douglas Sanderson, Ronald J. Cooke, and Al Palmer—set novels in the city where they lived, playing it up with titles like *Sugar-Puss on Dorchester Street, The House on Craig Street, The Mayor of Côte St. Paul, The Crime on Cote des Neiges, Murder Over Dorval,* and *The Body on Mount Royal.* The urban grit in the fiction of Toronto's Thomas P. Kelley, Tedd Steele, Keith Edgar, and Horace Brown came from the streets of New York or, more often, some faceless North American city. No snide remarks, now.

The notable exception amongst Toronto's pulpists is Hugh Garner, who used the city as the setting of *Cabbagetown, Present Reckoning,* and *Waste No Tears,* his infamous "Novel about the Abortion Racket." And who can forget *The Door Between,* Danny Halperin's sole Toronto-set novel? Not me. His best, it lingers as one of the most peculiar novels I have ever read. Now we have *Die with Me, Lady,* the only novel that transplanted British newspaperman Ronald Cocking set in the Ontario capital.

We begin at the corner of Queen and Bay, opposite Old City Hall, where withered and weathered newsie Timmy McGuire sells the day's papers. Ask for the *Star* and press a wadded bill into his palm and he'll hand you a well-folded copy containing a cocaine supplement. As evening begins and the business crowd thins out, old Timmy packs up and takes the streetcar east, past Union Station, past the grain elevators, to the island ferry. He's being followed and he knows it. He'd call out for help, but what's the use? "There was tomorrow, and the next day. The little man's heart contracted at the thought of the constant terror. Anything was better than that—anything."

Timmy is resigned to his fate, but still tries to dodge it. Aboard the *Sam McBride*, hoping to reach his modest Centre Island rental alive, he seeks safety in the toilet:

> "Come here, Timmy."
> The little man turned, trying to peer through the blood-red mist that was fogging his sight. It was Him, of course.
> Then he felt his wrist being gripped, and his forearm was suddenly bare. A sharp pain, a little pressure.
> "There, Timmy. That was painless, wasn't it?"
> The sleeve of his jacket was pulled down, and then he was being pushed through the open doorway.
> "Go back to your seat, Timmy. You'll need to sit down in a minute."

Exit Timmy McBride, dead by morphine; enter Al Morley, drunk as a skunk. Al works the police beat at the *Toronto Daily News*; Timmy would've sold thousands of his words. A pilot during the war, McBride spent three years as a McGill med student before drink got the better of him. Now he works in a field that "places a premium on failure," one that "has gathered unto itself the refugees from more different professions than any other occupation except prostitution."

His words, not mine.

Al's losing money playing poker with a morality squad cop when the call comes in about Timmy's death. They make their way to the morgue, Al blathering on about some of the stuff he learned in med school:

> He fell silent, suddenly nauseated with his own inane conversation.
> The siren cut a noisy swathe for the car as it rolled down Bay Street.

All at once he hated the solid smugness of the city. He felt as though he wanted to get a giant sledgehammer and smash the stony temples of industry; crack them into a billion pieces.

I'm going crazy, he decided dispassionately.

It was at this point I put down the book and placed orders with UK booksellers for Cocking's other novels. I then wrote a few friends advising them to get the book while there were still copies to be had.

My enthusiasm was premature. Never have I seen a book fall apart quite so dramatically and melodramatically. Narrative decay sets in when Al breaks into dead Timmy's home and encounters a girl "in a cool green linen suit that set off her copper-coloured hair, cut short like a boy's in the new style." She is Valerie, the virginal daughter of import-export business tycoon Sir Wilfred Cremore. Next thing you know, Al has it bad. He turns from hard liquor to ice coffee, becomes a regular visitor at the Cremore mansion, and sits like a puppy at Sir Wilfred's feet. Al's amusing enough as a drunk; sober he's a bore. But things hit rock bottom for the reader when Al declares his love for Valerie and they share their first embrace. This is the type of writing that would one day turn Harlequin into Canada's richest publisher:

There was a mighty thundering in his ears, and his whole body was filled with the warmth and sweetness of her.

After a while he said, with his mouth still touching hers: "I never knew this could happen to me. You read about it, and you hear about it, but I never knew that it could happen to me."

She was crying, silently, and the tears ran down salty on his mouth. He kissed her again, marvelling at the fierce intensity with which she gave herself. She reached up and put her arms around his head, pulling his mouth closer to her...

Presently she lifted her face away a little.

"It's for ever and ever," she said softly. "You read that in books, too, don't you? But I've always waited for this, because I knew one day it would happen. Now—it had to happen this way. Forever may not be very long, darling, but that doesn't matter. We know what it's like to have found what some people call Heaven. But Heaven was never like this."

Call me a cad, but I much prefer this passage from earlier in the novel:

"Why," Patti said softly, "our boy sounds all tuckered out." She climbed up on the stool beside him. "Maybe I ought to take you back with me and get you relaxed."

"Maybe," Al said, and his throat and mouth went dry at the thought. "Maybe."

"Finish your drink, honey," she said urgently. "I can't wait. God! The things you do to me shouldn't happen to a dog."

"You either got it," said Al, "or you ain't." Then he turned towards her. I'm sorry, Patti, I'm just a trifle stewed."

"You're a doll," she said, staring at him. Her mouth was red and very moist. "You're a doll, Al," she repeated. "Let's go, huh?"

"Where'll we go?" Al asked. She was very lovely, he thought. Her figure was perfect.

"We'll go up to my room, Al," she said softly. "I'll pour you a drink, and we'll talk—then I'll relax you. Huh?"

Okay, let's remember that this is meant to be a mystery. Who killed little Timmy McGuire and why? Our reporter hero doesn't do much to find the answers; instead he visits, revisits, and revisits Sir Wilfred, his editor, the morality squad cop and a Mountie named Summers to compare notes. He doesn't know a lot, but what he does know is enough to make a couple of parties very unhappy. Kidnapped once, shame on the crooks; kidnapped twice, shame on Al.

"For a reporter, you ain't smart," observes Sir Wilfred's dimwitted muscleman.

No, no he's not. Frankly, I doubt he was ever accepted at McGill.

Of Sex and Drugs and Montreal

Hot Freeze
Martin Brett [pseud. Douglas Sanderson]
New York: Dodd, Mead, 1954
246 pages

It was cold; bitterly paralysingly cold. There was a dampness in the air that bit into the marrow of your bones and stayed there. The red in the thermometer was below zero and still dropping steadily, and the weather forecasts offered no immediate hope of a let up. The city lay rigid under the stiffening blanket of snow. The air as you breathed it felt solid.

Though a transplanted Brit, Douglas Sanderson really knew winter and he really understood Montreal. *Hot Freeze* was his third novel; the first, *Dark Passions Subdue* (1952), was his one stab at a work of "literature." When it failed, Sanderson turned to writing crime novels, beginning with *Exit in Green* (1953), a "Martin Brett" mystery set in the Laurentians. With *Hot Freeze* he hits his stride, introducing us to Michel Garfin, a no-nonsense Montrealer of French and Irish heritage. Mike, as he's known, was a member of the RCMP until he was caught bedding the wife of the man he was supposed to be chasing. Now he makes a modest living as a private detective—Mike prefers "inquiry agent"—working out of an office in the city's east end.

Here he's summoned to upmost, uppermost Westmount by the exquisite Vivian Remington, who is troubled by her son, Gerald. She wants to know the source and destination of the great wads of cash that have been passing through the young McGill student's hands. No sooner is the private dick hired than the rest of the household arrives home. Mrs Remington covers by introducing Mike as an interior decorator, there's some talk about lampshades, he's invited to dinner, but no hilarity ensues.

After, Mike offers cash-rich young Gerald a lift:

"Enjoy the dinner, Mr. Garfin?"

I never cheat a client. I had a job. I said: "The name's Mike. No, I was bored as hell."

It hit the mark. He patted my knee. We became pals. "Me, too," he said. "Let's counteract it with a little excitement. Two guys like us could have a lot of fun together. I know some very nice interior decorators. What do you enjoy, Mike?"

"Almost everything. But maybe you and I wouldn't agree on the ultimate enjoyment."

"You never know," he murmured. "Sometimes it takes time…"

The pair drive north to a barbotte joint, where Gerald places a series of losing bets and irritates our inquiry agent with yet another none-too-subtle pass.

"I know a couple of dames who'll suit us fine," I said coldly.

His eyebrows went up and suddenly he began to laugh. "Dear Mike, you said that with positive defiance. Did you think a woman would frighten me as I frightened you? Come don't be so constrictedly old-fashioned. Something for everybody is my motto. Flesh, fur or feathers, I take them all. And they remember it."

There's a decent amount of sex in *Hot Freeze*, but to catch it you have to be alert. It usually appears out of nowhere and is over in less than a sentence. Here Garfin forces Felicity, a delicate blonde thing, into a cab after the stabbing death of her butch-lesbian lover: "She fought for about twenty seconds and then the thaw set in. She melted like hot ice-cream and came back at me like a Hoover."

Yep, Felicity and Vivian Remington's daughter, too. But in his own strange way Mike always stays true to his girl, Tessie, who listens when he's low, dishes dough when he's broke, and lets him shack up with her "when the occasion arises, which is often."

"Sin Took Over When The Sun Went Down" was the cover pitch of the 1955 paperback edition. This is true enough, I suppose, if one considers pre-dinner cocktails, heroin, cocaine, gambling, and sex outside of marriage to be sinful. The greater sin, murder, takes place whether the sun is up or not. An awful lot of people are offed in *Hot*

Freeze, most due to their involvement in the drug trade. The first to go is Gerald. I was sorry about this —there aren't many sexually aggressive nineteen-year-old bisexuals in mid-twentieth century CanLit. I'd have missed him more had it not been for the number of equally unfamiliar and unusual characters in the novel. Herein lies Sanderson's great strength: his Montreal is not only very real, but is populated by characters that are anything but types. Nothing is spelled out, they emerge over time, revealing more of themselves with each appearance. This alone is enough to get me to pick up Sanderson's other three Mike Garfin novels.

I mean, I just gotta know: is Mike's girl Tessie a hooker or something?

Dark Blondes

The Darker Traffic
Martin Brett [pseud. Douglas Sanderson]
New York: Dodd, Mead, 1954
213 pages

There are seven female characters in *The Darker Traffic*, but the woman on the cover isn't one of them. I'm not so sure about the man, either—and that sure isn't Montreal in the background. Yet the city and its island provide the setting for this, the second novel to feature the adventures of Mike Garfin, private detective.

I left off my review of the first, *Hot Freeze*, wondering whether Garfin's girl, Tessie, was a hooker. The answer comes about a fifth of the way into *The Darker Traffic*, when the private dick talks about marriage:

"It has to come some day. It's been a long time now, nearly two years since we met at that party."

"Yeah," Tessie said bitterly, "and nearly five years since I was a clever little girl who thought she'd found a way to make a hundred dollars. There was only going to be one time. I needed the dough. Two months later I didn't have an excuse any more and I was still doing it. Still am."

There's no room for ambiguity in *The Darker Traffic*; not as far as Tessie and her chosen occupation are concerned. There can't be. Where *Hot Freeze* covered the drug trade, this novel is all over prostitution. It begins with a visit to Garfin's office by "blindingly blonde" Gertrude Hess, moves to a Lakeshore mansion just west of "the township of Pointe Claire," then the roundabout by Dorval Airport and a roadside café on Highway 20. These are the details to which a reader like myself, who was raised just west of said township, cling.

A prostitute is murdered at that roadside café. Her prone body is placed under the carriage of a large truck and is then run over by an unsuspecting truck driver. I spoil things a bit in writing about the squished girl, doing so only because she appears to have been an Eastern European immigrant. *Plus ça change… Чем больше все меняется.*

There's more Montreal, including a scene that begins with Garfin leaving a drug store at the corner of Ste-Catherine and Peel. He's chased that time, but for much of *The Darker Traffic* the private detective is the pursuer. Though at a disadvantage, Garfin makes good use of what little he has in his arsenal by drawing on his friendship with Police Captain Masson and an exhaustive knowledge of women's clothing and undergarments. I imply nothing here, and point out that Russell Teed, David Montrose's rival Montreal private dick, has an appreciation of fine interior decoration and design.

The Darker Traffic doesn't quite compare to Montrose, but then it also pales when placed beside *Hot Freeze*. The latter's characters, quirkiness, and quips are less in evidence here; instead we have a fairly straightforward mystery that just happens to be set in the country's most fascinating city. Fortunately, the generic dust jacket does not reflect this.

Return to Miss Moneypenny's Fishing Lodge; Or, Billy's Bad Trip

Return to Rainbow Country
William Davidson
Don Mills, ON: PaperJacks, 1975
186 pages

In my aging mind, *Adventures in Rainbow Country* is forever linked with Gerry Anderson's *UFO*, both of them television shows that came and went when I was in third grade. In fourth, fifth, and sixth grades I bought a *UFO* Viewmaster set, a SHADO Interceptor, and a SHADO tank. I don't think *Adventures in Rainbow Country* had similar product, but I could be wrong. Truth be told, I never gave the show much thought. I didn't even know about *Return to Rainbow Country* until last year when I came across a copy at a sidewalk sale to support our local library.

Adventures in Rainbow Country holds interest for certain people; it has a fan site and a Facebook page. My pal Chris, a Bond fan from way back, cares because it featured Lois Maxwell (née Hooker), the Kitchener native best remembered for playing Miss Moneypenny.

Of course, we don't remember her as Nancy Williams. Maxwell wasn't the star of *Adventures in Rainbow Country*. Sure, she was in every episode—all twenty-six—but the show's star was Robert Cottier. A good-looking kid plucked from a Toronto private school, Cottier played Nancy's son, Billy.

Billy Williams. William Williams. Created by William Davidson.

Davidson wrote several things for television, including episodes of *The Littlest Hobo* and *The Forest Rangers*, but *Adventures in Rainbow Country* dominates his résumé. I don't think he wrote another novel, but then I doubt *Return to Rainbow Country* was ever intended as a novel in the first place. Visit the Canadian Film Development Corporation fonds at York University and you'll find an unproduced Davidson script with the very same title.

Return to Rainbow Country centres on a son's quest for his father, though this isn't at all apparent at first. The story opens with fifteen-year-old Billy piloting a boat into the choppy waters of Georgian Bay for two American fishermen. After that, he hitchhikes ninety or so kilometres to the courthouse in Gore Bay. There's a bit about an attempted murder trial that has something to do with the Ojibway bear walk curse, but all these things are incidental.

To get to the heart of *Return to Rainbow Country* you have to know something about the series' premise. I admit I was unaware, and blame Davidson for not following Sherwood Schwartz's example in setting it down in the opening theme. Readers of *Return to Rainbow Country* will find it in this passage—*my favourite*—on page 24:

> Nancy Williams was removing a pan of butter tarts from the oven when the boys walked in. She was a soft, appealing woman in her mid-forties with long auburn hair and a willowy figure, capable and hard-working, but a city girl who never really adjusted to the north. She had agreed to stay on at the lodge when her husband had disappeared, only because it was important to Billy.

Billy's father—Frank Williams—didn't take off with a softer, more appealing woman in her mid-twenties, rather he vanished while looking for a hidden mountain of gold in a part of North Ontario known as Wilderness Valley. This was two years ago.

There is a town in North Ontario, everybody knows, everybody knows, but in truth Neil Young is getting all nostalgic about a place that's just a couple of hours northeast of downtown Toronto… and you drive more east than north to get there. Billy's North Ontario, Rainbow Country, hugs the coast of Georgian Bay. In our world, Wilderness Valley is the name of a Michigan resort located one hundred or so kilometres southwest, but in the novel it's a place of mystery and danger that lies somewhere up an unidentified river. "My father left notes about how the Indians say Wilderness Valley is haunted by evil spirits," Billy tells his Ojibway pal, Pete. "There are legends about men who went up the river and never returned. Later their bones were found scattered along the shore."

Not much of a sales job. It doesn't help that Billy has tricked Pete into coming with him. He's also lied to his willowy-figured mom, who thinks that the two boys are off on a week-long canoe trip to a pleasant-sounding place called Smooth Rock Harbour.

Return to Rainbow Country is a screenwriter's novel. There's a respectable amount of action and dialogue, but little in the way of introspection. Description runs along these lines: "...he stopped at Pete's house, a bright blue and yellow frame building with flowered curtains, and spoke with his mother, a large plump woman with straight hair pulled back in a bun." Reading the thing was a bit of a chore, but I'm glad I persevered. The payoff came in the final third with something so unexpected, so unusual, that my description warrants italicization and a paragraph of its own:

Billy knowingly takes a hallucinogen. He trips out, becomes lost, finds his father's mountain of gold, dances with a girl with indigo eyes and nearly joins a commune.

Sounds incredible, I know. Could be that it never happened—Billy was high, after all—except that Davidson continues with the same bland omniscient narrator throughout. Nothing is seen through Billy's dilated pupils.

The most surprising adventure in Rainbow Country, it begins when Billy tears off the root of a small plant and pops it in his mouth. "It was something boys do," we're told. A man asks what Billy is chewing— something men do—and tells him to stop. "If you'd kept on chewing this another ten minutes you might have had some of the wildest nightmares of your young life."

Nightmares? Wild nightmares? The *wildest* nightmares? Who can resist? Not Billy. When no one is looking, he squirrels away a piece of root for future use.

Picture yourself on a boat on a river...

Return to Rainbow Country was published in 1975, a full five years after the show's last episode aired. Was anyone interested in the "television heroes in a new adventure"? How much did anyone remember of their old adventures? As I say, I didn't give the show much thought. Of course, by then I'd entered puberty.

Adventures in Rainbow Country had Lois Maxwell in it.

UFO had Gabrielle Drake.

EROTICA, PORN, PERVERSION, & RIBALDRY

Toronto's Tortured Sexual Souls

The Door Between
Neil H. Perrin [pseud. Danny Halperin]
Toronto: News Stand Library, 1950
160 pages

Sheila Grahame sings and plays piano in a Bloor Street bar. Classically trained, she's a squeaky clean "nice" girl whose idea of a torch song is "On the Sunny Side of the Street." For more than three years, Sheila has been travelling back and forth to Brookhaven Military Hospital, where boyfriend Bruce Darwin is being treated for "battle shock" suffered in the Second World War. The drive is tedious and the visits unpleasant, yet she's remained dedicated and faithful, certain that Bruce will regain his health and that one day they'll marry. As 1948 draws to a close, visions of matrimony and sugarplums nearly collide when she learns that Bruce is to be released. The good news is delivered by Emlyn John Davies, Colonel, Canadian Army Medical Corps:

"We shall not meet again. Only let me say that these trying years in which I have come to know you, you have given me pride in that friendship and a renewed faith in the Canadian woman. You know, many people said our women proved themselves—permit me to put it bluntly—tramps, during the war: they were promiscuous, they left their soldier-husbands, they carried on disgracefully. I never believed it true of as many women as they said and, knowing you, Miss Grahame, I know that there must have been hundreds, thousands of fine decent loyal women, the kind no one ever heard about. Yes, you have proved yourself selfless, devoted and sincere."

The colonel may have been impressed by the number—*hundreds! thousands!*—but in a country that then had a female population of over seven million, it sure doesn't seem that many. So, given the preponderance of promiscuous tramps, the reader might expect that it will only be a matter of time before poor Bruce becomes entangled. Who will it be? The pretty little waitress at the local diner? Clara, the flirtatious boozy floozy? Exotic Vera with her sexy Viennese accent and "outrageously high heels"? Bruce seems immune to all, in part due to his fear of other people—a "frightened rabbit," he sneaks in and out of his rooming-house hutch—but also because of his morning trysts with Sheila on the couch at her Sherbourne Street apartment.

Colonel Davies would be so disappointed.

Still, Sheila remains a "nice" girl, as evidenced by her unspoken "no marriage, no bed" rule. Bruce knows that she's nothing like those "oversexed sluts," the "promiscuous lower-class girls he had known carnally in school out Winnipeg way." As for the women he'd slept with during the war—in England, France, and Belgium—they were nothing but "berouged machines geared to satiate the temporary pangs of male desire."

The pleasant, if mundane routine of sex, toast, and coffee is shaken when Felicia Clark moves into Bruce's rooming house, taking the room not just next to his but connected to it by a locked door. She is a wicked woman, a violent femme fatale. How does Bruce know? Well, he's never seen her, but he can hear Felicia and her lover Eric through the open transom above "the door between":

> It was like living alone on a desert island and finding a fantastic book of photographs of nude women; the conversation he had heard induced in Bruce a kind of masturbatory traumerei [sic], a hazy eroticism that made him long to possess Felicia as this unknown, this Eric, must have possessed her.

The experience leaves Bruce "rigid all over, his body stiff with the ache of longing." He soon tires of cheerful Sheila and her "radiant, clean, healthy, decent" looks. He wants a costumed woman, an exotic woman, a woman like Felicia with her "lewd unheeding ruthless" desires. After an unsatisfying tumble on the couch, Bruce begins to retreat from Sheila and the rest of the world. He spends much of 1949 holed up in his room, eavesdropping on Felicia and her new lover, Mike, all the while recording his thoughts in a journal:

7th Sept, 1949: Listened again today. They were making love. Mike is rather good at it, I gather. Felicia was wonderful. What a grand performance!

Dark, disturbing, and violent, this is a far cry from staid, post-war "Toronto the Good"—it's perhaps for this reason that Perrin adds a curious quirk. Bruce goes for walks through Queen's Park, listens to CKEY, eats at a diner on the corner of College and Spadina, and yet this city on the shores of Lake Ontario is referred to as Yorkton (and, once, as New Yorkton, though I'm betting this was the publisher's error).

Oh, one last thing—the street Bruce lives on? Willcocks.

Climax! A Happy Ending

Closing *The Door Between*, I note that the novel was once listed in Ireland's Register of Prohibited Publications. How an obscure Canadian paperback came to the attention of that country's Censorship of Publications Board remains something of a mystery, though I'm led to believe it had something to do with an alert customs officer. That the Board placed it on its Register is more easily explained. Yes, *The Door Between* features pre-marital sex, voyeurism, and at least a couple of allusions to masturbation, but there's a good deal more to cause a censor to pop his monocle. Moving past the well-scrubbed, antiseptic couch romps shared by Bruce and Sheila, we find relationships in which sex and violence are invariably entwined.

The first glimpse we're given of these comes courtesy of Clara, Bruce's downstairs neighbour, who gets off on being knocked around by her husband. The morning after Bruce's arrival, the nightgown-wearing battered wife corners Bruce in the rooming-house hallway, teasing: "Bet you'd like to beat the hell out of me, wouldn't you?"

Jump to Vera, who shares a loveless sex life with Jake, one of the three men in her fawning entourage. "It is zee glandular love," she sighs. "I suppose it will have to do until zee real love comes along. Some day he vill come to me, zee lover I need. He vill be strong and filty; he vill beat me and kiss me and feel everything—everything!" When one of her lapdogs dares describe her as a masochist, she responds: "I am not to be labelled. You can say I am zee masochist, I am zee sadist, I am zee pervert—anything that pleases you. But all I really am is zee voman. How do you explain zat?"

Zee voman from Vienna is more easily understood, I think, than the ending of Perrin's novel. The climax is spoiled somewhat by the back cover, which tells us that the door between Felicia and Bruce will be opened, adding: "From that moment until the fateful New Year's Eve of 1949–50, Felicia and Bruce were hopelessly entangled in a strange love too powerful, too demanding, for either of them to fight it."

As I say, spoiled *somewhat*; the description is far from accurate. Felicia and Bruce don't meet until the final chapter, and their sexual entanglement lasts barely five pages. That strange, powerful, demanding love they share? Well, even Bruce knows it doesn't exist.

After a few days with Felicia, thoughts turn increasingly to Sheila. Bruce sends her a Christmas card, they make plans to meet on New Year's Eve and he dumps Felicia. The reunion is delayed by inclement weather slowing traffic along the Queen Elizabeth Way. As Bruce awaits Sheila's arrival, Felicia brings a man back to her room. Bruce breaks down the door, throws Felicia's pick-up down the stairs and starts slapping her around. The much-delayed Sheila chooses this moment to arrive at the rooming house:

> Again Bruce hit Felicia, and then again. Then he raised his fists and showered them on her, blow after blow. Moaning softly in pain, Felicia went down at his feet. Bruce's fingers, quivering, grasped her throat and began to strangle her.
>
> "I hate you," he whispered. "I hate you!"
>
> Sheila sprang forward into the room.
>
> "Bruce!" she cried.
>
> He stopped, turned to face her, still holding Felicia's throat between his hands, dragging her after him.
>
> "Sheila!"
>
> "Let her alone, Bruce. Come with me."
>
> "Sheila, I—"
>
> "Please, Bruce. Drop her!"
>
> Automatically, Bruce did as he was told. Felicia crawled away from him, whimpering into a dark corner of the room.

The pair leave the rooming house, presumably stepping over the man Bruce attacked, who's lying still, an "inert lump" at the bottom of the stairs.

"Something has happened to me here in this house, Sheila," said Bruce. "Something weird and wonderful."

"I don't care what it was, Bruce, so long as we are together."

"Kiss me, Sheila."

They kissed and there were tears in Sheila's eyes.

"I want to marry you," said Bruce. "Will you marry me?"

"Oh, I will, darling! Just give me half a chance!"

That little bit of awkwardness out of the way, the newly betrothed join happy, singing young people walking down Spadina Avenue. Bruce spots Vera and her pals, grabs Sheila's hand, and begins to run, yelling: "Hey, gang, wait for me, wait for me!"

These are Perrin's last words, bringing to an end one of the most peculiar Canadian novels I've ever read.

How do you explain zat?

Sexy Stuff from Bizarro Superman's Creator

Touchable
Les Scott and Robert W. Tracy
[pseud. Alvin Schwartz]
New York: Arco, 1951
184 pages

Alvin Schwartz died at his Chesterville, Ontario home on October 28, 2011, weeks short of his ninety-fifth birthday. I'd only just encountered his name—courtesy of my pal Stephen J. Gertz—but I've read much of his work. Schwartz was one of the foremost figures of the comic book's Golden Age, writing adventures for Superman, Batman, Wonder Woman, the Flash, Green Lantern, and Captain Marvel. He's probably best remembered as the father of Bizarro Superman, an accomplishment that should be overshadowed by his 1948 existential novel *The Blowtop*, inspired by his friendships with Jackson Pollock and Willem de Kooning.

A lesser book, *Touchable*, the story of a small-town girl who runs off to the corrupt and corrosive big city, follows a post-war pulp template. Anyone looking to read this novel is well-advised to ignore its jacket flap, which gives a detailed rundown of what's in store for heroine Ruth.

How much Schwartz had to do with *Touchable* is anyone's guess. His pseudonym appears on the front of the book's dust jacket, but not the spine; the title page credits only co-author Les Scott. Another of Scott's Arco titles, *Lady of the Evening* (1952), features the very same ingredients—sex and drugs and Greenwich Village—but in different qualities.

In *Touchable*, the sex begins on page two, when eighteen-year-old Ruth quite literally takes a tumble in the hay. Drugs don't appear until the mid-point, when she's offered a reefer by lipstick-lesbian Tony. Here marijuana proves to be a gateway drug, "the first turning of the key that unlocks a gate of terrors." Next thing you know, poor Ruth is turning tricks and mainlining horse supplied by her pimp.

The one thing that sets *Touchable* apart from *Lady of the Evening* is an odd account of the 1930 Ohio Penitentiary fire. Fourteen pages in total, it provides a detailed description of the institution, events leading to the disaster, the fire itself and the aftermath. For the first and only time, Ruth disappears from the narrative and attention shifts to her imprisoned boyfriend, Blackie… only we don't see much of him either. It all reads like something lifted from another work. Perhaps it was.

I imagine a good deal of fun and frustration could be had studying Alvin Schwartz's œuvre. Here's hoping someone does just that, and is able to figure out who—Schwartz or Scott—deserves credit for this novel's final line:

Chin up, her breasts pointing bravely, she walked back to the Inferno.

Canada's First Olympian

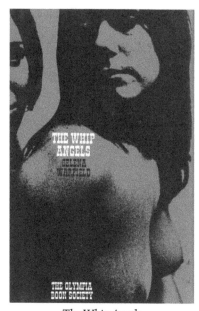

The Whip Angels
Selena Warfield
[pseud. Diane Bataille]
New York: Olympia Book Society, 1968
184 pages

Patrick Kearney's authoritative *The Paris Olympia Press* (2007) informs that the notorious Parisian publisher of Jean Genet, Samuel Becket, and Henry Miller also published books by three Canadians: Diane Bataille, John Glassco, and Jock Carroll.

Little has been written about Diane Bataille, the first to have been published. It's a shame, really, as the few words that have been set down about her point to a most extraordinary life. She was born Princess Diane Kotchoubey de Beauharnais on June 4, 1918, in Victoria, the daughter of Prince Eugene Kotchoubey de Beauharnais and his wife, Helen Pearce. Michel Surya's otherwise thorough biography of the princess' second husband, *Georges Bataille, la morte à l'œvre*, errs in recording her birthplace as Vancouver, and covers family history in four unsatisfying sentences. We learn, for example, that Bataille's Russian father, forced to flee Germany at the onset of the Great War, "crossed the Atlantic and reached Vancouver." A little more detail would be appreciated. *The Whip Angels* itself receives no mention in *Georges Bataille*; indeed, there's no indication that the princess, very much a ghostly figure in the biography, ever wrote so much as a word, never mind a work of pornography.

Make no mistake, *The Whip Angels* is pornography. The story of a girl's crude introduction to things sexual, it's not much more than a collection of encounters, each more adventurous, unconventional, and graphic than the last. First published in 1955 as part of Olympia's infamous Traveller's Companion Series, it was banned by French authorities the following year.

I chased down a copy after reading this passage in Mavis Gallant's *A Fairly Good Time*:

"Does he still keep books in the hamper?"
"Only *The Whip Angels*. We know it by heart…"

I recommend *A Fairly Good Time*.

A Canadian Fifty Shades? S&M From M&S?

A Stranger and Afraid
Marika Robert
Toronto: McClelland & Stewart, 1964
320 pages

My title is a cheat, a lame attempt to draw attention to one the finest novels I've yet discovered through this casual exploration of Canada's suppressed, ignored, and forgotten. That Marika Robert's *A Stranger and Afraid* is so very good and so very remarkable had me wondering about its descent into obscurity. A quick tour of my immediate circle, a bookish lot, found not a single soul who had so much as heard of *A Stranger and Afraid*, yet it was published by McClelland & Stewart, once the great Canadian publisher. The work was brought to American readers by Doubleday, which pitched it as "A NOVEL OF PARIS TODAY."

It isn't.

A Stranger and Afraid is very much a post-war novel, and Paris features only in the first half. It begins in the spring of 1949 with Kristina, our narrator, attending an elegant party on the banks of the Seine. A Hungarian refugee, young and beautiful, she is far too naive to be on her own:

> I was not yet eighteen, hungry-looking, long-legged, and skinny. My unruly hair, cropped by a refugee barber—who might have been a bank director at home—was always a mess. Though several people had commented on my budding beauty the bud was still very much closed.

Cut off from her mother and the wealth and privilege of her early years, Kristina is very much adrift. Guidance, of a sort, has been provided by friend Georgette, a flaky *femme fatale*, but Kristina doesn't have the confidence to follow her example. Here it's worth noting that she's wrong about her beauty. It has indeed begun to bud.

It's at the party that Kristina meets André Duval, a sophisticated parvenu two decades her senior. Though a snob of the highest order, it gradually becomes clear that he's naught but a gigolo to a beautiful wealthy woman who lives with a cuckolded husband in the South of France. Lucky André has parlayed her gifts into what must surely be the most lucrative black-market racket operating in Paris. André does have his pretentions, and he introduces Kristina to the world of culture that her parents enjoyed before war and displacement, all while using her as a mule in his operations. The first time she disappoints, André applies belt to backside.

In *Toronto: A Literary Guide*, Greg Gatenby describes *A Stranger and Afraid* as "the first S&M novel in Canadian history to be published by a mainstream house." I disagree. *A Stranger and Afraid* has less to do with Kristina's penchant for punishment than a displaced person's struggle for place.

The novel's second half opens with our heroine having left Paris for a new life in Toronto. There, she finds a job in an appliance company and a husband in its youngest executive. Whereas in Paris Kristina had thought the idea of Canada "rather repulsive," she quickly comes to love her adopted land: "It had accepted my roots, and it would nourish them and in time I would shed all my old leaves infested with nostalgia and grow new ones that no longer turned toward the east."

Living in comfort, she grows uncomfortable. Husband Neil, though loving, is more than a bit bland; worse, he's overly considerate, forever deferential and so very kind. Wouldn't hurt a fly. As their marriage enters year two, Kristina begins to look for a man who will dominate, going so far as to place a personal ad in the notorious *Justice Weekly*.

Anyone looking for titillation will be greatly disappointed; Robert is always quick to close the bedroom door. Her focus is on the power struggles that surround the act, not the act itself. It all makes for fascinating reading.

This is not to say that *A Stranger and Afraid* is without flaws. One curious aspect of the novel is the truly bad sentences that infect what, on the whole, is a very fine and polished piece of prose.

How to explain?

I suppose mother tongue may have something to do with it. Born in 1927 in Kosice, Czechoslovakia, Robert (née Barna) emigrated to

Canada in her early twenties. She wrote for *Maclean's* and *Chatelaine*, and seems to have been well connected; the reception for her second wedding, to George Sereny—two months after *A Stranger and Afraid* appeared in shops—was hosted by Pierre and Janet Berton. In 1973 she and partner Otto Pal opened the very posh Cafe Marika in the mall at 77 Bloor Street West. She died on May 27, 2008, in New York City, where she and her husband had been living. According to her obituary, she had intended to return to Toronto.

Sadly, she left us with just one novel. Sadly, we're not giving it the attention it deserves.

FUTURE PAST

Global Warming as Nationalist Dream

Erres boréales
Florent Laurin [pseud. Armand Grenier]
[Montreal]: [Ducharme], 1944
221 pages

Graced with a cover that appears every bit the sorry result of an elementary-school geography assignment, this is one peculiar-looking book. The interior is nicely laid out, quite professional in appearance—but then we hit the drawings. Twenty-seven in number, nearly one per chapter, they're the work of author, journalist, and sometime-civil servant Armand Grenier. It's no great compliment to describe Grenier as a much better writer than illustrator; *Erres boréales* is a pretty poor novel, but it is interesting.

Set in the year 1968, the book presents global warming in the most positive light, a great achievement made possible through a network of gigantic radiators installed beneath the Labrador Sea. The project is part of a nation-building exercise. In Grenier's post-war world, Quebec has left Canada, taking with it not only the territory granted in 1898 and 1912, but the eastern islands of the Arctic Archipelago. The old Dominion of Newfoundland would appear to have ceded Labrador. That Grenier is vague here is odd because, *Erres boréales* isn't so much a novel as a travelogue taking the reader through the wondrous land created by those humongous heaters. Lest we become lost, the book features a tipped in map.

Our journey begins in Quebec City. Montreal, though it appears on Grenier's map, is neither visited nor mentioned. Never mind, the ultimate destination lies in the islands of the Arctic; this new New France stretches north, not south. Amongst our eager travelling companions is Louis Gamache, a man who last visited these lands when they were still covered by snow and ice.

The ten years since the *"reseau d'appareils électroniques"* were switched on have seen sudden, dramatic changes. There has been no downside. Sea levels pose no danger, weather patterns have only improved and the Gulf Stream continues to warm Europe. The Arctic, however, has melted, revealing fertile soil and many sources of rich minerals. Palm trees now grow on the shores of what was once known as Baffin Island.

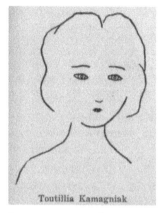

Toutillia Kamagniak

As is typically the case with utopian literature, Grenier focuses very little attention on the people in the land he describes. That said, every journey is touched by romance. In *Erres boréales*, this comes when Louis Gamache encounters Toutillia Kamagniak. An "Esquimaux" cutie-pie, she is as two-dimensional and poorly realized as her portrait suggests.

Toutillia lives with her family in one of the stone structures referred to as the *"anciens iglous."* No, not pools of water. Stone structures that owe more to California's Huntington Mausoleum than anything found in the Canadian North.

Erres boréales is ultimately a Victorian throwback. In Grenier's mid-twentieth-century world, the environment is something to be conquered for economic gain. This view is stated quite clearly in reference to the Northwest Passage: *"la disparition des glaces a rendu au rôle économique qui lui revenait."* The melted north is a territory to be colonized—its people, like Toutillia, are to be converted into good, God-fearing Catholics. But take away Grenier's naïveté concerning climate change and we see something rather insidious. The Esquimaux remain, absorbed and forever altered by this New France. They seem happy enough, but where are the Cree, the Huron, the Montagnais, and the Abenaki? Like the anglo Quebecers, who are also absent, their place names and history have been disappeared on that tipped-in map.

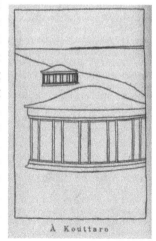

À Kouttaro

SF, Not S/M

The House that Stood Still
A.E. van Vogt
Toronto: Harlequin, 1952
224 pages

A few pages into *The House that Stood Still*, Allison Stephens, lawyer for Arthur Tannahill, stumbles upon a drama being played out in one of his client's many buildings:

> Nine men and four women were standing in various tensed positions. One of the women, an amazingly good-looking blonde, had been stripped to the waist; her ankles and wrists were tied with thin ropes to the chair in which she sat sideways. There were bloody welts on her tanned back, and a whip lay on the floor.

Spicy stuff, so it's little wonder that Harlequin exploited the scene for its cover. American publisher Beacon went even farther with the revised, 1960 edition, replacing the original title with something more suggestive.

How long before folks who'd bought these books felt they'd been had? Sure, Beacon's pitch line, "I have come to pay my debt—in the way I've discovered men prefer," features in the novel, but it's just about the hottest thing you'll find.

The first third of *The House that Stood Still* reads like a noirish mystery. There's an encounter with a California cult, a groundskeeper is murdered, a woman is shot, and an elevator operator is found stabbed to death.

Stephens does his best to ward off an aggressive DA who seems intent on pinning at least one murder rap on Tannahill. But as the lawyer grows closer to Mistra Linett, the "amazingly good-looking blonde" he saved from further flogging, things get strange. Turns out she's hundreds of years old and that her swanky, ultra-modern apartment is really a spaceship. That whipping Stephens interrupted? It had to do with a disagreement over what to do in the event of an expected "atomic war." Should Mistra and her fellow Methuselahs try to prevent the conflict or relocate to their base on Mars? At the centre of all this is Tannahill's ancient radioactive house, which has somehow bestowed eternal life upon Mistra and the gang.

These revelations don't raise so much as an eyebrow with Stephens. A dim bulb, he's much more shocked by the murders than all that stuff about eternal life, imminent atomic war, and a base on Mars, never mind the ancient robot brain from another planet. This is not to say that Stephens isn't a thinker; to the contrary, he's forever thinking:

> As they embraced, the thought came to Stephens: "Is she trying to buy my help with her body?" It was an idea he held only for a moment before dismissing it as irrelevant. In a way, it was true. But the fact was, temporarily at least, this woman was his without reservation. She was obviously caught up by love desire, and he was the fortunate recipient. He could even believe that she had not for years been stirred to such a response as she was making on him.
>
> For a while, then, he had no thought, only awareness of the physical contact with her, and of a mounting feeling of excitement. Presently, he wondered, could a mortal man really love an immortal woman? Instantly, he didn't wish to think about that. This was now, not some future time when he would be grown older, and she still young and beautiful and eternally desirable. Here and now, this was an act of love between a virile man and a healthy woman, who, with every meeting, roved that they enjoyed each other immensely. It was pleasant to realize also that there had not yet been a prudish moment between them.
>
> When they finally dressed...

How hot was that?

Our hero's greatest weakness is that, for all his thinking, he's incapable of reaching any real conclusions. As the novel progresses, Stephens is confronted by a growing list of events he finds baffling. Though he moves with great purpose, breaking into private property, stealing documents, and digging up graves, the lawyer is never able to figure out what the hell is going on.

Neither can the reader.

The House that Stood Still is unintelligible. Blame lies, at least in part, with the original editor and all those who've followed. One simple example of the mess left behind: early in the novel, Stephens returns home and changes into his pyjamas. Mistra, again in distress, appears at his door. Stephens helps her, returns to his bedroom, and then changes into his pyjamas. This error appears in the first edition, and is repeated right up to the most recent 1993 Carroll & Graf edition. This was back when van Vogt still had roughly seven more years to enjoy this mortal coil; it wasn't too late to whip things into shape.

I apologize for that last sentence.

Post-Apocalypse in Pink

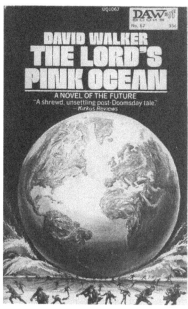

The Lord's Pink Ocean
David Walker
New York: Daw, 1973
160 pages

David Walker sold an awful lot of novels in his time, but nothing I've read has been particularly memorable. His most successful book, *Geordie* (1950), the sentimental story of a simple, scrawny Scot's transformation into an Olympic hammer-thrower, sold in the six figures. Quite the accomplishment for a writer working out of St Andrews, New Brunswick. In belated recognition, I think, Walker was given back-to-back Governor General's awards for the novels that followed, *The Pillar* (1952) and *Digby* (1953). *Geordie* was adapted for the screen—a weak film starring the wonderful Alastair Sim—and in 1966 spawned a sequel, *Come Back, Geordie*. Such was the original's success that two decades later its title continued to grace the covers of Walker's novels.

I'm not so sure that *The Lord's Pink Ocean* would have appealed to the audience that had been so captivated by the sentimental, uplifting story of Geordie MacTaggart. This is a novel of the seventies, a bleak work of science fiction set in a world deadened by shocking pink algae. The cold waters of the Arctic and Antarctic protect several thousand survivors, but this is not their story. Instead we have the Parkers and the Smiths, two farm families eking out a living in a secluded valley that overlooks what was once the city of Boston.

Yes, a secluded valley above Boston.

The Parkers are black, the Smiths are white; the Parkers have a boy, the Smiths have a girl; father Parker hates father Smith and vice versa. There's all sorts of stuff going on here, but for what purpose?

My reaction to *The Lord's Pink Ocean* mirrors that of William French, who in the September 12, 1972, edition of the *Globe and Mail* wrote:

I thought for a while that Walker was writing a satirical novel—that would make it more bearable. He could easily be poking fun at religion, which plays some part in the plot, or science fiction—pink algae, indeed—or industrial society, scientific progress and pollution. But the horrible realization dawned that he was serious.

French goes on to poke fun himself at Walker's dialogue, providing this example: "Now be good sports and give our floats a mighty shove. Toodle-oo, then."

Those are the words of an Inuit Anglican minister preparing to fly off in his pontoon plane.

Like so many post-apocalyptic fantasies, *The Lord's Pink Ocean* works only if one doesn't pause to think. In this, film has an advantage—zombie headshots do distract—but with a novel read over the course several evenings, questions come to mind. For example, how is it that people born just a few years—or is it months?—after the collapse of civilization know next to nothing about "The Time Before"? How do two estranged men, each raised without religion, develop an identical system of belief? Why is it that they speak like nineteenth-century Mennonites, while their teenager children speak like... well, teenagers? And what's with that altitudinous valley anyway?

French titled his review "Blushingly Bad." A bit harsh, perhaps. *The Lord's Pink Ocean* is nothing more and nothing less than a middling genre novel. Might we expect better from a Governor General's Award recipient? Yes, but let's also remember that Walker was honoured in the same decade that saw the award go to Igor Gouzenko and Lionel Shapiro.

I chose to read *The Lord's Pink Ocean* because I thought it would be quirky enough to hold my interest. I mean, just look at the title. Maybe I made a mistake. A friend's mother recommends Walker's 1960 novel, *Where the High Winds Blow*, but I think the time has come to leave the author behind.

Toodle-oo, I say.

At Long Last, Lunacy

"TERRIFYING!"

The Last Canadian
William C. Heine
Markham, ON: Pocket Books, 1974
253 pages

In the opening chapter of *The Last Canadian*, protagonist Gene Arnprior leaves his suburban home and speeds along the Trans-Canada toward Montreal. A to B, it's not much of a scene, but the image has remained with me since I read this book at age twelve. This was the first novel in which I encountered a familiar landscape. Of the rest, I remembered nothing... nothing of the sexism, the crazed politics, or the absurdity.

Penned by the then editor-in-chief of the *London Free Press*, it begins with late-night news bulletins about mysterious deaths in Colorado. Gene recognizes what others don't and takes to the air, flying his wife and two sons to a remote fishing camp near James Bay. As a virus sweeps through the Americas, killing nearly everyone, the Arnprior family live, untouched, for three idyllic years, before coming into contact with a carrier. As it turns out, what doesn't kill you makes you stronger; Gene lives on, but must bury his wife and children.

The Last Canadian is a favourite of survivalists everywhere. Someone calling himself Wolverine writes on the Survivalist Blog:

> The immediate response reaction is instructive. Second there are the North country [sic] survival techniques. Third there are psychological factors of being a survivor in a situation where most others die. And there is more, dealing with post-disaster situations, though I won't go into that because it would spoil the book for you.

I won't be as courteous. Spoilers will follow, but first this complaint: the title is a cheat. Gene is not "The Last Canadian"—there are plenty of others—rather, he considers himself such because his citizenship papers came through the day before the plague struck. Gene is an American who came north for work. He'd enjoyed his time in Canada, where he made many friends and "had come to understand the Canadian parliamentary system, and agreed that it was far more flexible and effective than the rigidity of the American system of divided constitutional responsibility."

Reason before passion.

Is it then surprising that, there being no parliament, he's drawn back to the United States? Heading south, Gene resists all invitations from the Canadians he meets; he considers them "eccentric" for choosing to stay put, supporting themselves through farming and whatever might be found in local shops. There's much more excitement to be found south of the border.

First, he stumbles into a Manhattan turf war—but that's hardly worth mentioning. As a carrier, Gene succeeds in killing a number of Soviet military types in Florida. In doing so, he becomes Enemy #1 of the USSR. They send frogmen assassins, set off bombs, plant land mines, and lob nuclear missiles in his general direction, but still Gene beetles on. When a Soviet submarine destroys his Chesapeake Bay home, killing his girlfriend, however, Gene seeks revenge.

Though he has no evidence, Gene comes to blame the Soviets for the plague (in fact, it's a rogue Russian scientist), and dedicates himself to infecting the USSR. He begins with a short-wave radio broadcast directed at the Kremlin: "If the Russian people were half as smart as your literature says they are, they'd have tossed you out long ago. Because they haven't, I have to assume they're as stupid as you are."

You see, because they are stupid, Gene has decided that all citizens of the Soviet Union should die. He cares not one bit that the plague will spread beyond the borders of the country, killing the rest of Asia and Europe, never mind Africa.

It's all crazy, but the reader isn't surprised. Though Heine spills an awful lot of primary colours in an effort to paint the man a hero, concern has been growing for quite some time. Remember when he hit his wife, just so she'd understand the gravity of their situation? How about when he threatened to tie his young son to a tree and whip him until he couldn't stand—all because he'd fallen asleep while tending a fire? Then there's that little glimpse of Gene's psyche provided when his new love,

Leila, tells him a horrific story of being kidnapped, beaten, and raped repeatedly by a psychopath:

> "You can't imagine the things he made me do. And he killed a man to get one of his girls."
>
> Gene felt another chuckle welling up. In the few years he'd spent in Korea and Japan, he'd read about most of the sex things there were to do, and tried a few himself. He stifled it, however, recognizing her revulsion.

Yep, pretty funny stuff… and don't forget to add that boys will be boys.

Intent on killing billions, Gene makes his way up the Pacific Coast, dodging Soviet and American forces before crossing the Bering Strait into the USSR. Hundreds of Americans and an untold number of Russians die as a result. His journey and life are finally ended by a clusterfuck of nuclear strikes—Soviet, Chinese, American, and British—that obliterate the Anadyr basin.

Lest the reader agree with the Soviets that Gene has become a madman, Heine is at the ready to set things right. You see, Gene's actions are perfectly understandable; the British prime minister tells us so.

We're left with the image of radioactive clouds composed of the people and terrain of Anadyr. They drift across Canada, sprinkling poisoned dust over the land. Some settles on the graves of Gene's wife and children:

> In time the rains washed the radioactive dust down among the rocks and deep into the soil. Something of Eugene Arnprior, who had suffered much and had done more to serve mankind than he could ever have imagined, had come home to be with those he loved.

Thus ends what I believe to be the stupidest Canadian novel written to date.

A Tremendous Canada of Darkness

For My Country
[Pour la patrie: roman du XXe siecle]
Jules-Paul Tardivel
[Sheila Fischman, trans.]
Toronto: University of Toronto Press, 1975
250 pages

The man who wrote this book believed novels to be instruments of the Devil, "weapons forged by Satan himself for the destruction of mankind," but as he explains in his preface, "it is permitted to capture the enemy's war machines and to use them to assault his own ramparts." Taken in this context, you could say that *Pour la patrie* was written by someone who didn't quite know what he was doing. This is not to say that Tardivel was unskilled; as a journalist, editor, and publisher he certainly knew how to wield a pen. What's more, he was a master of the French language, which he defended with zeal in tracts like *L'Anglicisme voilà l'ennemi* (1880). Finally, as a deeply religious and conservative Catholic, he showed no reluctance in firing his enemy's war machine.

Tardivel's targets are easy to identify; *Pour la patrie* is very much a black-and-white story. The dark side is led by Aristide Montarval, a French Satanist who is charged by Beelzebub himself with destroying the Catholic faith in its very last place of influence: the province of Quebec.

Old Nick's timing couldn't be better.

Pour la patrie was published in 1895 but is set fifty years in the future. In this not-so-wondrous world of 1945, an England weakened by "secret societies" watches powerlessly as its empire grows smaller by the day. Ireland has its independence, Australia has rid itself of the Crown, there are rumblings in Scotland and Germany gains ground daily—quite literally—as it takes over what little remains of the African colonies.

Seizing the opportunity offered by an undisclosed diplomatic indiscretion, the United States has succeeded in demanding that Westminster cut ties with Canada. The plan, hatched by Freemasons, is to invade and annex, but this is delayed by yet another war with Spain and troubles along the border with Mexico.

The mess leaves Canada with a constitutional crisis as it looks to replace the Governor General with... well, Tardivel never quite addresses the issue. All the reader really knows of the constitutional proposals is that they number three: the status quo, legislative union, and separation. Led by Prime Minister Sir Henry Marwood, the governing party promotes the first option.

Dry stuff, I know, but remember that there is great evil at work. As a Freemason, and therefore a Satanist, Marwood is only pretending to support the status quo; in fact, he's working under Montarval's guidance to bring a legislative union that will rid Quebec of both the Church and the French language.

Marwood's foe is charismatic separatist Joseph Lamirande, a wealthy medical doctor who sits as the Member of Parliament for Charlevoix. A pious soul, he has as his ally lifelong friend Paul Leverdier, editor of *La Nouvelle-France*, an independent newspaper not unlike Tardivel's own *La Vérité*.

As might be expected, the Freemasons do their level best to kill both men, only to be thwarted time and again. The earliest attempt results in the poisoning of Lamirande's lovely wife, Marguerite.

God is on his side, of course. As Lamirande prays for his wife before a statue of St Joseph—after whom he was named—cold, white marble becomes flesh and blood. The husband of the Blessed Virgin Mary gives the separatist leader a choice:

"Joseph, if you insist on the temporal grace you ask for, it will certainly be granted. Your wife will live. But if, on the contrary, you leave everything to the will of God, the sacrifice of your domestic happiness will be repaid by the triumph of your homeland."

Understandably, Lamirande is tempted to ask God to spare Marguerite, but the good woman talks him out of it:

"It is not only a question of our country's prosperity and material greatness but of the salvation of many souls over the centuries.

Because if the secret societies continue to flourish it will be the ruin of our religion. That thought has sustained you in the painful struggles over these past few weeks, and it sustains me now. Think what good can be accomplished in return for a few years of miserable life! It is not often that a woman can save her country by dying!"

And so, she does.

And because she does, the ending comes as no surprise.

The great Henri Bourassa found Tardivel's novel unreadable, but I got through it all, including the chapter in which Lamirande's eight-year-old daughter relates her understanding of the catechism. Of course, I had a certain advantage over Bourassa in reading this nineteenth-century *roman du XXe siècle* in the twenty-first century. It is always interesting to look back on a future that never was. Tardivel's Canada of 1945 is one of electric lights and trains that move between Ottawa and Montreal in under two hours, yet most personal travel still takes place by horse and buggy. I was most interested in his descriptions of the "telephone-telegraph," a machine that enables the user not only to speak to another at a distance, but is also capable of transmitting facsimiles of handwritten letters and documents.

I used to have one of those.

Still don't have those trains though. I blame Ottawa.

A Man, a Plan, a Dam—Labrador!

FERMEZ LA PORTE ON GÈLE

par René Carrier

Le barrage de Belle - Isle

Fermez la porte, on gèle
René Carrier
Westmount, QC: Desclez, 1981
298 pages

Winters have been pretty rough of late and we have only ourselves to blame. Had we paid heed to René Carrier, the good folks of Happy Valley-Goose Bay might be downing margaritas and playing beach volleyball as I write this.

Appearances to the contrary, this is a Victorian book. Author Carrier may have been born a couple of decades after the old queen died, but he carries the attitude that characterized her time on the throne. *Fermez la porte, on gèle—Close the Door, We're Freezing—*is about the command of nature. This is Man as master of his dominion... or a corner of his dominion... or a corner of the Dominion of Canada. It holds the distinction of being the only book-length argument for damming the Strait of Belle Isle.

Fittingly, M Carrier's idea stretches back to Victoria's reign. He credits civil engineer Charles Baillargé with having first proposed the barrier, in 1887, but I've seen the idea laid out in earlier documents. The October 1878 edition of *Harper's New Monthly Magazine* claimed that such a scheme would "ameliorate the climate of Canada." In closing off the strait, the cold Arctic current would be "diverted past Newfoundland and directed ocean ward, leaving the portion of the Gulf Stream which finds its way into the St. Lawrence to exert its genial effect unimpaired." In other words, the Gulf of St Lawrence would become considerably warmer, transforming our smallest province into something resembling a Caribbean island.

Popular Science Monthly, October 1921

It all seems the stuff of a Bruce McCall fantasy, especially when one recognizes that such a structure would not only have to withstand the force of the current, but the two hundred thousand tonne icebergs it carries. Never mind, in 1909 a group of British investors known as the Labrador Syndicate began lobbying Newfoundland to build just such a barrier.

Popular Science Monthly, October 1921

The October 1921 issue of *Popular Science* put it that the proposed structure would forever change the Dominions of Newfoundland and Canada. American journalist Walter Noble Burns, best known as the author of *The Saga of Billy the Kid*, wrote with seeming authority:

> The Strait of Belle Isle, a narrow channel separating Newfoundland from Labrador, is a hole in the wall of the Atlantic seaboard that is mainly responsible for the bleak winter climate in Eastern Canada. Plug up this hole, and Eastern Canada and New England would have a climate as mild and delightful as that of the Carolinas.

This change in temperature would see Montreal become the new New York, while in the Maritime provinces great metropolises would grow. Burns described the proposed causeway as a "solid strip of stone and concrete ten miles in length and fifty feet wide," allowing a railway to run between Quebec City and St. John's. Newfoundland's capital would be transformed into a great shipping port. The distance from Liverpool to St. John's, the reporter noted, was a thousand miles shorter than that between the English city and New York. In the midst of all this enthusiasm, Burns allowed that the diversion of the Arctic stream just might cause England's climate to resemble that of Labrador.

Oh, well.

Black Tuesday brought an end to the Labrador Syndicate. I don't see that anyone said anything much about damming the strait until M Carrier's book. Neither meteorologist nor climatologist, the author was a graduate of Université Laval's school of commerce. A retiree, he had spent much of his working life as an assistant general manager at Vachon Inc in Saint-Marie de Beauce. This connection with Jos. Louis may go some way in explaining the strange conclusion to the book's cover copy: *"Le fermeture du détroite de Belle-Isle est d'après lui le seul gâteau de fête digne de la population des cinq provinces canadiennes de l'est."*

Fermez la porte, on gèle puts the author's commerce degree to good use. This is a book written with business in mind. In its 298 pages, M Carrier provides a convincing, remarkably detailed analysis of all aspects of the project.

But don't take my word for it—I have no mind for numbers—look to Roger D'Astous, the architect behind the Château Champlain and Montreal's Olympic Village. So captivated was M D'Astrous that he established la Fondation de la Grand Jetée de Belle-Isle Inc/The Great Bel-Isle [sic] Crossing Foundation Inc. Or how about Pierre Lajoie, president of the Group LMB, who, four years after the book's publication presented the Mulroney government with a proposal for a 15-kilometre barrier modelled on M Carrier's. Price: $7 billion.

Again, I have no mind for numbers; the one thing I took away from *Fermez la porte, on gèle*, is this: It can be done. That said, what troubled me was the effect such a change might have on our ecology. M Carrier devotes just twenty-seven pages, less than ten percent of the book, to *considérations écologiques*, most of which has to do with anticipated benefits to the gulf's herring stocks. But what of the other creatures... creatures like my UK cousins?

GOTH

Falling Hard for May Agnes Fleming

The Midnight Queen
Mrs May Agnes Fleming
New York: Hurst, [n.d.]
256 pages

Canada's earliest best-selling author, no one has been so forgotten as May Agnes Fleming, right? So how is it that I spent nearly seven years exploring this country's suppressed, ignored, and forgotten books before reading any of hers? The simple fact is that, for all my hunting, I just never came across any of them. Oh, they're out there—loads are listed online—but they're not making their way into our used bookstores. Not the ones I haunt, anyway.

Patience lasts only so long. Last month I bid two Yankee dollars for a nineteenth-century copy of Fleming's seventh novel, *The Midnight Queen*. As it turned out, I was the only one who bothered. Shipping set me back a further twenty-five.

A story of the Plague Year, *The Midnight Queen* takes place over the course of one remarkably eventful evening. It begins with a chance encounter between young Sir Norman Kingsley and his friend Malcolm Ormiston in a darkening London thoroughfare. Sir Norman has made preparations to flee the afflicted city and advises Ormiston to do the same. However, his friend has fallen in love and cannot be moved. The object of his desire is a woman of exquisite figure and great mystery. An enchantress, she is known only as "La Masque"—so named because her face is invariably hidden behind a veil of black velvet. Ormiston seizes upon any excuse to visit, and so encourages Sir Norman to make use of the lady's services as a soothsayer.

With a servant serving as usher, the pair are introduced to a room appointed with the very finest Goth fixings. La Masque enters and entreats Sir Norman to gaze upon the water held by an ebony cauldron sitting in the centre of the room. What follows delights and disturbs. He sees first an extravagant gathering presided over by a woman whose beauty surpasses any of his dreams. A dungeon cell is the setting of the next scene. The woman reappears. Sir Norman draws his sword and strikes her heart. This is followed by an image of two men lying on the street.

"Do you know those two last figures?" asked the lady.
"I do," said Sir Norman, promptly, "it was Ormiston and myself."
"Right! and one of them was dead."

Sir Norman and Ormiston have no sooner left La Masque's abode—without paying, I note—when they witness a shrieking woman run from a nearby house. Inquisitive souls, the friends enter the building to find a lifeless figure in a glowing bridal gown of white satin. Further inspection reveals a mark of the plague, but Sir Norman is more concerned by the dead woman's resemblance to the one he saw himself kill minutes earlier.

Conveniently, a plague cart happens by. Sir Norman reluctantly assists in placing the bride upon the pile of other plague-ridden bodies. Such is the woman's beauty that Sir Norman decides to follow the cart to the plague pit—the one in Finsbury Fields, to be precise—so that he might gaze upon her face one last time.

Ormiston here proves what a good friend he is:

"Oh! if you are determined, I will go with you, of course; but it is the craziest freak I ever heard of. After this, you need never laugh at me."
"I never will," said Sir Norman, moodily; "for if you love a face you have never seen, I love one I have only looked on when dead. Does it not seem sacrilege to throw any one so like an angel into that horrible plague-pit."

A rhetorical question, clearly.

Just as the nameless bride is being readied for the old heave-ho, she comes to life. Unfortunately, upon seeing her surroundings, she again loses consciousness. With Ormiston's help, Sir Norman carries the woman back to his home. The pair then set out to fetch a doctor, only to return to an empty house.

In her *Dictionary of Canadian Biography* entry, Fred Cogswell praises May Agnes Fleming for plots "as ingenious and satisfying as those of Wilkie

Collins." This one involves a secret court composed of highwaymen, an evil dwarf prince, handsome triplets and their disfigured half-sister, Charles II in disguise, and the presidency of the yet-to-be-born United States. One character will be beheaded, another will die of fright, a couple more will be run through, and, as might be expected, many will be taken by the plague. Sir Norman is the unfortunate witness to the suicide of a woman who throws herself into the pit:

> He saw her for a second or two heaving and writhing in the putrid heap; and then the strong man reeled and fell with his face on the ground, not fainting, but sick unto death. Of all the dreadful things he had witnessed that night there was nothing so dreadful as this; of all the horror he had felt before, there was none to equal what he felt now. In his momentary delirium, it seemed to him she was reaching her arms of bone up to drag him in, and that the skeleton face was mopping, and mowing, and grinning at him on the edge of the awful pit.

It's one hell of a ride. Not wanting to let go, I became wistful reading the final page.

And so, flush with new love for an old author, I turn again to online booksellers—and throw buckets of money at postal services.

A Nineteenth-Century Céline Dion and Her Horrible Hunchback Husband

"The Lane that Had No Turning"
*The Lane that Had No Turning
and Other Tales Concerning the People
of Pontiac*
Gilbert Parker
New York: A.L. Burt, 1900
359 pages

To think I nearly set this aside!

A historical novella of old Quebec, "The Lane that Had No Turning" begins with an awful lot of backstory and a presumption that the reader is familiar with "Valmont, the bizarre but popular Napoleonic pretender." Well, this reader was not only unfamiliar, but had to poke around a bit to discover that the character and accompanying plot elements are derived from Parker's 1895 novel, *When Valmont Came to Pontiac.*

Don't know it? Not to worry, everything you do need to know can be reduced to three sentences: Pontiac's aging Seigneur has let it be known that his estate will go to Englishman George Fournel. The old man dies, no documentation can be found, and so everything goes to direct heir Louis Racine. He's a lawyer.

The eyes fairly glaze over... until this:

On the very day of his marriage Louis Racine had made a painful discovery. A heritage of his father's which had skipped two generations, suddenly appeared in himself: he was becoming a hunchback!

Wow! Didn't see that coming.

"Terror, despair, gloom and anxiety," begins the next sentence. Turns out that Racine's bride, beautiful Madelinette Lajeunesse, the local blacksmith's daughter, is recognized throughout the world as "the greatest singer of her day." Three months into the marriage, the songbird leaves Quebec on a European tour. Her groom delays his departure with a story that all sorts of seigneurial matters require attention. The truth is that Louis, who has somehow succeeded in hiding his condition, looks to arrest his "strange growth" with a secret surgical operation.

It's a failure.

Madelinette returns from Europe to find a hunchback husband of twisted mind and body. She retires from the stage to devote herself to keeping Louis in check. You see, the seigneur is unstable, as evidenced by his attraction to the days of old. He flies the flag of the golden lilies, maintains a guard in the uniforms of New France, and works assiduously to rid Pontiac of those of English and Irish heritage.

But Madelinette cannot be ever-present. She manages to stop her husband from killing a man, then races through the Quebec countryside to save the seigneury but cannot prevent her husband's second, successful, murder attempt. Like the nineteenth-century heroine she is, Madelinette will stand by helplessly as a suicide takes place on the other side of a locked door.

Throughout all her trials, I couldn't help but liken Madelinette, a woman from rural Quebec whose pipes are celebrated the word over, to Céline Dion.

Of course, the greatest Quebec singer was actually a Jewish poet from Montreal.

Everybody knows.

Alberta Gothic

Cattle
Winnifred Eaton
New York: A.L. Burt, [c. 1925]
294 pages

There's an award-winning book waiting to be written about Montreal's Eatons. Sixteen in all, headed by artist-father Edward and his Chinese wife Lotus Blossom, they were anything but the typical Victorian Canadian family. The children were raised in poverty—again, Edward was an artist—but managed to do fairly well for themselves. Sara performed on stage, Grace practised law, and Edith, a journalist, holds the distinction of being the first Asian-North American writer of fiction.

It was the eighth Eaton child, Winnifred, who had the greatest public profile. Casting herself as Nagaskai-born Onoto Watanna, she exploited the public's fascination with things Japanese in a series of romances with titles like *The Wooing of Wisteria* (1902), *The Heart of the Hyacinth* (1903), and *Daughters of Nijo* (1907).

A late career novel, in a great many ways *Cattle* marked a departure for Eaton. Here her fragrant, falling cherry blossoms are replaced by grain and the harsh, hardscrabble reality of prairie life. The first of her novels to be set wholly in Canada,—Alberta to be precise—it is populated by an odd assortment of Americans, Scots, Chinese, and English remittance men. Ontarians, too.

Alberta is, in a way, a land of sanctuary, and upon its rough bosom the derelicts of the world, the fugitives, the hunters, the sick, and the dying have sought asylum and cure.

Our heroine, Nettie Day, is one of a very few characters to have actually been born in the province. A "slow-moving, slow-thinking girl, simple-minded and totally ignorant of the world," she cares for nine siblings on her widowed father's failing ranch. When Dad dies, all but

Nettie are dealt to neighbouring farms and orphanages. She has no other choice but to work for Bull Langdon—"I'm willin' to take her along with her dad's old truck"—who's looking for a girl to help his sickly wife with housework.

A former schoolteacher, Mrs Langdon is perhaps the most positive figure in all of Canadian literature:

> She had an ingenious faith, imbedded from tracts and books that drifted into her hands in her teaching days; she denied the existence of evil, pain or illness in the world, and when it pushed its ugly fist into her face, or wracked her frail body, she had a little formula that she bravely recited over and over again, like an incantation, in which she asserted that it was an error: that she was in the best of health, and that everything in the world was beautiful and in the image of God.

After a few months, Bull sends his frail wife off to rest in Banff. No sooner is she gone than he rapes fifteen-year-old Nettie; the next day he informs her that she will be the next mistress of his ranch.

Cattle is extraordinary in that it is far more brutal and disturbing than any other Canadian novel of its time; that it is by a woman who'd made a career writing romances makes it all the more so. Amongst its characters we find a self-loathing, androgynous "man-woman" and a "half-breed" bastard boy whose father's beatings have rendered him "half-witted." That father being Bull Langdon.

There are many deaths, including that of another of Bull's illegitimate children, an infant he kidnaps and all but tosses to his hired hands: "... there was a great swelling on the forehead, where he had fallen off the seat of the car to the floor. Its whole body, in fact, was bruised from the cruel bumping of that long mad ride."

I haven't mentioned the Spanish Flu pandemic or that a character is gored, thrown, and rent to pieces by a prize Hereford bull.

While Eaton's dark story is in no way a *roman à clef*—thank goodness—it draws on knowledge gained through her second marriage to Alberta rancher Francis Reeve. She published just one more novel, *His Royal Nibs* (1925), also set in Alberta's cattle country, before heading off to Hollywood.

Yes, Hollywood.

Now, who's going to write that book on the Eatons? Why hasn't it been written already?

Crazy, But that's How it Goes

Crazy to Kill
Ann Cardwell
[pseud. Jean Makins Pawley]
Winnipeg: Harlequin, 1949
191 pages

One of the earliest Harlequin paperbacks—the twenty-second to be precise—for years I'd all but ignored *Crazy to Kill*. Oh, the cover is memorable, but no more so than *Corpse on the Town* and so very many others from the publisher's early years. What encouraged me to at long last delve into this mystery novel was the discovery that "Ann Cardwell," Jean Makins Perkins (1902–1966), lived her life in Stratford, Ontario, a mere twenty kilometres from my home.

As the rebellious, eccentric daughter of Supreme Court Justice J.C. Makins—once of Makins and Hanley, Barristers, Etc.—Mrs Perkins enjoyed an obvious advantage over many other mystery novelists. What's more, writing seems to have been in her blood; James Reaney was a younger, distant cousin. Though the two never met, the award-winning poet and playwright would one day turn *Crazy to Kill* into a well-received opera.

Yes, an opera.

Reaney once described *Crazy to Kill* as a "book about Stratford," a statement I'm at a loss to explain. The novel takes place entirely at Resthome, a mental institution catering to the wealthy just outside the fictional town of Fairburn, New York. Our narrator, elderly spinster Agatha Lawson, has been a patient for ten uneventful years. However, just as her release looks imminent, bad things begin to happen. First, young John Lennox, the son of the head doctor, is found unconscious at the bottom of a gravel pit. Nurse Jones nearly succumbs to strangulation. Nurse Zimmerman lies in the glow of a pink bed light, "her pretty throat cut from ear to ear."

The bodies really begin piling up. The problem is that they're just that: bodies. Cardwell's greatest weakness is that she has difficulty giving flesh to characters. The most notable exception is Agatha Lawson herself. For an explanation as to why our narrator stands out, we look to cousin James, who frustrates in telling us that the author "felt an identity with Angela Lawson."

Whatever does he mean?

The Harlequin edition of *Crazy to Kill* promises a clever novel laced with black humour:

> Here is a gory, murder-filled mystery story, yet so amusingly told that the reader will constantly chuckle when he is not shuddering!

And at times it delivers:

> The jagged edges of the stone had done awful things to Tim's skull. Lieutenant Hogan said that it had taken a great deal of strength to bash in Tim's head because of its extreme thickness.

But for the most part the humour amounts to nothing more than a series of scenes in which a little old lady, Agatha, bests and belittles a none-too-bright detective.

In promising a *mélange* of gore and chuckles, Harlequin misses the big selling point: here we have a psychological mystery, set in what one character uncharitably calls "a nut house," and told by one of its patients. *Crazy to Kill* certainly has its moments, and in those moments one can see a better novel within. But let's recognize this as a debut novel and look forward to her maturing talent.

Cousin James suggests we'll be disappointed.

To the Big House... Or Not

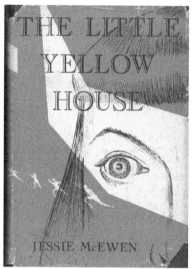

The Little Yellow House
Jessie McEwen
Toronto: Ryerson, 1953
249 pages

Mark Crosbie is a damaged war vet. A few years back, whilst downing Messerschmitts over Denmark, his plane caught fire. Mark managed to parachute to safety and—more luck—found sanctuary in a *little yellow house* inhabited by an exiled German university professor and his beautiful daughter. Sadly, the airman's injuries necessitated the amputation of a leg; happily, he and the beautiful daughter, Adella, fell for one another.

This novel opens two years after the war's end with our hero standing on the deck of a ship bound for Canada. Poor Mark is returning to Toronto empty-armed, having spent a frustrating few months travelling through Europe in a failed search for Adella and her scholarly father. Mark hasn't even settled into his deck chair before he's approached by Charlie Griswold, a boozy friend of his cousin Alec. In the manner of drunks everywhere, ol' Charlie latches onto his semi-acquaintance and begins to babble: "Got hitched in Lun'on a month ago and she's the fines' bit o' luggage I ever did see. Ain't nuthin' like her in the whole wide world."

The bit o' luggage—name: Margery—isn't so great, but there's something about her that reminds Mark of Adella.

Sadly, Charlie's honeymoon is short-lived. On the sixth night at sea he corners Mark. "She says she's going to dish me when we dock," mutters Charlie. "Says she only fastened on to me for a free ride."

The unhappy newlywed tries to enlist Mark's help in discrediting Margery: "Swear you know she's a flossie, fleesie or a what-have-you." In exchange, Charlie will give the goods on Alec. Mark refuses and returns to his cabin. A few hours later, he's awoken with the news that Charlie has gone overboard.

But wait, there's more.

It seems that Mark has long been suspicious of his cousin. This may have something to do with Alec's father, Alexander, who decades earlier embezzled money and property from the Crosbie family company. Alec's sister Monica, a columnist for the *Toronto Daily Graphic*, is so worried that her brother inherited Dad's dishonest nature that she has set up a secret account to cover anticipated legal fees. She's also written a drama about a man caught stealing from his children. Efforts to sell the play brought her into contact with Isy Lerman, "a famous New York play agent," to whom she is now engaged. Monica is about to leave Toronto to marry her fiancé when she's stopped by Alec. Her fears have come true: Alec has been stealing from the family firm, just like dear old Dad, and now needs her help.

Hold on, there's still more.

Alec is playing for time, and has managed to secure a good chunk of it in thwarting Mark's European search. Just as the one-legged veteran began his hobbling through Copenhagen, Cologne, Paris, Bruges, and who knows how many towns and villages on the Rhine, he had pal Charlie whisk Adella and her father off to Canada. They've spent the ensuing months at Ruthven House, the long-neglected, seldom visited Crosbie family estate in rural Ontario. An odd place, "almost like a castle," it comes complete with a tower and hidden dungeon, but no telephone. Adella and her dad are cut off, and dare not venture outside as Alec has warned them of the deep hatred Canadians have of Germans.

Alec dispatches Monica to keep an eye on his Ruthven House house guests, trusting that she will stick by his story that Mark has been committed to a psychiatric hospital.

When Mark arrives back in Toronto, he's told by Alec that the missing Monica "has cracked up, gone to pieces."

It's a lot to take in, especially because the reader has only three chapters in which to do so. Things get easier but less interesting in the fourteen that follow as Mark and Monica struggle with indecision. The one-legged war hero tries to convince himself that Alec is good—"*Alec is good.* Mark said to himself. *Alec is very good*"—in the face of overwhelming evidence to the contrary. When he finally does admit to himself that Alec is not good, Mark doesn't know what to do. Meanwhile, Monica spends some two hundred or so densely packed pages debating whether she should come clean with Adella and the professor:

She would tell; she could not tell; Monica Crosbie still was a creature divided. That she would tell—and the resolution was firm—caused her heart to swell with delight. That she could not tell —and she had tried and failed—caused her heart to shrink and tighten with misery. King Solomon could not have divided the baby for the disputing mothers more evenly than she was cut, Monica thought.

From chapter 14, this is one in a great number of angst-ridden paragraphs that I can't be bothered to count. Was it not enough to have read them? I trudged on as the book's editor fell by the wayside. This later passage is typical:

> The inability to tell was an enormous, throbbing pain that took such fierce possession of her that, no matter with whom she was when it gained possession of her that, she rushed to Alec where he still cowered in the bedroom.

After the title page, after the copyright information, after the table of contents, the reader encounters a stark statement on an otherwise blank page:

This is the story of a crime.

But which one? When time finally runs out for Alec, it's revealed that his criminal acts are plentiful—arson and attempted murder figure—yet he faces no charges because... because... Well, you must understand that as the wealthy son of a convicted man he was greatly disadvantaged.

I didn't buy it. Call me a law-and-order type if you will, but I think some sort of police investigation was warranted. Besides, I'd really like to know just who killed Charlie Griswold and why.

Ontario Gothic Romance
(With the Scent of Brut)

spine tingling...
don't read this book late at night

SATAN'S BELL

JOY CARROLL

Satan's Bell
Joy Carroll
Markham, ON: Pocket, 1976
190 pages

Summer reading from my four-teenth year, a time when the black spines of mass-market horror paper-backs ran across my bookcase. They're all gone now, sold long ago for pennies on the dollar. I know I enjoyed these books, but can't remember much about them. The only thing that stayed with me about *Satan's Bell* was its setting: Lake Huron and Georgian Bay. Somehow this seemed much more interesting than, say, Amityville, New York.

Narrated by its heroine, twenty-two-year-old secretary Polly Harris, the novel opens with the funeral of a murdered teenage runaway. The dead girl was found by a lost fish-erman on a secluded private island where the lake and bay meet. Its owner, mysterious billionaire Justin Cavell, is charged with murder.

Polly's pragmatic boss, small-town lawyer Matthew Mackay, is hired as a consultant by Justin's high-powered Toronto legal team, which in turn brings her into contact with the accused. From the beginning, she's convinced of his innocence:

> Why would a man like Justin Cavell kill a young girl and leave her lying around on his property? In the first place, he was young, hand-some, and rich. He would have been able to find dozens of beautiful women in his world, and he was not a stupid man. One would have expected something cleverer than this awkward plot.

Indeed, why murder a missing juvenile delinquent when you could bump off the daughter of Princess Grace?

The billionaire is acquitted and begins dating pretty Polly, bringing the book's finest sentence:

> His handsome face was very close to mine, I could feel the warmth of his breath, smell the faint scent of Brut that he always wore, and see the tender concern in his blue, blue eyes.

Three weeks into the relationship, she's invited to spend the weekend with Justin and his twin sister Theodora at their Cavell Island castle. Polly has only just arrived when the supernatural intrudes on what, to this point, has been a rather conventional romance novel:

> It was while climbing the staircase that first time that I became aware of the spirit… What some people would call a "ghost," I suppose, although I have never thought that an adequate word.
>
> I must explain here that I have a peculiar talent that for the most part I keep secret from my friends. I discovered when I was a child that I could "see" things that other people could not. Evidently, I was born a sensitive or psychic.

Polly's "peculiar talent" allows her to witness past events in the castle's history, all of which centre on what she believes are an earlier Justin and Theodora and their quest for eternal youth. A bit thick is our Polly; patently obvious though it may seem, she can't quite figure out that her Justin and the Victorian Justin are one and the same.

Justin is handsome and charismatic, Theodora is beautiful and cold, and Matthew is Atticus Finch. Only Polly—simple, virginal Polly—appears as something other than a cardboard cut-out. Given the premise, the most curious aspect of *Satan's Bell* is that its heroine seems much older than her twenty-two years; indeed, she appears to hearken from an earlier time. There's her name, of course —I've yet to meet a baby boomer named Polly—but also her prim and proper behaviour and speech. This small-town secretary comes off a bit like Ruth Wilcox in *Howard's End*.

It's hard to think of Polly as anything but an odd bird, yet I don't think this is the author's intention. Or is it? You see, it's important to the plot that Polly continues to love Justin even after she realizes that he's a one hundred and twenty-five-year-old serial killer. The teenage runaway was killed in an attempt to prolong his youth, but Justin now knows that he can only achieve this goal by murdering someone who's in love with him.

I'll spoil things here by revealing—*surprise!*—that this never happens. As a sword is poised over Polly's neck, Matthew shows up, revolver in hand. Justin dies, Theodora dies, and Cavell Island sinks into Lake Huron.

The supernatural elements out of the way, *Satan's Bell* returns to being a conventional romance novel for one final, rushed chapter. How rushed? In the third to last page, Matthew turns up unexpectedly at Polly's door with news that he has inherited a vast estate in Nova Scotia:

> "I probably didn't tell you, but my mother married again a few years ago, and the man had money. My mother died and now her second husband has died. He's left me with the estate."

On the penultimate page, he proposes. Polly is set to turn him down, but then, on the last page, he takes her in his arms:

> When Matthew kissed me, I felt the rising of that same passion I'd had for Justin. A fantastic gush of feeling, an excitement I'd never expected to feel again. And with Matthew, of all people. It was the most astonishing thing!
>
> "Matthew, I *love* you!" I cried.
>
> And we both laughed and cried at the same time, standing there by the lake.

Oh, Polly, you're mistaking lust for love. My thirteen-year-old self could've told you that.

THE MILLARS

Munro, Bellow, Millar, Macdonald, and Identity

"A thrilling story told with consummate skill."
—*New York Times*

I DIE SLOWLY
(THE DARK TUNNEL)

KENNETH MILLAR

LL 52

A NOVEL OF OUTRAGE AND FEAR

I Die Slowly [*The Dark Tunnel*]
Kenneth Millar
New York: Lion, 1955
222 pages

"You look like an American and you act like one."

"How does an American look and act?" I said, for the sake of continuing the conversation.

"Well, tall and healthy and quite—neither beautiful nor ugly."

–Kenneth Millar's *I Die Slowly*

I have never before read a story which so piercingly and succinctly examined the terrors and hopes through which the intellectual and emotional life of Canada apparently must still, forty years after my graduation from UWO, find its way.

–Kenneth Millar on Alice Munro's "The Beggar Maid"

Alice Munro's 2013 Nobel win forced our media to recognize 1976 recipient Saul Bellow. Qualifiers came quickly: Munro was the first Canadian woman; Munro was the first Canadian-born writer to set her work in Canada; Munro was the first Canadian who'd lived her life in Canada.

Jared Bland and Sandra Martin didn't vacillate, beginning their joint *Globe & Mail* story by declaring Munro the first Canadian accorded the honour. Bellow's name didn't appear until the third to last sentence (and even then only in parentheses):

(Saul Bellow, a previous Nobel laureate, was born in Quebec, but moved to the United States while young and self-identified as an American; so entrenched was he in American letters that he lends his name to the PEN/Saul Bellow Award for Achievement in American Fiction.)

And Lord Stanley of Preston was a great Canadian.

More nonsense was provided by Cathal Kelly of the *Toronto Star*: "Bellow was born in Lachine, Que., but moved to the U.S. as a child and lived there his entire life."

Mr Kelly is one of the paper's sports columnists.

The fault, of course, lies with the keepers of the canon who embrace Louis Hémon (twenty months in Canada) and West Coast squatter Malcolm Lowry, while dismissing Bellow entirely. Understand, I'm not trying to argue that the author of *Mr. Sammler's Planet* wasn't a lion of American letters, but that the child is father to the man. Let's at least acknowledge that the nine years Bellow lived in Canada—his first nine—were formative. Dr Spock tells us so.

Kenneth Millar's situation is just as muddy. His California birth appears to have kept him out of *The Oxford Companion to Canadian Literature*. How else to explain the entry for Kitchener-born wife Margaret? Millar was an infant when his Canadian parents returned home. He lived in Ontario, Manitoba, and British Columbia, and attended the University of Waterloo (né College), the University of Western Ontario, and the University of Toronto. By the time Millar returned to the States, in his mid-twenties, he and Margaret had already started their respective writing careers.

"We had a very Canadian eagerness to make something of ourselves," he wrote of those years.

The question of identity is key in *I Die Slowly*, and draws much from the author's life. Millar's first novel, it was written while he was studying at the University of Michigan. The setting is Arbana, a stand-in for Ann Arbor. Millar's narrator is Robert Branch, an associate professor at Midwestern University. Like the author, Branch visited 1937 Nazi Germany; unlike the author, he met and fell in love with a beautiful, crimson-haired actress named Ruth Esch. This is all backstory. The novel opens in the autumn of 1943 (the time of composition) and a glorious Detroit day spoiled when Branch is rejected by the United States Navy (as had happened to Millar). Much worse is yet to come, but the associate professor's spirits are lifted heavenward—fleetingly—by the news that Ruth, with whom he had lost all contact, has somehow managed to make her way to Canada and will be arriving by train within hours to teach at Midwestern U.

What are the chances!?

It seems that Dr Herman Schneider, head of the Department of German, had had Miss Esch as a pupil at the University of Munich. Good on him for helping her out. Herr Doktor Schneider invites Branch over to his house for dinner, after which they're to make their way to the station to meet Ruth.

Bolstered by the talents of his German cook, Schneider proves a passable host. However, son Peter commits a terrible *faux pas* in very nearly killing Branch with a sabre. When the doctor tries to murder Branch with his car, the associate professor begins to think something is up.

The real nightmare begins when Ruth finally appears, sucking face with Schneider's son. Allowing for six years spent in a Nazi prison, the actress looks much the same, but has hardened on the inside. In short, she's a character acting out of character. Not at all the girl Branch once knew, she joins the hunt to kill him.

The pace of that chase is fast and there is strength in the details. Branch's visit to a bootlegger's shack-cum-brothel, at which he takes refuge, endures. One often makes allowances in reading first novels, but this isn't really necessary here. Yes, the coincidence in Ruth taking a job at Midwestern University is great, but we've all encountered something similar. Sadly, the cover illustration spoiled things a bit for this reader.

Perhaps I've said too much.

Margaret Millar's Great
Toronto Murder Mystery

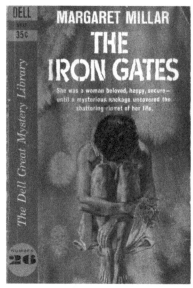

MARGARET MILLAR
THE
IRON GATES

She was a woman beloved, happy, secure—
until a mysterious package uncovered the
shattering secret of her life.

The Iron Gates
Margaret Millar
New York: Dell, 1960
222 pages

Boris Karloff thought this was a great mystery, and so do I. Does that convince? What if I add to the book's list of fans Anthony Boucher and Louis Untermeyer, who joined the actor in selecting *The Iron Gates* for Dell's Great Mystery Library?

Margaret Millar's sixth novel, *The Iron Gates*, was the one that really made her. With the proceeds of its sales, she bought a house in Santa Barbara, sharing it with husband Kenneth, far from the cold of Canadian winters past.

The book begins at the season's first snowfall, in the expansive Toronto home of gynaecologist Andrew Morrow, wife Lucille, daughter Polly, son Martin, and Edith, the doctor's spinster sister. Snow aside, the day promises to be memorable: Polly's fiancé, Lt Giles Frome, will be meeting the Morrow family for the first time. What does he encounter? Edith, for one, who insists on making a speech as he walks in the door:

> She blushed and gave Giles an embarrassed and apologetic smile. "I know how sentimental that sounds but I think it's true, we are a happy family. Of course we have our lapses. Polly is invariably rude and Martin's high spirits are a trial..."
>
> "And Edith gets maudlin," Polly said.
>
> "Oh, I do not," Edith said. "And Andrew can never find anything and then gets cross, don't you, Andrew?"
>
> "I may become justifiably irritated," Andrew said, "but never cross."
>
> "As for Lucille..."

Yes, what about Lucille? Stepmother to Polly and Martin, they've never really warmed to her. Lucille had once been a neighbour and friend of their mother. In fact, the first Mrs Morrow was returning from a visit with Lucille when she was killed by an axe murderer. Her bloodied body was found the next day in High Park. The scene of the unsolved crime is laid out in what is perhaps the least helpful of all Dell mapbacks.

Giles Frome never has the opportunity to develop his own feelings about Lucille because the lady vanishes the very next day. Late that afternoon, a shabby little man appears at the front door with a small package for Lucille. Annie, the most eager of the Morrow help, carries it up to her mistress' room. Moments later, there's a scream. Annie races back. From the other side of the locked door Lucille orders her away. Annie does as she's told, but returns a few minutes later to find her mistress gone.

Enter Inspector Bascombe, Sergeant D'Arcy, and, finally, Inspector Sands, all of the Toronto Police. It's the experienced Sands, veteran of Millar's *Wall of Eyes* (1943), who tracks the missing woman to the Lakeview Hotel. Now quite mad, Lucille is whisked off to an asylum, the ambulance passing the slumped figure of the shabby little man dead in the alley of a morphine overdose.

In 1945, the year *The Iron Gates* was first published, Warner Brothers bought the rights and hired Millar to work on the screenplay. The role of Lucille was offered to Bette Davis, who turned it down for reasons that would spoil in the sharing. Barbara Stanwyck committed, but nothing came of it. This may be just as well. To quote the first-edition dust jacket, *The Iron Gates* is a "psychological thriller." Much of what makes the novel so very good has to do with the depiction of Lucille's less-than-lucid thoughts. We've all seen just how difficult it is to adapt these sorts of things to the screen. That said, I couldn't help but think of David Cronenberg, particularly his brilliant adaptation of Patrick McGrath's *Spider*, when reading passages like this:

The fat pink sugar bowl was passed. Lucille would not touch it, its flesh was too pink, too perfect. Not real flesh at all, she thought, but she knew it was because she could see it breathing.

Miss Eustace's spoon clanged against the grains of sugar. "One or two?"

"One"

"There. Stir it up before you drink it. No, dear, stir it up first."

She picked up her spoon, dreading the feel of it. Everything was alive, everything hurt. She was hurting the spoon, and though it looked stupid and inert it was hurting her in return, digging into her fingers.

"Not so *hard*, Mrs. Morrow."

Round the cup the spoon dashed in fury and pain, stirring up the hot muddy waves and all the little alive things. She swallowed them, in triumph because she had won, and in despair, because, swallowed and out of sight, they would take vengeance on her.

Everything was alive. The floor that hurt your shoes that hurt your feet. The napkin that touched your dress that pressed against your thighs. Pain everywhere.

No privacy. You could never be alone. You always had to touch things and have them touch you.

Cronenberg is a Toronto boy, and this is very much a Toronto novel. You don't have to be particularly familiar with the city to recognize the department store in which Polly and her fiancé shop as Eaton's. The Arcadian Court, the Savarin Tavern, and the White Spot (site of the city's first gangland murder) all receive mention. Giles takes out a room at the ill-famed Ford Hotel.

The Iron Gates is a great mystery. I don't mean to suggest that it isn't flawed; the mystery surrounding the first Mrs Morrow's murder unravels in an unlikely manner.

That's it.

The Iron Gates is a Great Mystery. Remember, Boris Karloff thought so. He had his own comic book, you know.

Margaret Millar's Great
Michigan Murder Mystery

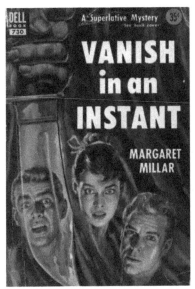

Vanish in an Instant
Margaret Millar
New York: Dell, [1953]
224 pages

Roughly halfway through *Vanish in an Instant*, protagonist Eric Meecham gives pause:

> He wanted to hear more about Loftus and Birdie, as if Loftus's relationship with his wife and mother might explain more about the murder of Margolis. Yet he was sure there was no link except the psychological one—the effect of A and B on C had determined C's conduct toward D.

I was right there with him. In Margaret Millar's mysteries we come to care not so much about crimes committed—here a married playboy is stabbed several times in the neck with a hunting knife—as we do the characters. Their lives hold the greater intrigue.

A lawyer, Meecham has been hired to defend Virginia Barkeley, the sole suspect in the murder of Margolis, the butchered playboy. She was slip sliding drunkenly through slushy snow not far from the cooling corpse when police picked her up. A California girl living in the Millars' fictional Arbana, Michigan, Virginia is far from home and out of her element. Her flat-roofed house of redwood and fieldstone sits in snow and ice; dead plants can be viewed from both sides of its enormous plate glass windows. Icicles fringe the barbecue pit.

The California-style bungalow is as much a mistake as her one-year-old marriage to staid medical doctor Paul Barkeley; Virginia's mother would tell you as much. She's flown in from the West Coast, paid companion Alice Dwyer in tow, to set things right. Though there's no need, really, because a leukemia-stricken odd bird named Earl Loftus soon confesses the whole thing. "Since I was going to die anyway," Loftus tells Meecham, "I thought I would take someone with me—rid the world of someone it would be better off without, some incorrigible criminal, perhaps, or a dangerous politician. But when the time and opportunity came, it was Margolis. I wish it could've been someone more important. Margolis was very third-rate."

I was reminded of the dying Dennis Potter's dream of murdering Rupert Murdoch.

Earl's suffering isn't just physical. As his health deteriorates, the ghost of a failed marriage haunts, and worries over the alcoholic mother he's been supporting become unbearable. The pitiable, self-confessed killer is far from alone. *Vanish in an Instant* is crowded with suffering souls. Have sympathy for Dr Barkeley, who has hired Meecham to defend his straying barfly of a wife. Spare some thought for Earl's aforementioned mother, a once-respectable woman who dove into drink after being abandoned by her spouse. Then there's Mrs Margolis, who, having accepted her husband's philandering, must now come to terms with his murder. We don't even see the Margolis children, but know that they too are in a bad state; just look at the lady snowman left on their front lawn:

> One of her charcoal eyes had fallen out of her melting socket. She had a witch's nose made out of a carrot and a moist beet-mouth, and stuck in her chest was a long dripping icicle that gleamed in the light like a stiletto with a jewelled handle. The snow lady seemed to be aware of her wound; her blurred beet-mouth was anguished, and her single eye stared helplessly into the night.

Vanish in an Instant is a horribly dark and depressing novel of failed marriages, yet in the midst of all the despair, love blossoms between Meecham and Alice Dwyer.

Why?

I suggest an editor's influence. I suggest there was pressure to inject just a bit of hope and light into an otherwise overwhelmingly bleak novel. How else to explain the sudden, unexpected declarations of love that mar chapter fifteen (of twenty-five)?

Would I believe in a love at first sight?

Yes, I'm certain that it happens all the time... but not like this:

"Oh, Meecham, I *love* you."

"At this point I think I think I might kiss you, if I didn't have one foot in the grave."

"I didn't say you have one foot in the grave. I said you weren't very young and adjustable and—"

"I accept your apology."

He took her in his arms and kissed her for a long time, feeling that he had never kissed a girl before, it was so strange and perfect.

She looked very solemn. "I will love you forever, Meecham."

This is the very worst I've seen of Millar's writing. Lasting three or so pages, I could stomach it, and I'm betting you would, too, only because this is one of the finest Canadian novels of the fifties.

There has never been a Canadian edition.

The Air Up North

An Air that Kills
Margaret Millar
New York: Random House, 1957
249 pages

An Air that Kills opens with a seemingly trivial conversation between husband and wife. The former, Ron Galloway, is preparing to leave his Toronto home for a weekend of fishing with his buddies on Georgian Bay. Meanwhile, wife Esther rustles around the room in a pink taffeta dress.

"I'm sick of my hair like this," she said. "I think I'll become a blonde. An interesting psychic blonde like Thelma."

"You're psychic enough. And I don't like phoney blondes."

"What about natural ones like Thelma?"

"I like Thelma alright," he said obstinately. "She's my best friend's wife. I have to."

"Just all right?"

"For Pete's sake, Esther, she's a fattish little hausfrau with some of her marbles missing. Even *your* imagination can't build her up into a femme fatale."

"I guess not."

"When are you going to get over these crazy suspicions?"

"Dorothy…" She swallowed as she spoke the name, so that he wasn't sure until she repeated it. "Dorothy had no suspicions."

We will learn that Dorothy is Ron's first wife, just as we will discover that Esther's suspicions are justified. Thelma Bream is pregnant with Ron's child, an unfortunate situation of which he learns on his way north. Best friend Harry Bream awaits at the lodge, as do second-tier friends Bill Winslow, Joe Hepburn, and Ralph Turnee, a professor of economics at the University of Toronto. A flurry of phone calls follow when Ron fails to show. Seemingly inconsequential events come together—a dog is struck by a car, a Mennonite girl discovers a driving cap—leading to the discovery of Ron and his Cadillac convertible at the bottom of a small lake just outside Meaford. A suicide note arrives by post a few days later.

It often seems there's no real mystery in this mystery novel, just a whole lot of domestic drama. Esther struggles in adapting to dual roles of grieving widow and betrayed wife, while the Breams battle and a baby is born. Harry clings, Thelma rejects and things become increasingly unpleasant. Though it's not expressed in so many words, the author having a subtle touch, the second-tier friends breathe a collective sigh of relief when Harry is transferred to the United States. Thelma, who has spent much of her life pining for warmer climes, ends up in southern California.

It doesn't end there, of course. It never does.

The Trouble with Charlie

The Fiend
Margaret Millar
New York: Dell, 1966
224 pages

"Even by Mrs. Millar's usually high standards, *The Fiend* is something extraordinary," Anthony Boucher wrote in the *New York Times*.

It is.

Here's why: the primary character, a registered sex offender, is the most sympathetic.

This is a novel of many characters and many marriages, all of them unhappy. The Brants, Ellen and David, fight over money. Neighbour Howard Arlington fights with wife Virginia over the attention she gives Jessie, the Brants' daughter. Mary Martha, Jessie's friend, is being used as a pawn in a particularly acrimonious divorce. Her mother's lawyer, Ralph MacPherson, *was* married, but his wife died. A middle-aged widower, he attempts to stave off loneliness by keeping early nights and a dog.

Ben Gowen was married too, but his wife left him when scandal struck the family. His younger brother, Charlie, was convicted of something having to do with a young girl. Now thirty-two, Charlie has done his time and is back living with Ben in the modest house they inherited from their parents.

Charlie has a job in the stockroom of a paper-supply company. When not at work, he can often be found across the street from a local playground, sitting in his parked car. The vantage point provides a fairly inconspicuous view of young Jessie. Charlie is very concerned about Jessie. He worries that she takes too many risks on the jungle gym. Her young body is so very thin and fragile. Her flesh shouldn't be that exposed. It's very upsetting.

Charlie used to spend his evenings at the public library. It was there, about a year ago, that he met a reference librarian named Louise Lang.

She's thirty-two, single, and has "a tiny figure like a girl's with the merest suggestion of hips and breasts."

Charlie and Louise are a couple thanks in large part to Ben. It was Ben who told Louise about Charlie's past problems, though exactly how much he disclosed is unclear. What is clear is that Ben sees in Louise someone on whom he can unload the burden of being his brother's keeper. He hopes for marriage. Louise dreams of matrimony, and pushes Charlie to propose.

But why would Louise want to marry a registered sex offender? Why tie yourself to such a socially awkward man? What about his increasingly frequent psychotic episodes? My first thought was that Louise was blinded by desperation, seeing only an escape from her unpleasant parents. I should know better. There's never anything so uncomplicated or overt in a Margaret Millar novel. The Brants' marriage won't be made healthy through money. Virginia Arlington's focus on Jessie proves selfish. Divorce doesn't really explain Mary Martha's unhealthy home life. Adults use children in unhealthy ways throughout this novel. It's very upsetting.

Why would Louise want to marry Charlie? Because she loves him. That the reader comes to understand and believe this speaks to Millar's talent.

It is something extraordinary.

MOORE

Disowned and Distant

Unlike Graham Greene, who never disowned his "entertainments," Brian refused to talk about his thrillers and in his later years he vainly hoped that nobody would unearth these ephemeral works or decipher the pseudonyms. I personally could never understand this. From the very beginning it was obvious that he had mastered the genre. The books were immensely readable and his genius for atmosphere, dialogue and plot was everywhere evident, but when I said that to Brian it only irritated him.
—William Weintraub, *Getting Started: A Memoir of the 1950s*
(2001)

The last time I saw Brian Moore he was sitting alone in a damp bar overlooking Vancouver's False Creek. I felt he was owed a drink. Just thirty minutes earlier he'd completed a reading at one of the worst literary events I'd ever attended. The reading itself, from *The Statement*, had gone quite well, but it was followed by a deeply cringeworthy Q & A.

It began badly, with a woman who asked about his work habits. This is, I believe, is the most common query posed at such events, often by audience members seeking some sort of formula that will magically transform them into writers. In this particular instance, a rough description would not suffice; what this woman wanted were details, dammit. Her follow-up questions—and there were many—invariably began: "So, you're saying I should...."

Next up was a man who had some extremely complimentary things to say about Margaret Atwood. Praise served as preamble. After assuring the author that he and Atwood were very much in the same league, the speaker blamed Moore's relatively low profile on the fact that his novels were published by several different houses. "Your agent should attend to this," the author was advised.

It ended with an animated, wildly overdressed man delivering a lengthy monologue on Canada as a "rabidly anti-Catholic country."

"Is Canada an anti-Catholic country?" was Moore's brief, yet polite response.

Filing out, I repeated this question to my companion, a member of the Church of Rome, who countered that our then-prime minister, Jean Chrétien, was a Catholic (as had been seven of his nineteen predecessors). Though C of E myself, I breathed a sigh of relief.

At some point in all this mess, Moore happened to mention *The Revolution Script*, his 1971 novel about the October Crisis. It was, he'd said, a mistake to have written the book. Moore had already disowned his pulp novels; was he now starting to distance himself from other works?

Brian Moore was Graham Greene's favourite living novelist, and as one might expect, his bibliography is both impressive and long. Ignoring the pulps, from 1955 until his death he averaged something approaching a book every two years. Here's the list that was included in Moore's 1988 novel, *The Colour of Blood*:

The Lonely Passion of Judith Hearne
The Feast of Lupercal
The Luck of Ginger Coffey
An Answer from Limbo
Canada (with the Editors of *Life*)
The Emperor of Ice Cream
I Am Mary Dunne
Fergus
The Revolution Script
Catholics
The Great Victorian Collection
The Doctor's Wife
The Mangan Inheritance
The Temptation of Eileen Hughes
Cold Heaven
Black Robe

And here's what was printed seven years later in *The Statement*, the book he was obliged to promote that grey Vancouver afternoon:

The Lonely Passion of Judith Hearne
The Feast of Lupercal
The Luck of Ginger Coffey
An Answer from Limbo
The Emperor of Ice Cream
I Am Mary Dunne
Fergus
Catholics
The Great Victorian Collection

The Doctor's Wife
The Mangan Inheritance
The Temptation of Eileen Hughes
Cold Heaven
Black Robe
The Colour of Blood
Lies of Silence
No Other Life

Note that *The Revolution Script* has disappeared, as has *Canada* (1963), a non-fiction title he wrote for money "with the Editors of *Life.*" I very much doubt that this was an oversight. Once published, the titles had always been recognized in similar bibliographies until *Lies of Silence* (1990), when they disappeared, never to be included again.

I'd be proud to have written either.

Brian Moore's True First

Sailor's Leave [*Wreath for a Redhead*]
Brian Moore
New York: Pyramid, 1953
160 pages

Brian Moore holds a place as the most versatile of our novelists, moving with ease through seventeenth-century New France, nineteenth-century Algeria, Vichy France, and Jean Drapeau's Montreal. Moore wrote of missionaries, monasteries, revolutionaries, and cowards. He had an unusual talent for depicting women, one unmatched by any other male writer I've read. Moore's debut novel, *Judith Hearne,* brought us the first of these convincing characters. Mary Dunne followed, as did Sheila Redden and Eileen Hughes. The last was Emmeline Lambert, heroine of *The Magician's Wife,* his final book.

Of course, *Judith Hearne* wasn't really his first novel, rather it was the one that he chose to recognize as such. It is a small secret that, between 1951 and 1957, Moore published seven pulp novels. They had wonderful titles such as *French for Murder, A Bullet for My Lady,* and *This Gun for Gloria.* Some were published under his own name; others appeared under the *noms de plume* Bernard Mara and Michael Bryan. As a young man, I collected them all—a long and frustrating hunt in the days before the Internet—but never read a word.

Something to do with respect for the man, I suppose.

Moore's good friend William Weintraub encouraged a change of mind. Bill has read the books, and describes them as good fun.

And so, ten years after Moore's passing, I turn to his pulps. The first, *Wreath for a Redhead,* was published in 1951 by Harlequin several years before the publisher zeroed in on the romance market. My copy appeared in 1953 as *Sailor's Leave,* an American mass-market paperback that owes its existence to the good work of Willis Wing, Moore's New York agent. The novel's hero is John Riordan, a "prairie sailor" who is travelling by train from Halifax to Montreal. At a stop in Levis, he encounters Joan Harlowe, "a redhead, tall and with a beautiful build." What follows is, of course, a pick-up—made possible through some seductive talk of Ottawa, Halifax, Saskatchewan, Nova Scotia, and "Muskoka Lake." The couple ends up in a low-grade Montreal hotel where the softness of Joan's thighs makes Riordan dizzy. They dine at a French restaurant on Mountain Street, after which Joan vanishes, leaving the sailor with a mystery. Joan reappears a day or two later, but only long enough for Riordan to rip off her silky delicates. She's next found murdered. Riordan is, of course, fingered for the crime.

Those with an appreciation of Moore's talent are certain to be disappointed. The writing follows a strict formula the novelist once laid out in a letter to Mordecai Richler: short sentences, short paragraphs, short chapters. "Imitate Hemmy with more sock and bash!" Moore advised his friend.

And so, we find passages like this:

Something cooks here, I told myself. The dame has plenty of money, or someone in this joint has. Yet ever since I came in, she's been behaving like a shoplifter with the loot under her skirt. She's sure acting like somebody who's got something to hide. And it wasn't her sex.

There's not much sex in *Sailor's Leave*, I'm afraid; Moore leaves that to the imagination:

"Help me with these buttons," she said, pulling at her housecoat.

CHAPTER SEVEN

Afterwards, when we lay on the rug, she filled me up on her biography.

Up?

Sailor's Leave—Wreath for a Redhead, if you prefer—has just enough quirkiness to interest the very dedicated Moore enthusiast. For example, Riordan learns he is wanted and follows the manhunt through the dailies, but only the *Gazette*—Moore's employer at the time—is mentioned by name. He places Maurice Maeterlinck's *The Life of the Bee* in the library of a gay photographer and has Riordan read *Mutual Aid*, the 1902 anarchist classic by Peter Kropotkin, in order to pass the time.

Of *Sailor's Leave* and the other pulps, Moore once said, "I did all these things for *Judith Hearne*." And it is in this, I suppose, that this novel's true value lies.

No Gun for Gloria

THEY SET OUT TO MURDER GLORIA—
AND I SET OUT TO CATCH THE SLUGS

25¢

THIS GUN FOR GLORIA

by BERNARD MARA
Author of A BULLET FOR MY LADY

This Gun for Gloria
Bernard Mara [pseud. Brian Moore]
New York: Gold Medal, 1956
144 pages

As titles go, *This Gun for Gloria* is right up there with *Wreath for a Redhead*, Moore's first pulp. No one can resist that caption:

THEY SET OUT TO MURDER
GLORIA—AND I SET OUT
TO CATCH THE SLUGS

Much more exciting than, say: GLORIA'S MOM WANTED TO KNOW WHERE SHE WAS—AND I SET OUT TO FIND HER.

American Mitch Cannon is our narrator and hero. Not so long ago, Mitch was *wunderkind* of the newsroom, rising quickly through the ranks at a wire-service agency. Then came a brief, ill-advised marriage to Nancy, a junior reporter intent on sleeping her way to the top. Mitch quit it all and made for Paris, where he hoped to reinvent himself as a freelance journalist. It didn't go well. When we catch up with Mitch at his Left Bank hotel, he has perhaps fifty dollars to his name. In walks Dorothy Gaye, an attractive older woman wearing a Dior suit with a tight black skirt. She also has a sapphire-blue mink stole, but it's not worth dwelling on these details. Still smarting from Nancy, Mitch isn't much interested in women. Dorothy—Mrs Gaye—isn't interested in him either, except as a man who might be able to find her missing daughter, Gloria.

No private dick, Mitch is polite in declining the work, but changes his mind after finding a wad of bills Mrs Gaye left behind in his bathroom. He decides to use the money to travel to Berlin, where there's a big story he's looking to break.

Forget Berlin. Forget Gloria, too. What's most interesting in *This Gun for Gloria* is the tour of the seedy side of Paris provided by Mitch's search. There's a nightclub where sadists hook up, a sweat-filled jazz cellar, an Arab drug kingpin, an Amazonian German mule, Senegalese strong-arms, and a wealthy, worn-out prostitute, her once-handsome face a "mired field where expensive cosmetics blurred and wasted into a stained palette of colours."

This Gun for Gloria features some of Moore's best pulp writing, much of it focused on the callow, spoiled, and pretentious American kids who fill clubs and cafés. Pushing through the crowd, I found I didn't much care about ever finding Gloria, though I did begin to wonder about the title.

This Gun for Gloria? Just two guns feature in the novel, neither of which belongs to Mitch. While one errant shot is fired, they're used in the main to intimidate and pistol whip. No one, Mitch included, catches a slug.

This isn't to say that our hero doesn't suffer. He's twice knocked out and endures several beatings, but, as convention dictates, he soldiers on without breaking stride. And, as per the norm, he falls in love with Caroline, the most sensible, least spoiled of the young Americans. That's not her on the cover. It's not Gloria, either—she's a blonde. I'm not even sure that that's Mitch. The only person he ever carries is Papa Houdin, an elderly, one-legged book pedlar who gets run over by a taxi.

Of the seven Moore pulps, *This Gun for Gloria* is the best, but I can't help but leave off with a final complaint: only one person "SET OUT TO MURDER GLORIA"—and he used a wrench.

Murderers Move in on Montreal... Again

Intent to Kill
Michael Bryan [pseud. Brian Moore]
New York: Dell, 1956
191 pages

Hired assassins travel to Montreal tasked with killing a foreign leader. These barest of narrative bones will seem familiar to anyone who has read *The Executioners* (1951), the second of Brian Moore's disowned thrillers, but *Intent to Kill*, sixth of the disowned, is markedly different.

A much better novel, to be sure, it relies less on convention. The hero sets the tone. Where *The Executioners* had untethered tough guy Mike Farrell, *Intent to Kill* gives us young Dr Robert McLaurin, a straight-laced American surgeon who has come north to study at the feet of Dr McNeill at the Canadian Neurological Institute.

Whether McNeill is modelled on Wilder Penfield (probably), or the Canadian Neurological Institute is really the Montreal Neurological Institute (it most certainly is) matters because *Intent to Kill* ranks amongst Moore's very best thrillers. All comes down to research. Its air of authenticity and authority had staff at the Institute convinced that "Michael Bryan" was one of their own.

The facility plays host to nearly all the action. The assassins' target is Juan Menda, the centrist president of an unnamed South American country, who must undergo surgery to repair damage sustained in a previous assassination attempt. Meanwhile, wife Carla waits in her hotel room, bored by Montreal, hating the winter, and casting about for a temporary bed partner to keep her warm. In these three ways she has something in common with Margaret, Dr McLaurin's wife. Margaret has just returned from visiting friends with benefits in Boston, and is now stepping up an ongoing campaign to get her husband back south and into a lucrative, if inconsequential practice. Margaret's latest move involves blackmail: if her demands are not met, she'll tell McNeill that her husband is having an affair with fair Nancy Ferguson, yet another of the Institute's unselfish doctors. Not true, of course, but Margaret's threats force McLaurin to recognize his love for lovely Nancy.

Meanwhile, the hired assassins—also American—sit in the Windsor Hotel, waiting for the right opportunity.

It was one of Moore's contentions that murder happened far too easily on page and screen. The killing of Herman Gromek in *Torn Curtain*, for which he wrote the screenplay, shows us the reality. Not even the seasoned assassins of *Intent to Kill* have an easy time of it. They do their homework, wait for the right moment, and botch the job—a failure that can only make the next attempt more difficult.

I've written often, always with envy, of the days when talents like Ted Allan and hacks like Ronald J. Cooke could simply dash off a paperback for quick and easy cash. *Intent to Kill* is from those times, and is of those times, but it's also in another league. Care went into its composition. Most writers would take pride in having their name on its cover, but then so very few writers can compare to Moore.

The Last of a Paperback Writer

Murder in Majorca
Michael Bryan [pseud. Brian Moore]
New York: Dell, 1957
158 pages

Murder in Majorca features no murder. There is a death, but it's an accident.

Moore's working title was *Free Ride Home*. The free ride is offered to Isabel Kenner, the estranged wife of aspiring journalist Chuck Kenner. Home is the United States. Isabel and Chuck met two years ago in Paris; she was a student, he an ex-serviceman with dreams of becoming a foreign correspondent. What little money they had was quickly spent, though there were efforts to economize. The couple relocated to Spain because the living was cheaper, eventually ending up in Majorca (the cheapest of the cheap).

"It had begun gaily, like a ride on a carrousel. But the carrousel slowed down."

It was in Majorca that their relationship came to an end. Chuck made arrangements for Isabel to return home on a free Pan Am flight from Paris to New York. His story was that he knew someone who worked for the airline.

At the *aérogare*, Isabel met a man who handed her a first-class ticket, two ten-dollar bills and a small package she was to deliver to someone who would identify himself as "the bridegroom." No mule, she returned, package in hand, to Majorca.

And that's just the backstory.

The action begins with Isabel's return. At the airport she meets Gregory Fall, an American magazine photographer who has arrived in Majorca on assignment. Neither realizes it immediately, but Greg's contact is none other than Isabel's ne'er-do-well husband, Chuck.

Murder in Majorca was the seventh and last of Moore's disowned paperback thrillers. In his true bibliography, it follows *The Feast of*

Lupercal, which ranks amongst the best novels I've ever read. Though Moore wasn't aiming quite so high here, I don't hesitate in saying it's one of the finest thrillers going. He shows off his talent by telling the story from various points of view. Isabel, Chuck, and Greg make three, but there are many more. As in the real world, some are more interesting than others. Compare Maggy, who might be dismissed as a bit of a tramp, with former Waffen S.S. officer Helmuth Freitag. The latter is as sinister and complex a character as one could hope to find. Lest things become too dark, kleptomaniac Aimée David provides tragic/comic relief.

Moore's next novel, *The Luck of Ginger Coffey*, earned his first of two Governor General's Awards. Decades passed before he returned to the thriller. There were occasional flirtations with the genre, but these were at the suggestions of others.

After Vladimir Nabokov turned him down, Alfred Hitchcock approached Moore with the idea of a cold war thriller. The resulting film, *Torn Curtain*, led to a falling out that gave birth to fat, flatulent Bernard Boweri in Moore's 1970 novel, *Fergus*.

In 1971, he published *The Revolution Script*, but blamed that misstep on Jack McClelland.

The first Brian Moore book I bought upon publication was 1985's *Black Robe*, a historical novel set in seventeenth-century New France. The next, *Colour of Blood*, was his first thriller in three decades. *Lies of Silence* and *The Statement* followed. They're the sort of books Graham Greene would have described as "entertainments." *Murder in Majorca* is very much in their league.

I'm betting Greene wouldn't have written it off, despite the title.

POLITICS

A Forgotten Fuss

The Land of Afternoon: A Satire
Gilbert Knox [pseud. Madge Macbeth]
Ottawa: Graphic, 1925
352 pages

The Parliamentary Librarian chased after "Gilbert Knox." Conservative MP Alfred Fripp joined in the hunt, intent on having the author deported to who knows where. The clergy condemned, Ottawa echoed with talk of lawsuits, an election was fought and a government fell. In the midst of it all, the woman behind the pseudonym suffered a nervous breakdown and was sent to a Toronto nursing home.

All these years later, it's a little hard to see what the fuss was about. Such is the fate of the *roman à clef*. The decades flow, carrying away souls who had once served to inspire characters and all who knew them.

The Land of Afternoon features some very unflattering portraits of the granddaughters of Thomas MacKay, the man who built Rideau Hall: "two sisters with generous florid cheeks and rotund figures, who, to quote Azalea Deane, seemed to lie flatly on the surface of every social function, rather like cream on a pan of milk."

Ella Beatty Harriss couldn't have been happy with Mrs Hudson, the character for which she served as a model:

> Mrs. Hudson loved her husband with a sort of cantankerous affection that was like the rubbing of a brass bowl to make it shine. She was always prodding him, or polishing him, or smacking at him with her hands or her tongue. Marriage had robbed her of the joy of believing him a genius, but she was fond of him in her peculiar, rasping way.

Before digging into and around this novel, I'd never heard of Ella Beatty Harriss, nor Thomas MacKay and his rotund granddaughters, but ignorance didn't rob me of delight in the reading. *The Land of Afternoon* is an extremely entertaining book. Its witticisms have stood the test of time for the simple reason that social pretention remains much unchanged.

The centre of the novel, a comedy of manners with no stock characters, is held by Marjorie Dillings and her husband Raymond, Conservative MP for the western riding of Pinto Plains. A young couple blessed with unattractive and unruly children, they arrive in Ottawa in the years preceding the Great War. Raymond, who won Pinto Plains thanks to his oratorical skills—words he delivered with hand on hip—makes an impact in the House of Commons. This, in turn, attracts the attention of the Honourable Member for Morroway, cabinet colleague Rufus Sullivan, who worries that the newly minted western MP might prove an impediment to his own interests. He sets out to destroy Raymond by sending beautiful bohemian temptress Hebe Barrington his way.

Such an attractive figure! I'd have been tempted myself, but Raymond remains flaccidly unmoved. In those fleeting moments he manages to raise his eyes away from Shakespeare and Hansard, Raymond's gaze drifts toward Azalea Deane, the spinster he has selected as his personal secretary. The physical opposite of Hebe, she's a plain little thing with freakishly large hands and feet. Raymond isn't a palm partialist or foot fetishist, but a sapiosexual. "He could not for the life of him, [sic] visualise her features, but he could bring to mind many an illuminating twist in her thoughts." Raymond is attracted to Azalea's mind, which he considers "bi-sexual" in that it is, in his opinion, masculine.

The realization that he loves Azalea disturbs the politician. Love has never factored much in Raymond's life, least of all in his marriage: "With the simplicity that marked so many of his social adventurings, he believed that when he could support a wife and family he should marry; and he chose the least objectionable—and most desirable externally— woman of his acquaintanceship."

Dull is Dillings; so dull that he very nearly drags down the novel:

In the abstract, Dilling saw men as trees, walking, but women he saw scarcely at all. Emotionally, he was vestigial. Artistically, he was numb. Beauty in any form registered only through his outward eye. He missed the inner vision that should have quickened the soul.

Readers in 1925 would have recognized the Member from Pinto Plains as once-and-future prime minister Arthur Meighen, MP for Portage la Prairie. Like Raymond Dillings, Meighen had the gift of oratory; the man's first electoral victory came when he secured the presidency of his collegiate's debating society. The two share a reverence for Shakespeare—Meighen's best-selling work was a book on the bard titled *The Greatest Englishman of History*.

Contemporary reviews appear to have been either deferential or fearful; I've not seen one that so much as mentions the Meighens. Not one dares describe the Dillings marriage as loveless.

The first title issued by Ottawa's legendary, ill-fated Graphic Publishers, *The Land of Afternoon* was published in October 1925, the very month of the federal election in which Meighen's Conservatives returned to power. Talk of the town—Bytown—spread across the Dominion and the Atlantic; articles about the *roman à clef* were published in London and Paris.

By end of year, sales had numbered fewer than two thousand copies. In this respect, at least, it was a truly Canadian *succès de scandale*.

Author and Publisher as Forgotten Men

Forgotten Men
Claudius Gregory
Hamilton: Davis-Lisson, 1933
444 pages

Christopher Ward is a young man of wealth and privilege. The son of a steel-mill owner, he lives life adrift until he happens upon an impromptu meeting of unemployed men in a public park. Wonderment is reawakened. He devotes his life to some hazy idea called "the Cause," becomes close friends with the unemployed Peter Bronte, is mentored by holy man Reverend John, and meets a prostitute named Mary. "Mary. That is my mother's name, too," Christopher says when introduced. Well before he amasses his group of twelve, known as the Society of Forgotten Men, the reader senses that things are going to end badly. It comes as no surprise when he's betrayed by Society member Jude Braithwaite and arrested while having supper in a modest eatery.

A familiar story, of course, though the reader is left wondering at the charge: sedition. Christopher is long on describing the suffering of the workingman, short on its causes and silent as to its solutions. This isn't to say that the messianic figure hasn't proposed something, but that Gregory, for all his verbiage, chooses not to reveal the goal of the Society of Forgotten Men. Christopher's thoughts provide the merest of hints:

> Beginning. "In the beginning." But, of course, everything must have a beginning. It was plain now, quite plain, the task he must undertake, the part he must play. Millions of forgotten men were depending upon them, men whose very souls had been exploited because they did not understand what was theirs by right. Yes, there was a thought in that. One should say, by birthright. There it was again. A man's birthright: something which came to him in the beginning.

There were millions of men who would be powerful enough, once they understood, to select leaders among themselves to govern, to select men incapable of being influenced by the taint of party politics. He had no socialistic ideas; that was not the thought.

If that is not the thought, what is? The answer, invariably is cloaked. We see it in the part of the previous passage where Christopher dreams of leaders untainted by party politics. To put it more plainly, the publisher's next book was *Is Fascism the Answer?*, a work praising Benito Mussolini, penned by Brampton police magistrate and corporal punishment enthusiast S. Alfred Jones.

Gregory dedicated *Forgotten Men* to its publisher, Thomas Dyson Lisson, adding a dense three-page acknowledgement devoted to "the man whose collaboration gave the story." Here Gregory tells us something of the novel's failure by revealing that the plot was woven around Lisson's "outstanding thoughts," as expressed in self-published brochures, such as *Did You Ever Look at It this Way?* (1931) and the more ominous-sounding *Eventually You Will Look at It this Way* (1933).

Forgotten Men was the first book for both Gregory, a transplanted Brit, and Lisson, co-owner of a successful Hamilton printing business. Despite their friendship, the author's next two novels, *Valerie Hathaway* (1933) and *Solomon Levi* (1935), were published by other houses. All were reviewed in the pages of the *New York Times*, yet Gregory's life, literary career, and death in 1944 were ignored by the dailies in his adopted city of Toronto. Lisson, on the other hand, received some notice. On September 13, 1918, the *Globe* reported that he may have thwarted a dastardly German plot to poison the good citizens of Hamilton.

On December 4, 1932, Lisson's Hamilton printing plant was damaged in a fire so spectacular that it made the front pages of the Toronto papers—"Exploding Celluloid Showers Hot Glass Upon Firefighters," reads the *Globe* headline. Three years later, he returned to the front page as co-founder of the short-lived Reconstruction Party, lead by temperamentally difficult once-and-future Tory H.H. Stevens.

Lisson's own writing attracted little attention, though the arguments set forth in his 1937 pamphlet, *Gold*, were considered and dismissed by *Globe*'s mining editor. Sadly, my search for his self-published titles hasn't borne fruit. Just as well—having read the ideas put forth in *Forgotten Men*, I don't imagine *Birth Control and Scrap Labor-Saving Devices* is nearly as interesting as the title suggests.

A Communist's Bodice Ripper?

The Governor's Mistress
Warren Desmond
[pseud. Dyson Carter]
Toronto: News Stand Library, 1950
160 pages

Oh, yes, a bodice *is* ripped, but I'm not so sure this novel quite fits the genre. There's little romance in *The Governor's Mistress*, and passion, though present, is not as pervasive as cover copy would have you believe.

VIRILE—VIOLENT—WARM—WICKED—
This was Angeline

Virile? Can a woman be virile? The OED answers in the negative. But then Angeline isn't violent either. She *is* warm though… and, it's implied, wicked in the sack.

Angeline—referred to as "Angel" on the book's back cover (and nowhere else)—is Angeline Paradis, a beautiful English spy who's sent into the heart of seventeenth-century New France. Hers, cover copy tells us, "is a tale kept out of school-books." Makes perfect sense; after all, Angeline was the creation of the author, and exists nowhere outside this book. She moves through pages populated by figures from our history, and it's here that this novel begins to falter. There's a supposition that the reader will know these men—they are all men—that is misguided. Frontenac? Yes. Radisson? Yes. But how many of us are familiar with the scandal and intrigue surrounding François-Marie Perrot, who served as governor of Montreal from 1669 to 1684?

This Montrealer recognized his name.

That's all.

Pity the poor American reader, who I'm assuming has been taught little of the political machinations of New France. After all, it was to these folks that *The Governor's Mistress* was marketed. Its author, Dyson Carter, a card-carrying member of the Communist Party of Canada, hid behind the pseudonym Warren Desmond only so that the novel might be sold south of the border.

The Governor's Mistress isn't so much a bad book as an irritating one. Stuff happens, but often offstage. When Radisson is put on trial for treason, an event that never actually occurred, he escapes the courtroom by painting his face with ghoulish features: "Thus had Radisson used the phosphorus oil he brought with him from Rupert's workshop." And thus we hear for the first and last time of Rupert's workshop.

Ultimately, *The Governor's Mistress* is a grand disappointment. The Harlequin set will find little in the way of romance, those seeking something spicy will be left dangling, and readers like myself, who'd hoped for an oddball Marxist reading of life in New France, will be met with nought but paper, ink, and glue.

Dyson Carter's Long Exercise in Political Pathology

Despite Moscow's best efforts, it wasn't until a decade or so after the collapse of the Soviet Union that I first became aware of Dyson Carter. *Northern Neighbors*, "Canada's Authoritative Independent Magazine Reporting on the U.S.S.R.," which he edited for some thirty-two years, wasn't something I saw on newsstands. I didn't notice his books, including those published by the Communist Party of Canada, though they were distributed in the thousands at home and abroad.

In my defence, I point out that Carter is not found in *The Oxford Companion to Canadian Literature* or W.H. New's *Encyclopedia of Literature in Canada*. He is very much a forgotten figure, something reflected in his *Canadian Encyclopedia* entry, which has yet to record his death.

Further defence: Nearly all of Carter's books were published before I was born. What's more, his moment in the sun came decades earlier. In 1940, Carter published *Sea of Destiny*, a much-discussed work in which he warned that, undefended, Hudson Bay could be used by the Nazis for an invasion of North America. The following year, months before the United States entered the Second World War, Carter predicted the development of the atomic bomb. It would, he claimed, bring a sudden end to the conflict.

Carter's first novel, *Night of Flame*, drew considerable praise from the *New York Times* and the *Globe and Mail*. In the *Ottawa Citizen*, reviewer W.J. Hurlow described Carter as possessing a talent "only a little down the street from genius… We cordially hail Mr Dyson Carter as a Canadian writer of brilliant possibilities."

Possibilities require opportunities, and for a Communist like Carter these became fewer with the advent of the Cold War; just look what happened to *Night of Flame*. The 1942 first edition was published in New York by Reynolds and Hitchcock. Four years later, the novel was reissued in Canada by Collins White Circle. But by 1949, when American paperback giant Signet looked to do likewise, the book's authorship had to be hidden behind a *nom de plume*.

Margaret's Marriage in Mass Market

Margaret Trudeau: The Prime Minister's Runaway Wife
Felicity Cochrane
Scarborough, ON: Signet, 1978
173 pages

Anyone needing a reminder of the crap once thrown at Margaret Trudeau need only look to Kate McMillan and the pseudonymous comments made at her Small Dead Animals blog. Revelations of Mrs Trudeau's decades-long struggles with bipolar disorder have brought neither compassion nor reconsideration—but did serve as something to chew, digest, and defecate.

Margaret Trudeau: The Prime Minister's Runaway Wife is a product of a more civil time. It presents as a sympathetic account, all the while promising to dish the dirt. In the end, however, this is a book that teases, but never delivers. "The *full*, completely uncensored story of Margaret Trudeau's relationship with the different members of the Rolling Stones," ends up being little more than an overview of the seating arrangements at the band's 1977 El Mocambo gigs. Felicity Cochrane wasn't there, yet she still manages to paint a memorable scene:

This was the Stones' first club appearance since 1964, and as in the past, Jagger eventually whipped up the crowd into a convulsing hysteria with jerks of his hips, thrusts of his pelvis, and grasshopper-like gyrations guaranteed to induce mass orgasm.

Sounds messy.

The author next provides details of the painstaking preparations made to fête Peter Rudge, "manager of the Stones" (touring manager, actually) on his birthday. Mrs Trudeau didn't attend the party, but never mind.

Want to know why Pierre Trudeau didn't marry until his fifty-third year? The cover copy promises the answer.

Here's what Ms Cochrane has to say on that topic: "It has always been a mystery why Pierre didn't marry. It will always be open to speculation."

Thin stuff for a thin book; it contains nothing that hadn't already been reported at the time of its August 1978 publication. And yet, the author tells us that she spent "almost a year in interviews and research." Cochrane can't tell us who she spoke to—"for obvious reasons"—but does express appreciation for the Greater Vancouver Convention and Visitors Bureau. I doubt this was reciprocated. Here's the author on Margaret Sinclair Trudeau's birthplace:

> Vancouver, where the Sinclairs settled, is a port city in the southwest corner of British Columbia, on what is now called the Pacific Rim. It was discovered by a British naval officer, Captain George Vancouver, in 1792, became a British colony in 1859, and was admitted into confederation in 1871. The original name of the city was Granville, but this was changed to Vancouver in 1886.

I count five factual errors. How about you?

We're also told that Vancouver has a daily called the *Providence*, that its West End is comprised of highways and modern shopping complexes, and that the "famous Lion's [sic] Gate Bridge links West Vancouver to the lower mainland."

Great swaths of this one-hundred-and-seventy-four-page book are devoted to an overview of the Canadian parliamentary system, the office of prime minister, and the early history of Simon Fraser University (also located in the southwest corner of British Columbia, on what's now called the Pacific Rim). Cochrane quotes liberally (no pun intended), lifting passages from dozens of news stories, all the while criticizing journalists for not having been more dogged in their pursuit of *scandale*.

Strange this, because without the uncredited, unacknowledged work of the fourth estate, Cochrane would have no book. She brings nothing to the table, and yet her author's bio claims she was once a reporter for *Newsday*. A Progressive Conservative, in the 1965 federal election Cochrane challenged veteran Liberal Stanley Haidasz in the riding of Toronto-Parkdale. She placed a very distant second, but made the papers just the same by breaking her leg in a fall down some slippery polling station steps on election day.

After the fall, Cochrane jetted around the globe promoting Canadian honey, cheese, and maple syrup for the Federal Department of Trade and Commerce. She also served as chaperone for 1966 Canadian Dairy Princess Gaylene Miller, but I think the most interesting point in her career began in 1970, with her role as "personal manager" for Dianna Boileau, whom she billed as "Canada's first sex change." Two years later, Cochrane wrote Dianna's story, *Behold, I Am a Woman*. It was published by New York's Pyramid Books, whose copywriters penned this pitch:

> The story you are about to read will quite possibly shock you in its brutal frankness and graphic descriptions. It will startle you as it reveals a way of life and a way of sexual being that seem [sic] beyond the range of the normal imagination. And it will move you to a new kind of realization of the torments a sexual deviant must suffer in our society—as well as the hope that new medical techniques offer a person like Dianna, to at last find fulfillment.

Margaret Trudeau was Cochrane's second and final book. And not a happy experience, it seems. Even as the paperback was hitting the stands, Ms Cochrane was complaining that Signet's lawyers had made her take out the juiciest bits. Could *Margaret Trudeau* have been a better book? Did Felicity Cochrane dig up anything new? Shall we give her the benefit of the doubt?

Nearly four decades later, we know it wasn't Margaret and Mick, but Margaret and Ronnie—both said so in their respective autobiographies. So should we have read anything into this?

> The following day, a small get-together was held in the Rolling Stones' suite at the Harbour Castle Hotel. Margaret joined the group, sitting on the edge of the bed, and proceeded to watch the hockey game on TV, at the same time playing with Ron Wood's seven-year-old son. One guest who was there recalls that the little boy gave the impression he already knew Margaret quite well.

Condemned By Coren

How Do You Spell Abducted?
Cherylyn Stacey
Red Deer, AB: Red Deer College
Press, 1996
135 pages

Newspaper columnists don't always write their headlines, but I think Michael Coren had something to do with this one:

TAXES FUND OFFENSIVE CHILDREN'S BOOK ABOUT ABUSIVE FATHER:
Suddenly your dad is no longer a man to be loved or trusted.

Published in the July 31, 1996 edition of the *Financial Post*, the column that followed lit a fire beneath the seat of Alberta backbencher Julius Yankowsky, who called for the book to be banned and its publisher's funding to be pulled. The MLA aped the columnist, repeating Coren's assertion that it was "hate literature," all while acknowledging that he hadn't actually read the thing. After all, *How Do You Spell Abducted?* is 135 pages long, and some of the words have eight letters. Just look at that title!

A few months later in *Books in Canada*, Coren reported that the controversy he'd started over *How Do You Spell Abducted?* had been "so much fun"—his words, not mine… as are these:

> It begins with bad old Dad, divorced from good old Mum, forcing his way into his ex-wife's bedroom and screaming at her until she weeps. He then kidnaps the kids and they are so terrified they think he might kill them all and then commit suicide.

Well, no.

Dad never forces his way into any room, least of all his ex-wife's bedroom. Mum does indeed weep, which has been known to happen in divorces. Dad leaves with the kids on what is meant to be a vacation, but it soon becomes clear that he has no intention of returning. That stuff about the kids being "so terrified they think he might kill them all and then commit suicide" was fabricated by Coren; it isn't in the book.

Michael Coren was once employed by the Sun News Network.

Not to be outdone or ignored, in the August 19, 1996 *Western Report* an anonymous reporter bravely worked to fan dying embers with the claim that "the fictional father threatened to kill or prostitute his progeny." It's a lie, plain and simple, but then the late magazine was never tied to the truth. More lies follows: "Her book features three other men: a crabby oldster, a fat and stupid state trooper and a good Samaritan who has been unjustly denied legal access to his own children."

There is no "crabby oldster" in the novel. The state trooper, girth never mentioned, is pretty sharp. The good Samaritan—name: Dusty Andover—is a very fine and generous gentleman. He has never been denied access, legal or otherwise, to his children, though there is estrangement. Dusty's adult offspring (no sexes mentioned) begrudge his having spent their inheritances in fighting their mother's cancer.

How Do You Spell Abducted? is a rotten title, but the book isn't half bad. The characters, particularly the father, are well drawn. The plot is believable, disturbingly so, though the resolution is forced and fantastical.

I can say these things because, you see, I've read the book. I have Michael Coren to thank for bringing it to my attention.

POP & PULP

Whatever Happened to Jimmie Dale?

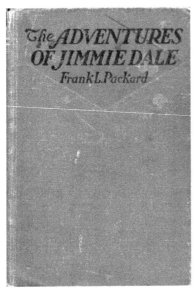

The Adventures of Jimmie Dale
Frank L. Packard
Toronto: Copp Clark, 1917
468 pages

This was my fourth Packard. Put in context, it's like tackling John Buchan's *Witch Wood*, *Castle Gay*, and *Sick Heart River* before *The Thirty-Nine Steps*. The Adventures of Jimmie Dale is the real entry point to Packard; it's his best-known book, his best-selling work and it introduces his most popular character. As with Buchan and Richard Hannay, Packard returned to his hero repeatedly throughout his career.

Jimmie Dale owes everything to his late father, who made millions manufacturing the finest safes money could buy. You might say the fortune came through protecting those of others. Jimmie himself dabbled in sketching and writing before turning to breaking and entering. Donning a black silk mask, he'd sneak into the expansive homes of New York's well-to-do, crack open their safes, and affix a diamond-shaped grey seal in place of a *carte de visite*. Nothing would be taken—Jimmie has never wanted for anything—the thrill was payment enough.

One night, however, all went horribly wrong. Jimmie's secret identity as the "Gray Seal" was discovered by a mysterious, unseen woman who threatened to expose him unless he turned his talents toward combatting crime. So the millionaire playboy did just that—leading to even greater thrills.

There are comparisons to be made. Jimmie Dale follows Baroness Orczy's Scarlet Pimpernel by some ten years, though I'd argue he's had a far greater influence. For one, the Gray Seal's adventures take place in a contemporary setting, not some fanciful, idealized past. There's a gritty reality in Packard's depictions of New York's impoverished and its criminal class, aided, I think, by the access he was granted to NYPD stakeouts and raids. Then there's the Sanctuary, a secret lair where Jimmie transforms into Larry the Bat, to all appearances a down-and-out cocaine addict who moves through the city's underworld. As both Larry and the Gray Seal, Jimmie wears a wide leather belt holding the tools of his crime-fighting trade.

Walter Gibson acknowledged his debt to Packard in creating the Shadow. That Batman co-creator Bob Kane never said a thing is unsurprising; he was a bastard.

Walt Disney was a huge Gray Seal fan, and would re-enact scenes of Jimmie's adventures for his staff. I've seen a nice photo of Uncle Walt with a copy of *Jimmie Dale and the Blue Envelope Murder* (1930) on his desk. In 1952, Disney purchased television rights to the adventures and tried to interest NBC in a series. Too dark. Seems no one was ready for a hero pretending to be a coke addict.

I'm making a lot of the Disney connection because *The Adventures of Jimmie Dale* is well-suited for today's television landscape. The novel's structure owes much to the fact that it initially appeared in serialization. The first part, "The Man in the Case," details ten intricate and brilliantly executed adventures, each instigated by the mysterious woman. It's episodic, yet there's character development and an overarching narrative. The second part, "The Woman in the Case," consists of one long adventure in which the mystery of the mysterious woman is finally solved.

The mystery the reader is left with is how such an influential character could be so forgotten. Why has there been no revival? How is it that *The Adventures of Jimmie Dale* is out of print? Most of all, why did it take me so long to get around to reading it?

Am I the Only One Laughing with Leacock?

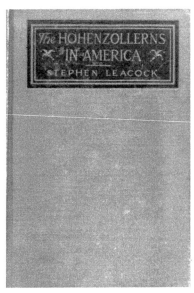

*The Hohenzollerns in America;
With the Bolsheviks in Berlin and Other
Impossibilities*
Stephen Leacock
Toronto: S.B. Gundy, 1919
269 pages

Robertson Davies hated this book. "Leacock at his worst," he wrote in his ill-fated 1970 tribute to the man, adding: "Nevertheless, we may not dismiss it; he wrote it, and if we accept the sunshine, we must not shrink from a peep into the dank chill of his shade."

Centring on the lengthy title story, Davies' disgust is anything but unique. Biographers David M. Legate, Albert Moritz, and Theresa Moritz express similar opinions, while Ralph L. Currie, the first to pen a life of Leacock, chooses to simply ignore it. In her Leacock book, Margaret MacMillan complains that the story is "too broad and too crude." Writes the author of *Paris 1919*:

The title piece of his 1919 book, *The Hohenzollerns in America*, starts from the amusing conceit that the German royal family takes refuge in the United States as penniless refugees after Germany's defeat in the First World War but goes downhill because Leacock cannot keep his light touch. "The proper punishment," says Leacock in his preface, "for the Hohenzollerns, and the Hapsburgs, and the Mecklenburgs, and the Muckendorfs, and all such puppets and princelings, is that they should be made to work."

I'd like to break in here with a couple of comments, the first being that the title piece does not *begin* with a "light touch," but is heavy from the start. Note that MacMillan contradicts herself by quoting the story's preface. And while it's true that Leacock can be relied upon for a good-natured, inoffensive chuckle, his touch was not always light. Teetotals will confirm.

MacMillan continues:

> The resulting sketch is nasty and not at all funny. At its end, the former Kaiser, now a ragged street peddler in the Bowery, dies of his injuries after a traffic accident.

I myself found "The Hohenzollerns in America" nasty, funny, and fun. Anticipating Sue Townsend's *The Queen and I* (1992), it imagines the German royal family stripped of wealth and trappings, and forced to work "as millions of poor emigrants out of Germany have worked for generations past." The piece is presented in the form of a diary—Townsend would approve—kept by Princess Frederica, niece to the deposed emperor, beginning with her first day in steerage on a ship bound for New York. Once in America, the Hohens, as they are now known, do their best to reinvent themselves. A couple become waiters. Uncle Henry, once a Grand Admiral, finds a job as a stevedore while studying to become a Barge Master. Meanwhile, untrustworthy Cousin Ferdinand makes a killing in the schmatta trade, as reflected in the vaguely anti-Semitic dust jacket of the first British edition. One of their number, Cousin Willie, becomes an out-and-out thief.

The deposed Kaiser loses his mind and ends up hawking pins, ribbons, and baubles to amused folk who see him as a something of a character. In the princess' account, he doesn't die after a traffic accident, as MacMillan claims, but of injuries sustained after he runs into a line of cavalry horses at the unveiling of a monument "put up in memory of the people who were lost when one of our war boats fought the English cruiser *Lusitania*." Princess Frederica finds true love with Mr Peters, a very nice iceman.

"What makes us cringe as we read it is that Leacock has plainly aimed it at minds inferior to his own to feed a nasty kind of patriotism and mean triumph," writes Davies. Come now, most readers of Leacock can't quite match the man's intellect. This dimwit detected not so much as a dash of nasty patriotism, but rather savoured the stewing of the aristocracy. Such is my taste. Any country's aristocracy will do. I'm also happy to eat the rich, though Davies doesn't share my appetite: "Even when we try to consider it ["The Hohenzollerns in America"] as a part of an hysterical post-war relief, it is still bad Leacock, and the other things in the book, including the satire on plutocrats who profited from the war but sent their chauffeurs to fight, is no better."

No better? The piece to which Davies refers, "The War Sacrifices of Mr. Spugg," is just about the best thing Leacock ever published. This is fine satire:

> Although we had been members of the same club for years, I only knew Mr. Spugg by sight until one afternoon when I heard him saying that he intended to send his chauffeur to the war.
>
> It was said quite quietly, no bombast or boasting about it. Mr. Spugg was standing among a little group of listening members of the club and when he said that he had decided to send his chauffeur, he spoke with a kind of simple earnestness, a determination that marks the character of the man.
>
> "Yes," he said, "we need all the man power we can command. This thing has come to a showdown and we've got to recognise it. I told Henry that it's a showdown and that he's to get ready and start right away."
>
> "Well, Spugg," said one of the members, "you're certainly setting us a fine example."

You won't find "The War Sacrifices of Mr. Spugg" in any Leacock anthology; nor, for that matter, "War and Peace in the Galaxy Club," in which a series of ill-conceived fundraising events meant to aid the Red Cross only bring increasing debt. By the Armistice, the Club faces insolvency:

> Peace has ruined us. Not a single member, so far as I am aware, is prepared to protest against the peace, or is anything but delighted to think that the war is over. At the same time we *do* feel that if we could have had a longer notice, six months for instance, we could have braced ourselves better to stand up against it and meet the blow when it fell.

Both pieces come from the middle section of the book: "Echoes of the War." Given the title, should we really expect a light touch? It leads with "The Boy Who Came Back," an account of young nephew Tom's first dinner party as a returning war hero. The host is concerned that Tom will disturb the other guests with gruesome accounts of the war, and is then disappointed when he doesn't.

Tom had nothing to say about the Hindenburg line. In fact, for the first half of the dinner he hardly spoke. I think he was worried about his left hand. There is a deep furrow across the back of it where a piece of shrapnel went through and there are two fingers that will hardly move at all. I could see that he was ashamed of its clumsiness and afraid that someone might notice it. So he kept silent. Professor Razzler did indeed ask him straight across the table what he thought about the final breaking of the Hindenburg line. But he asked it with that same fierce look from under his bushy eyebrows with which he used to ask Tom to define the path of a tangent, and Tom was rattled at once. He answered something about being afraid that he was not well posted, owing to there being so little chance over there to read the papers.

When Tom finally breaks his silence, it is to talk about how his French comrades had really taken to baseball, his great passion in life:

It grieved me to note that as the men sat smoking their cigars and drinking liqueur whiskey (we have cut out port at our house till the final peace is signed) Tom seemed to have subsided into being only a boy again, a first-year college boy among his seniors. They spoke to him in quite a patronising way, and even asked him two or three direct questions about fighting in the trenches, and wounds and the dead men in No Man's Land and the other horrors that the civilian mind hankers to hear about. Perhaps they thought, from the boy's talk, that he had seen nothing. If so, they were mistaken. For about three minutes, not more, Tom gave them what was coming to them. He told them, for example, why he trained his "fellows" to drive the bayonet through the stomach and not through the head, that the bayonet driven through the face or skull sticks and, but there is no need to recite it here. Any of the boys like Tom can tell it all to you, only they don't want to and don't care to.

Dismiss *The Hozenhollers in America?* Never! I've enjoyed the sunshine, but within the dank chill of his shade exists a depth that makes me appreciate the man all the more. It's Leacock at his best.

Gloria Gets Groped

Manhandled

Arthur Stringer and Russell Holman

London: Readers Library, [c. 1924]

243 pages

Manhandled is a perfect example of why Arthur Stringer is so frowned upon by CanLit academics. It sprang not from the lush farmland surrounding Chatham and London, the hometowns of his childhood, but the offices of Famous Players-Lasky in downtown Manhattan. General Sales Manager Sidney R. Kent came up with the idea, Stringer was hired to add flesh, then everything was passed on to screen-writer Frank Tuttle.

Our Ontarian was given one thousand dollars for his efforts, along with the right to turn the tale into something of substance to sell to the glossies. The first the world saw of Manhandled appeared as a 26,000-word short story in the March 22 and 29, 1924 issues of the Saturday Evening Post. This novel is that short story, expanded by Russell Holman, a writer who had a talent for turning American silents into entertaining text.

Manhandled is a Gloria Swanson vehicle, written long before the word had ever been used in that sense. It tells the story of Tess McGuire, the orphaned daughter of a comedic vaudeville team, beginning with her childhood in Marysville, a picturesque New England town found only in popular fiction. Though raised by a cautious, conservative spinster aunt—think latter-day Marilla Cuthbert—Tess grows to become a beautiful, adventurous young woman who looks to live a life in the visual or dramatic arts. That pursuit takes her to New York, where she rents a room in the very same house as high-school sweetheart Jim.

Now don't you go spreading gossip; the most that happens between the two is a fleeting kiss. Jimmy aches to make Tess his wife, while she keeps putting him off: "I wouldn't be satisfied with what you can give me—yet. I may be selfish, but it's better that I should tell you how I feel about it. It'll save us both a lot of pain."

Harsh.

Tess wants to make it on Broadway, but doesn't really try. After her one and only attempt at getting an agent, she accepts a job selling "soiled" lingerie in the bargain basement of Thorndyke's. Tess may be a subterranean shop girl, but such is her beauty that she's soon drinking hooch with well-known figures like artist Robert Brandt, Wall Street banker Luther Swett, best-selling author Carl Garretson, and, of course, department-store heir Chip Thorndyke.

As Jim, the rube boyfriend, works nights on a carburetor that might one day make him rich, Tess is wined, dined, danced, and driven on innumerable automobile trips by men with wandering eyes and busy hands. Her only acting gig comes by accident, the result of imitating an exiled Russian aristocrat at a drunken party. A week later, passing herself off as countess "Madam Patovska," she's playing hostess, pouring tea at Manhattan's most exclusive dress shop.

Tess is forced to defend herself to Jim:

"Will you tell me what the successes in this town are founded on? As I begin to see it, they're founded on bluff. It's the best window-dresser that gets by. Ten chances to one your boss is getting by on the very same game. I know mine is. The mayor probably is. The lawyers and bankers and swells and business men certainly are. So, why shouldn't I do my little share of it?"

Garretson, "the jitney George Moore," is more understanding. "The forest is too thick for you to see the trees," he tells Tess. "But you're on your way through. And sellers in a brisk market don't stop to wash mud from their tulips."

Tess doesn't get it. She will, and we know she will. Sidney R. Kent's simple idea was to bring an oft-told story, that of a country girl at risk of being corrupted by the big city, to a new medium. His greatest contribution was a title that was sure to sell. CanLit academics will point out that it was a brisk market.

Never so Disturbing

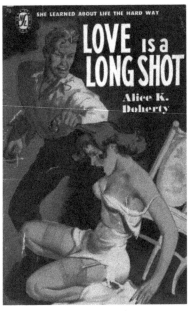

Love Is a Long Shot
Alice K. Doherty [pseud. Ted Allan]
Toronto: News Stand Library, 1949
160 pages

Can a writer, even a deceased writer, be stripped of the Leacock Medal? It's a fair question, particularly when one considers the late Ted Allan, who received the honour in 1984 for *Love is a Long Shot*. This slight, uninspired novel tells the story of seventeen-year-old David Webber and his sometimes ribald adventures tending the till in a thirties-era Montreal cigar store-cum-bookie joint. It features a cast of characters that are *characters*; each ultimately and invariably proving themselves loveable types despite earlier indiscretions. Readers familiar with *Lies My Father Told Me*, the 1975 film that earned Allan an Academy Award nomination, will recognize some of these folks, including David's frustrated inventor-father and his ideas for moveable cufflinks and permanently creased trousers.

This is not to suggest that there's anything deceitful here; not with the film, at least. The overlap between *Lies My Father Told Me* and *Love Is a Long Shot* is trifling, and in no way makes the latter ineligible for the Leacock. The medal's rules inform: adaptations are fair game, we need only discount works of which "significant or substantial parts have been previously published in book form."

Like so many tomes, the 1984 *Love Is a Long Shot* includes a list of the author's previous works. Allan's first novel, *This Time a Better Earth* (1939), is followed by *The Scalpel, The Sword* (1952), the commercially successful biography of Norman Bethune that he wrote with Sydney Gordon. There's *Quest for Pajaro* (1957), the science-fiction novel Allan published under *nom de plume* "Edward Maxwell," and his children's book *Willie, the Squowse* (1973). Also included is a comprehensive list of

Allan's plays and screenplays. What's missing is telling: an earlier *Love Is a Long Shot*.

Published by News Stand Library in September 1949, two months before newspaperman Al Palmer's *Sugar-Puss on Dorchester Street*, this *Love Is a Long Shot* holds the distinction of being the first pulp *noir* novel set in Montreal. Its setting is a Depression-era city that's as dark as the second *Love Is a Long Shot* is light. Where in the remake David Webber gets his job through a helpful, good-natured uncle, our desperate protagonist—recently orphaned teenager Katie Doheny—is out of options. Like David, she takes a job in a cigar store that's little more than a front for illegal gambling. The early pages of the girl's bleak world are broken by fleeting moments of black humour—all of which Allan reused in his Leacock-winning novel. Here, for example, is the most memorable, a comic scene that features Molly, the wife of the cigar-store owner. It begins with a boast:

> "Never wore a corset in my life. Never had to." She swaggered out from behind the counter. "If you don't believe me, feel," she said, offering me her hip.
> "I believe you," I said.
> "Feel. Feel. Don't be shy."
> I touched her quickly with the tips of my fingers.
> She started to laugh again, a loud, hearty laugh. "How old are you?"
> I dug the broom into the floor, pushed hard and told her my age.
> "I bet you never had a man."

The Molly of the 1984 *Love Is a Long Shot*, also married to the cigar-store owner, is equally proud:

> "Never wore a corset in my life. Never had to." Weaving from behind the counter, she offered me her backside. "If you don't believe me, feel."
> "I believe you."
> "Feel, feel, don't be shy." She wiggled her behind.
> I touched her hip quickly with the tips of my fingers. This made her cackle. You have to hear a woman with a bass voice cackle before you can believe the sound.
> "So help me, he's blushing. How old are you?"

"I'm twenty-one," I lied.

"I bet you're still a cherry."

Any further frivolity in the original *Love Is a Long Shot* is soon overwhelmed by the *noir*. The greatest difference between the two novels lies in their depictions of organized crime. While the Leacock-winning *Love Is a Long Shot* has the "syndicate" as a group of misbehaving boys, the 1949 original comes uncomfortably close to ugly reality.

Young Katie falls for "tall, rugged-looking, tanned" mob boss Hazen Black, a relatively young man rendered impotent by a life of debauchery. In what is surely one of the darkest scenes in Canadian literature, the appropriately named Black masturbates while instructing his henchman Herbert to rape Katie:

> Herbert grabbed me and held his hand over my mouth. I tried to bite it. "Go ahead," Black was shouting. "Go ahead, damn it, go ahead." His eyes looked insane. His breath was coming in short gasps, as if he'd been running. He was close to me, but hadn't touched me yet. "Go ahead. Pick up her dress... do it, do it, do it."

The original *Love Is a Long Shot* ain't that pretty at all—nor is it funny. Printed only once, in a fragile, disposable edition that credits the author variously as "Alice K. Doherty," "Alice H. Doherty," and simply "Alice Doherty," it slipped by the judges of the 1984 Stephen Leacock Memorial Medal for Humour.

The most one can say about the award-winning *Love Is a Long Shot* is that it was far superior to the previous year's winner, Gary Lauten's *No Sex Please... We're Married*. Allan didn't deserve the honour; the $3,500 cheque should have rightfully gone to fellow nominee John Gray, whose debut novel, *Dazzled*, had been issued by the anaemic Irwin Publishing.

It's a sad fact that the best novel Ted Allan ever wrote was one that he chose not to recognize. A cheap mass-market paperback issued under a pseudonym that the publisher couldn't get right, it has been out of print for over half a century.

Touched in The Head by a Telepathic Virgin

Soft to the Touch
Clark W. Dailey
Toronto: News Stand Library, 1949
159 pages

Caroline Prentiss entertains her male visitors—and she has many—in revealing robes and diaphanous negligees. She loves to kiss and encourages caresses, but don't you go getting any ideas about taking things further. At twenty-six, Caroline guards her virginity like no one else, convinced that it's tied, inextricably, to her independence.

Understandably, swains swarm, but quickly fall away in frustration. Only two, playboy Harvey Garrett and lawyer Larry Devlin, show any stamina. Both have been pursuing Caroline for years, each pitching woo and proposing marriage. With a girl on the side, Harvey has an easier time of it; poor lovestruck Larry has been leading the life of a celibate.

Caroline is content with the status quo. Montreal's foremost celebrity sculptress—no joke—she takes pride in her ability to make a good living without being tied to any one man. When not entertaining, Caroline throws off robe and negligee so as to admire her naked self in a full-length mirror. The reader is twice told that she's the spitting image of Virginia Mayo.

The great Thomas P. Kelley, King of the Canadian Pulps, once bragged that he never revised a work in progress. I don't mean to suggest that Clark W. Dailey—of whom there is no trace—is Kelley, rather that the two men held similar views when it came to composition.

The fourth of this novel's eight chapters begins with something of a revelation. The celebrity sculptress is shown to be struggling financially. The post-war art boom has proved to be more of a sharp crack, and Caroline is forced to sell her work at bargain-basement prices. Good guy Larry offers to pay her rent and bills, but Caroline hesitates. She fears the effect the loan—or is it a gift?—might have on their relationship. Ultimately, the sculptress accepts the lawyer's help.

Then something odd happens: *sans explication*, the narrator (omniscient) reverses things, revealing that the lawyer has been paying for everything, Caroline's car included, for many months. A couple of chapters later, the reader learns that she has been passing on wads of Larry's dough to support Harvey. In today's parlance we might describe this as a reboot, with Caroline reimagined as someone who never was a successful sculptor, despite her remarkable celebrity.

It's enough to make you want to throw the book against a wall. I didn't, because it was already coming apart, and also because the many weird digressions entertained. Here, our omniscient narrator goes off on an awkwardly constructed tirade about Dior's New Look:

> How many women try to keep themselves slim, and when they look like a sheet of paper set up on end, with but the merest suggestion of what could be an attractive pair of rising beauties, when what curves they have are shrouded by grotesque "New Look" clothing, when they can walk down the street looking exactly like almost every other woman, that is, they wear a smug expression, because they think they are beautiful! Gawdallmighty!—how the fashion designers and their partners in misleading "how to be smart" muck, the dress manufacturers, must smile as they purchase another yacht to set sail for Africa to get away from the horrible shapes they have been instrumental in creating, and to gaze in rapture and admiration upon woman as she was made to be—white, yellow or black!

The book is peppered with rants, observations, and other asides. The most repeated topic concerns "thought transference." Brace yourself, the narrator has some pretty harsh things to say:

> Concealment has destroyed in man the power of transferring his thoughts to another without speech. Man so seldom wants his thoughts revealed or known to another. He goes to considerable trouble to conceal them, and he has hedged himself around with so many lies and deceptions, that he has crippled his art altogether. The animals possess it still, because they neither deceive nor lie.

Sadly, *Soft to the Touch* isn't worth reading for the plot; I'm not spoiling anything by describing the drama that ensues.

Harvey tries to kill his rival with some sort of poison he brought back from the war. Larry makes it to a hospital, where he lies drifting in and out of consciousness. During one lucid moment he asks Caroline to marry him. The sculptress agrees, but only because doctors have told her that he is sure to die. The bedside ceremony is performed, after which Larry loses consciousness for what looks to be the very last time. Caroline is left alone with her dying husband:

> She was thinking. "How wonderfully he rallied after I held his hands for a long time. Perhaps…"
>
> She rose and, as before, took both his hands in her soft, warm ones. Then she drew all her inner forces and mental resources together and concentrated her thoughts on one short phrase, "I shall live." Perhaps if she could drive this straight from her brain into his, it would affect him.

Affect him it does! After a long night of handholding, Larry bounces back. The attending doctor, "wise, kind and clever, and a man very much interested in natural methods of healing," is pleasantly surprised. He sees nothing wrong with Larry wolfing down bacon, eggs and coffee with his new bride: "'Hurrah!' exclaimed Larry, 'our first breakfast together.'"

The last we see of Harvey, he's rushing off to the airport to catch a clipper to Bermuda. Larry is quickly discharged and returns to Caroline's Bishop Street apartment. The last pages of the novel are heavy with the promise of sex, but it ends before the act takes place. This reader didn't care; I'd grown bored of Caroline and her groping admirers. I do miss the haranguing narrator, though, even if he can't be trusted.

The Neons Go Up, the Nylons Come Off

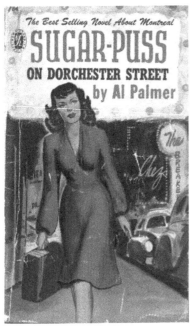

Sugar-Puss on Dorchester Street
Al Palmer
Toronto: New Stand Library, 1949
159 pages

Sugar-Puss is Gisele Lepine—not Gisèle Lépine—a farmer's daughter from the fictional Laurentian village of St Christophe. At thirteen, she's brought to Montreal for the St Jean Baptiste parade and is enchanted by shining pavement, neon signs, and snappy dressers. In an instant, Gisele's "neat and pleasant" home is "mentally transformed into one of bleak desolation." The next five years are devoted to fiscal prudence and self-betterment, all so that she might one day take her place amongst the city folk—not for her the life of a "farmette," "first a slave to a husband then to an ever-growing family."

Gisele is eighteen when her dream is realized. She returns to Montreal as a beauty blessed with large, firm breasts, "a legacy of her Norman ancestry," soft, brown skin that hints at Basque blood and feet that are "small and beautifully formed as are those of most French Canadian women."

Foot fetishists aside, who knew?

Montreal moves at a much different pace than quiet St Christophe. Gisele gets a job waitressing in a cheap restaurant, but flees after her oily Greek employer tries pawing her. In the next forty-eight hours, she becomes a chorus-line dancer, meets the love of her life, makes a BFF and loses her virginity.

> Events were piling up too fast for her to cope with. She couldn't think clearly. She closed her eyes tightly and shook her head to free some of the turmoil that raged within.

Next is a marriage proposal, the move to a luxurious apartment, a shoot-out with police, a death, another marriage proposal, a kidnapping, a car chase, a second death and, at the end of it all, a walk "into the brilliant sunshine of Dorchester Street." It's a helluva week.

This was Al Palmer's first book, published the year before *Montreal Confidential*. I'd have preferred the latter had it not been for the intriguing cover copy on *Sugar-Puss*: "He takes his readers behind the scene of a metropolitan newspaper. He takes them backstage to the city's leading night clubs and introduces them to the fabulous characters he knows so well."

Just who are these people? We meet Jim Schultz, a former boxer, who assures a nervous Gisele: "you're just as safe as if you were in yah mudda's arms. Safer unless yah mudda's got cauliflower ears." The "bistro bossman" of The Breakers—really Slitkin's and Slotkin's—Jim was almost certainly inspired by one of the owners, both former boxers. Or was the model Maxie Berger, a welterweight champion like Schwartz? And what about Gaston Courtney, the drug dealing night-club owner? Who inspired Diane and Trixie, Gisele's fellow hoofers?

These questions linger, as does this: "Sugar-Puss" or "Sugar Puss"? Picky, I know, but the inconsistency points to the News Stand Library's sloppy editing and production values. In my copy, the very first sentence fades into nothingness: *"Dorchester Street* spews out almost..." Almost what? The mystery is nearly enough to erase the image of vomiting asphalt.

The Man Who Hated Toronto

Present Reckoning
Hugh Garner
Toronto: Collins White Circle, 1951
158 pages

Tom Neelton has arrived too late for the party, but he doesn't care. It's the morning after V-J Day and he has just stepped off a train at Union Station. Outside, streamers hang limply from lampposts and confetti clogs the gutters.

What's he doing here?

Tom hates Toronto. Though born and raised in the city, "it had been something he had had to fight, an enemy of brick and stone and smug condescension." Tom's mother and father are dead. His nearest kin is a dishonest aunt with whom he made the mistake of storing his civilian clothes before shipping out. She'll claim that the moths got to them.

Again, what's he doing here?

At first, I thought the answer lay in Carol Berkett. Seven years ago, when he was twenty-five and she seventeen, they'd gone out for a bit. She'd even brought him home to meet her mom. Roast was served. Tom and Carol did some necking on the chesterfield. He never called on her again.

Now, he's thinking he made a mistake. Tom imagines a better life, one in which Carol would have been waiting at the train station. He returns to familiar digs, a cheap room in the Pentland (read: Warwick) Hotel, determined to track her down. But it turns out that she's not in the phone book. Her mom's not in the phone book, either. Then, "like a soft slap against his consciousness," it occurs to him that Carol might be married.

So he gives up and is soon snogging Margaret, the buxom blonde who works the front desk.

Tom guessed right about Carol. We know because Garner devotes several chapters to her marriage.

Happy?

Not unhappy. Husband George, a punch press operator, has come to accept that she doesn't share his passion for amateur radio. He sometimes gets a good chuckle out of *Blondie*, his wife's favourite comic strip. Carol, who often thinks of her brief romance with Tom, becomes much more contented after the birth of baby Harold.

Clearly, Tom and Carol are destined to meet, but this doesn't occur before the second half of the novel. Until then, the returning veteran kills time drinking with friends in the local beer parlour. Margaret decamps for Kamloops, Tom takes up with bohemian art school student Louise Kramer and Garner runs up his word count.

Biographer Paul Stewe is dismissive of *Present Reckoning*, focussing in on what he considers a melodramatic climax. In the monograph he penned for the *Canadian Writers & their* [sic] *Works* series, George Fetherling describes it as "a little novel which depends far too much on chance meetings, coincidence and on the double-whammy at the end and is nowhere near the level of Garner's best prose."

I agree with that last bit. That said, I count only two coincidences or chance meetings:

- Louise sees Tom in a museum one week, then spots him a library the next.
- Twelve months after returning to town, Tom encounters old flame Carol on the street.

These things happen.

I won't spoil the ending, other than to say that I found it believable, strong enough, more than a little upsetting and not the least bit melodramatic. But what I really took away from *Present Reckoning*—what's really of value—is its depiction of Toronto in the months after the war.

Carol, who lives in a new development, is ever aware of the prying eyes of neighbouring housewives. George's company prepares for the new peacetime economy. Over glasses of beer, Tom gauges the progress of a disfigured drinking buddy's reconstructed face. He'll also make the mistake of returning to an old haunt where he's confronted by "young punks in zoot-suit pants and girls in Eisenhower jackets." Tom later describes the scene to Carol:

"They danced differently than we did, wore their hair in brush cuts and feathered bobs, and stared at me standing on the sidelines as though I was a bouncer. I moved over near the orchestra and spent an hour or so listening to the music trying to recapture the feeling I had in the old days, but it was no use. I didn't belong there."

There's something not to like about *Present Reckoning*. It meanders in a way that had me wondering whether Garner wasn't drawing from unpublished stories and other jottings. After all, he'd done just that the year before with the pseudonymous *Waste No Tears*.

Again, I agree with my friend George that this is not Garner's best prose. And yet passages like this, in which newly arrived Tom is confronted by his first sight of the Royal York Hotel, are just about the greatest things he ever wrote:

The hotel—Largest in the British Empire—squatted sullenly against the opposite sidewalk, daring those leaving the station to pass it by without a glance. He forced his eyes along its self-satisfied exterior and thought back to the days of its opening fifteen years before. There had been much fanfare then, with big-wigs by the score. Ben Bernie's orchestra, a porter for every bag and doormen garbed in coachman's habit. During the depression the coachmen had disappeared along with many of the other opulent ostentations, and for years the edifice had gone on like a bankrupt dowager, bravely pretending that things had not changed and that its hundreds of empty rooms were full of guests. To him it symbolized the city: smug, part good taste and bad, a brave thing formed of a maladmixture of decency and sham.

What was Tom Neelton doing back in Toronto?
Better the hell you know.
He'll come to wish he'd never returned.

Toronto Noir, Montreal Noir, and the Dark Road Between

The name's Danny Keller, ex-convict, three years for manslaughter. I hit a man. He fell and struck his head on a fire hydrant. He was a rat. I'm not sorry he's dead, but I'd rather be dead beside him than do time again.

Not a bad beginning, but,as with so many post-war noir novels, the writer just can't keep it up. Twenty pages in, with three hundred to go, I'd become much more interested in the author photo.

Is it Louis Kaufman? Did Kaufman really serve in the RCAF as cover copy claims? Did he enjoy swimming, sailing, and pecking at the keys of a second-hand piano? Or are these just elements of Kaufman's Dan Keller, persona?

Flee the Night in Anger
Dan Keller [pseud. Louis Kaufman]
Toronto: Studio Publications, 1952
320 pages

And why take the name of your protagonist as a *nom de plume* when it's clear that Dan Keller, the ex-serviceman, and Danny Keller, the ex-con, cannot be one and the same?

I know nothing about the author, but believe I've got a pretty good handle on the protagonist.

Danny Keller is an unlucky man. After his stint in Kingston Penitentiary, he tries for a new life in Toronto, but finds that no one is very impressed with his criminal record. Desperate for work, Danny makes the mistake of considering a shady job. He becomes a bit hot-headed during the

job interview, and walks away convinced he accidentally killed his prospective employer.

An honest man would turn himself in, a dishonest man would skip town, but Danny takes a stupid man's route by keeping the appointment that had been arranged for him by the dead man. In a dark, wet cocktail lounge he meets "some looker; tall and supple, dressed in a light, filmy summer frock that did nothing to hide her assets and plenty to promote them." It's only then that Danny finds out the nature of the job: he's to retrieve a briefcase from the checkroom at Union Station. Simple enough, except the befrocked looker only has half of the check slip. Two days later, she shows up at his flat with the other half. She defrocks, they have sex, and he's off to Front Street.

Now the problem: *The two halves don't match!*

Danny phones his flat, but the babe in his bed doesn't pick up. On his return he finds that she has a hole "like a torn socket bereft of its eye" beneath her naked left breast. Our hero, fearing a set-up, moves the dead woman's body to her apartment then splurges on a Trans-Canada Air Lines ticket to Montreal.

"Montreal appealed to me as a good place to disappear from," he tells us. Don't you mean "in which to disappear," Danny? You're trying to disappear "from" Toronto.

Never the smartest guy in the room, it's only after our Danny books the flight that he remembers finding a bill from a Montreal lingerie store in the dead woman's apartment. Like many a rube before, he sets out to clear his name before the coppers—his word, not mine—slap on the cuffs. The task isn't nearly as unpleasant as it sounds. Danny enjoys a couple of tumbles with Belle Doan, a former burlesque dancer who's now a mob boss' wife, and has several similar encounters with a coltish, well-scrubbed girl named Joan. Think Ginger and Mary Ann… or Lili St Cyr and Madeline Kronby.

Flee the Night in Anger is unique in our post-war noir in that it moves back and forth between Toronto and Montreal. The pace is fast, and becomes even more so in the 1954 American "Complete and Unabridged" Popular Library edition, which cuts roughly a quarter of the original text. A lot of the sex is lost, including a pretty hot encounter in which we learn of Belle's masochistic tendencies. She likes to be knocked around. Die hard noir fans will want to read the Canadian edition, and may wish to skip the paragraphs that follow. There will be spoilers.

Three people are killed in *Flee the Night in Anger*. As befits a mystery, the deaths of the first two are explained in the closing chapter. For the third, the reader must wait for the very last page, in which the lead detective explains:

> As near as we can tell from the evidence, he tripped over the chair and put out his hand to save himself as his full weight fell on the seat of the chair, forcing it down. A broken spring inside the chair caught the trigger of the gun and fired it. The bullet hit him in the stomach; as he fell he pulled the gun free, upsetting the chair over himself before he died.

So you see it was just a freak accident. These things happen.

In the Canadian edition, Danny then heads upstairs for sex. The American ends with a kiss.

Encyclopedia Brown Spoils the Day

A Body for a Blonde
Ken McLeod [pseud. Kimball McIlroy]
Toronto: Harlequin, 1954
158 pages

Before starting out on this exploration of our forgotten, neglected, and suppressed, I'd read very few mysteries. There was an Agatha Christie, something by Margaret Millar and something else by Ross Macdonald, but most I'd read were written by Donald J. Sobol, the creator of Encyclopedia Brown. An admirer of the boy detective, I studied his every case during my days at Allancroft Elementary School. Pretty much everything I know about solving crimes comes from good, good Leroy Brown; and so, it's really to his credit that I was able to finger the murderer by page seven of this pre-romance Harlequin. I spent the rest of the novel wondering just how long it would take the characters to clue in.

A Body for a Blonde isn't nearly as startling or shocking as the publisher would have you believe. The man you see behind the door on the cover isn't being tortured; he's having a cold shower. The blonde isn't that of the title, but his pal's tiny, baby-faced girlfriend. She should be wearing more than a negligee.

A Body for a Blonde isn't startling or shocking, though it does contain a decent dose of humour. In the main, this is supplied by George Sloan, a hard-working, seemingly well-paid writer plying his trade in post-war Toronto. George has just finished his latest novel when two burly movers appear at the door, interrupting his celebratory drink. He makes a mistake in granting the men entry, then compounds it by allowing them to leave a heavy steamer trunk in his living room. After they're gone, George opens the trunk to find the cooling corpse of a dead man.

"Jee-zus!" says George.

His third mistake comes in picking up a gun that's lying on the body. It goes off, the cops rush in, and George is arrested for murder.

This would never happen in Idaville, Encyclopedia's hometown, but Toronto is different. George ends up drinking gin with jailer Joe in a holding cell. His one chance at salvation seems to lie with fiancée Mabel Jones, "a tall, beautiful, willowy girl who had paid her way through college by doing photographic modelling."

You know the type.

Former model Mabel is now a lawyer. Before she can get George off—nothing naughty implied—he makes a break that leads to her apartment and the shower scene so inaccurately depicted on the cover.

A Body for a Blonde is a book in which booze flows freely. George, Mabel, and their friends Roly and Rita spend about as much time drinking as they do trying to figure out who really dunnit. The whole thing comes off like a party game. There's a fair amount of ribbing and ribaldry throughout, as when attention turns to George's blonde bombshell of a neighbour—yes, she of the title—Estelle Hilton:

> Roly said, "I agree with George. I still see the thing just the way we had it figured out before. You two girls are just jealous of Estelle."
>
> Rita said, "Humph! That blowzy sex-bag? Nothing between her ears and everything between her..."
>
> Roly said, "Rita!"
>
> "Well, it's true. Just because she's got a lot of blonde hair on her head and sticks out in all the right places you dopes figure she couldn't possibly be mixed up in a murder."

Meanwhile, the cops are so convinced of George's guilt that they don't really bother to investigate and are therefore blind to strong evidence that might clear the writer.

The Toronto Police Service comes off poorly in this novel. It's only by getting a corrupt cop drunk on seized hooch that George is able to escape his holding cell. Minutes later, the murderer strikes again, killing within the very same police station. Whether sober or drunk, George moves freely through the city, climbing fire escapes, breaking into apartments, and strolling through the lobby of the Royal York Hotel. He's present for two police raids on Mabel's miniscule apartment, but is not found.

Worst of all, the murderer turns out to be a fairly senior member of the force.

Now don't go accusing me of spoiling the novel; at worst I've ruined the first seven pages. Encyclopedia Brown would agree. *A Body for a Blonde* is recommended, but not as a mystery. A light read, a fun read, and a bit of a ribald read, it should be kept away from the impressionable children of Idaville.

Dale's Dumb Luck; Or;
A Mountie Messes Up

Dale of the Mounted: Atlantic Assignment
Joe Holliday
Toronto: Thomas Allen, 1956
158 pages

First off, I should make it clear that the book I really wanted to read is *Dale of the Mounted: Atomic Plot*. Published in 1959, it involves a Pakistani scientist, East Indian religious fanatics, and a terrorist attack on Canada's Chalk River nuclear-research facility. I read *Dale of the Mounted: Atlantic Assignment* only because it turned up in our local library's most recent used-book sale.

That I haven't come across any others says something about the passage of time, I think. Dale of the Mounted books were once very popular, each landing in early November so as to take advantage of Christmas gift giving. Having been born the year the series ended, I never received one myself, but I remember a friend's older brother having a few.

Dale of the Mounted is Constable Dale Thompson. His "Atlantic Assignment" follows *Dale of the Mounted in Newfoundland* as the sixth adventure in six years. As in the previous book, Dale sets aside his Red Serge to adopt the guise of a journalist. Where in Newfoundland he was on the trail of Portuguese smugglers, here Dale investigates suspicious incidents that have taken place on HMCS *Pegasus*, Canada's newest aircraft carrier.

Was there really a time when it fell to the RCMP to investigate possible crimes of sabotage aboard Royal Canadian Navy ships? If so, would that task have been entrusted to a constable? And why is Dale a constable, anyway? After all he accomplished in the previous books, isn't a promotion long overdue?

These were the first questions that crossed my mind while reading *Dale of the Mounted: Atlantic Assignment*. Though never answered, by the end of the first chapter they'd been supplanted by another that I simply couldn't shake: How is it that Dale is still alive?

If *Dale of the Mounted: Atlantic Assignment* is anything to go by, the constable should've died in the series' first book. His end might have come at the hands of a foe, or while cleaning his gun, but he would be dead.

Dale never gets a chance to investigate past incidents. He's newly arrived on the aircraft carrier when a mysterious fire breaks out, destroying two planes. The challenge in describing what comes next involves time: Holliday is never terribly clear as to just when events take place in this novel. Instead, his narrative gets lost in irrelevant facts and figures. These aren't red herrings, but rather padding.

Dale learns all about sonobuoys, the *Habbakuk* Project, Pratt & Whitney Wright Cyclone engines, and a navigation and interception computer invented by an RCAF Wing Commander. One of the novel's one hundred and fifty-eight pages is devoted to the ins and outs of automobile ownership in Bermuda.

As the Mountie struggles to stay focussed, he's easily outpaced by his lone suspect, a mechanic named Joe DeMarco. The *Pegasus* loses three more planes, though this does not prevent the carrier from participating in a "United Nations sea exercise." The ship's commanding officer takes it all in stride:

> The plane was lost.
>
> When the young Mountie said how impressed he was with the part that aircraft carriers played in the war games Captain Grayson smiled. He liked anyone who thought that carriers were the finest things afloat.

Captain Grayson likes Dale so much that he readily follows the young Mountie's advice. When dynamite is discovered in DeMarco's toolbox, Dale suggests they play a waiting game:

> "I've a hunch that DeMarco can't plant any kind of time bomb unless he has plenty of time to do it. Unless I'm badly mistaken, the movies tonight will give him that big chance. Let us attend the movies. I'll keep within sight of DeMarco. I'll watch every move he makes. If he leaves the flight deck I'll follow him."

DeMarco does leave the deck. Dale follows but is knocked out cold (for the second of three times). The next morning, the mechanic manages a flight off the carrier, resulting in the loss of yet another plane.

Is a spoiler alert warranted? Is anyone thinking of reading this? If not:

As it turns out, DeMarco is one of two fifth columnists. The Mountie doesn't get either man. What happens is that the first saboteur kills the second, then plunges to his death in a kamikaze-like attack on the *Pegasus*. It's only through a bizarre accident that the carrier is saved. The attacks were the work of a Balkan "dictator country"—though why it targeted the *Pegasus* is anyone's guess.

The novel ends, improbably, with a chance meeting between Dale and the Secretary of State for External Affairs. I was distracted by the narrator's cock-up in referring to the latter as a diplomat—five times in less than a page—so didn't quite recognized its importance as a set-up for the series' next book. I was put right by the lamest of endings:

> Dale, at the time, gave the incident little serious thought, but it was fated to take him back into the heart of the Canadian Arctic, delving into the mysteries of The Dew line [sic], the secret Distant Early Warning radar system, whose development interested him more than one foreign diplomat. It would also give him an insight into important aviation tests.
>
> THE END

The promised adventure, *Dale of the Mounted: DEW Line Duty*, arrived in stores the following November. Five more adventures followed. The series ended in 1962 with *Dale of the Mounted in Hong Kong*, in which Dale is finally killed.

Okay, I don't know for a fact that he dies—but, really, dumb luck can only last so long.

Thriller Most Foreign

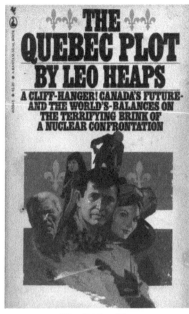

The Quebec Plot
Leo Heaps
Toronto: Seal, 1979
248 pages

This is a thriller written by a man whose own story reads like a thriller. A Jewish Canadian paratrooper in the Second World War, Leo Heaps fought in the Battle of Arnhem, was captured by the Nazis, escaped, joined the Dutch Resistance, and returned to fight another day. He served as an advisor to the Israelis in the War of Independence and worked on the International Rescue Committee during the Hungarian Revolution. Heaps was also the son of A.A. Heaps, a leader in the Winnipeg General Strike and one of the founders of the CCF. Anyone collecting Old Age Security today should raise a glass in his honour.

With a background like that it should come as no surprise that *The Quebec Plot* isn't just a thriller, but a *political* thriller. It begins with Marcel Legros, chief of the secret French intelligence agency—CEDECE—catching a plane at Charles de Gaulle Airport. Cut to Martinique, scene of a clandestine meeting between Legros and Gilles Marcoux, the Parti Québécois' newly installed Minister of the Interior. Our hero, Mark Hauser, makes his debut in Stowe, Vermont, where he's looking to get in some end-of-season skiing. Hauser is a Pulitzer Prize-winning senior journalist at a New York-based news syndicate. Far below him, in age and experience, is a colleague named Freeman. When the younger man breaks his leg while on assignment in Quebec City, Hauser is tapped to take his place. Good choice. The American-born son of a French Canadian and a German Jew, Hauser is bilingual and knows a good deal about Canada. It would've been his assignment from the start had the agency thought there was much of a story.

Just what is the story? Harry Consadine, head of the syndicate, explains: "This new Quebec party wants the province to separate from the rest of Canada. You know how insular we are down here, Mark. We've always taken Canada for granted."

Still do, apparently, which is why they sent Freeman with his schoolboy French, and why Consadine reassures his star reporter that he'll be back on the slopes in a day or two. With great reluctance, Hauser leaves Stowe and his newfound love interest, an intellectual ski bunny named Hilda Beane, for an appointment his boss has set up with Saul Klein at the Montreal offices of the Canadian Jewish Congress. Why? "The Jews are a seismograph. If they're leaving it's a sure sign something is wrong," Consadine tells him.

Klein is staying put.

The thriller only kicks into gear when Hauser leaves Montreal for Quebec City. Along the way, he picks up a hitchhiker named Paul Lejeune who's heading for a hunting and fishing lodge north of Lac St-Jean… or so he says. Hauser notices an automatic weapon with a folding stock sticking out of Lejeune's rucksack.

What Hauser doesn't know is that his passenger is really en route to a training camp belonging to something called the Quebec Army of Liberation. The Canadian government knows about the army, and is fairly certain that the bases exist, but can't seem to find any. Ottawa's doing much better with *L'Inflexible*, a French nuclear submarine it's tracking as it makes its way from Martinique to the Gaspé peninsula. Unbeknownst to the French, the Americans are following in their own submarine, *Wolverine*, which is equipped with a brand-new secret weapon.

Ignore the bit about the secret weapon. Ignore the cover copy about H-bomb missiles (we're never told exactly what *L'Inflexible* is delivering). The novel's most interesting parts centre on Hauser in Quebec City, beginning with his discovery that Freeman has disappeared from his bed at the Hôtel-Dieu hospital.

The Quebec Plot is taut, which is just the thing one wants in a thriller. I imagine it would've been tighter still had it not found its first home with London publisher Peter Davies. I blame the intrusive hand of an editor for its worst page. The first few of sentences should give you an idea:

The Canadian House of Commons rises majestically from atop Parliament Hill in Ottawa. It consists of an imposing series of three stone structures. Modelled on the Mother of Parliaments in

Westminster, the buildings are set in large grounds where every spring tens of thousand [sic] of multi-coloured tulips—an annual gift from Holland—burst from the exquisitely trimmed lawns. In the Centre Block are housed the Commons Chamber and the Senate. Above the main entrance itself the central tower rises several hundred feet like a cathedral belfry to where a giant clock melodiously chimes out the quarter hours sounding much like Big Ben in London.

I won't criticize Seal—McClelland & Stewart, really—for letting these lines stand, but will take it to task for ignoring typos, the British "tyre," and glaring mistakes like "Party Québecois."

Don't let that dissuade you from reading it. The separatist movement of the seventies inspired several Quebec-based thrillers. Heaps' followed others by old pros like Philip Atlee, Lionel Derrick, and Richard Rohmer. I expected little, yet found that *The Quebec Plot* rose high above the rest. Quite an accomplishment for a first-time novelist. The author's bio should've given me a clue.

The Paratrooper, the Professor, and the Publisher: The Prolonged Public Battle Over *The Quebec Plot*

The first review of my first book, *Character Parts*, was negative. The reviewer's disappointment had to do with my having written the book I wanted to write rather than the book he had wanted to read.

The second review of my first book was written by a man identified in same as the model for a thoroughly dislikeable character in George Galt's novel *Scribes and Scoundrels*. The reviewer made no mention of this, though he did question my existence.

"Do not respond," a senior writer friend advised.

I didn't.

The reviews that followed were very positive. I remember nothing of them other than that—very positive—but I do remember the two negative reviews in detail. For example, I can tell you that the first reviewer got the price and page count wrong. I can also tell you that I was taken to task for not including an index. The book has one, but he'd read an advance copy. His was an amateur's mistake, published in the closest thing Canada has to "the organ of the trade."

Bad reviews stay with you in a way good reviews don't. I know not to read them. I don't read good reviews, either. Every now and then I feel bad for not acknowledging a reviewer's kind words... and here I'm certain they are all kind words.

"Do not respond."

Good advice I pass on to others. And yet all these years later I still fantasize about taking on the critics in question, which is why I so enjoyed Leo Heaps' thrust and parry with Patrick O'Flaherty found decades-old editions of the *Globe and Mail*.

A professor at Memorial University, Patrick O'Flaherty was tasked with reviewing *The Quebec Plot* for the paper. I have no idea why; O'Flaherty doesn't appear to have reviewed thrillers in the past. Published in the July 22, 1978 edition, his opening sentence betrays a certain ignorance of the genre: "Leo Heaps, who has been reading James Bond stories and learning a little Canadian geography and history, has decided to write a thriller, some would say a *roman à clef* about the Quebec situation."

Ignoring the obvious (*The Quebec Plot* owes nothing to Ian Fleming), what irks is the insinuation that Heaps, then living in London, needed something of a refresher in things Canadian. This is the very same thinking that our dumbest cultural nationalists once employed against the great Mavis Gallant. Winnipeg-born Leo Heaps was educated at Queen's and McGill, and lived most of his life in Toronto. At the risk of being called racist—more on that later—I find this quip about Heaps "learning a little Canadian geography and history" a bit rich coming from a man whose early education pre-dated his province joining Confederation. It's not O'Flaherty at his worst, but it's pretty bad. His lowest and laziest comes when he quotes two lines of dialogue out of context:

- "I hope to God there's no armed revolution in Quebec."
- "Let's get down to business."

It's a cheap trick we've all seen before; indeed, Heaps himself recognizes it as such in his response. But before I get to that, O'Flaherty's conclusion is worth presenting in full:

And so, not all this story will appeal to Canadian nationalists. This may not matter a great deal, for as novelist Timothy Findley [sic] told us not long ago, we have plenty of wonderful Canadian fiction to read. Now let's see, where's the book I put down about a week ago? Something about a cardinal committing murder because he doesn't want the world to know about the discovery of the bones of Jesus. A Very Significant Book. When I finish that, I want to re-read a Great Novel from last year. About a woman who tries to copulate with A Great Big Bear.

Anyone out there for Little Orphan Annie?

Now, I'm the first to acknowledge that it's not always easy to come up with a decent conclusion to a review—look at mine for *The Quebec Plot* as evidence—but this one is a real head-scratcher. On the other hand, I'm no academic, which is why I so appreciated the University of Toronto's June V. Engel, who, in a letter in the *Globe and Mail* (August 1, 1978) refers to Prof O'Flaherty's conclusion as "incomprehensible."

Engel wasn't alone in her criticism of the critic. An earlier letter found in the July 28 edition describes the professor's review as "jumbled, incoherent." The writer was someone named Caruso, who may or may not have been an academic him or herself.

By that time, Heaps had responded to the critic. In the July 26, 1978 edition of the *Globe and Mail*, he shrugs off everything to do with his knowledge of Canada, associations with Ian Fleming, Marian Engel, Charles Templeton, and *Little Orphan Annie* creator Harold Gray, then makes a parting shot:

> I have been away from Canada for some time and have grown accustomed to having my books read by literate people who are concerned both with their prose and the philosophical content of their reviews. If Mr. O'Flaherty is a professor of English in Newfoundland, who is there to protect us from the academics who teach in our schools?

Fair question. I've been asking variations of it since my graduation from Beaconsfield High School.

Leo Heaps' letter drew no response from Patrick O'Flaherty, though Jack McClelland weighed in with a letter (August 4, 1978), which reads, in part:

> At first I thought it was a bad Newfie joke. Then my reaction turned from disbelief to anger. Mr. O'Flaherty's judgement, in my opinion, ranks slightly below that of a Rhesus monkey and I have nothing against monkeys.

Was the publisher being disingenuous? "It happens that although I am not the publisher, I have read *The Quebec Plot*," McClelland writes of a novel he would publish within a year. Might as well add that he also published the novel about the cardinal who doesn't want the world to know about the discovery of Jesus' bones and the one in which a woman tries to copulate with a bear.

Tellingly, it was not Heaps', but McClelland's, letter that brought a response from the professor. Notably tardy, here he is in the paper's August 24, 1978 edition:

> The letter from Jack McClelland (Aug. 4) comes out with abusive, racist talk—"Newfie," "monkey," etc. This letter, contemptible though it is, merits a few words of reply. In recent years I have reviewed a number of silly books published by McClelland and Stewart Ltd. rather harshly. Looking back over my reviews, my only regret is that they were not harsher. What does a reviewer do when he is sent a trashy book to review? Normally, I, for one, return the item to the editor with a note saying that it is not worth reviewing. But there is so much writing in Canada—especially at the "creative" level—and so much of it is published with the assistance of the Canadian taxpayer, that it is hard to resist occasionally damning bad books. And so I stand by my review of Leo Heaps' book.

I imagine the professor does so to this day, ignoring the simple facts that *The Quebec Plot* received no taxpayer support and was never sold as anything other than a thriller.

The last word is owed to Leo Heaps himself, as published in this letter in the September 4, 1978 edition:

> I cannot resist taking a parting shot at my friend Patrick O'Flaherty who reviewed my book *The Quebec Plot* in your columns. I will miss the professor from Memorial College, Newfoundland, at his departure.
>
> Professor O'Flaherty has in his letter to your newspaper on Aug. 24 presented such a perfect and inviting target that I felt it was irresistible. His remarks either hide a character of infinite subtlety and wit or one of enormous pomposity and self-righteousness. Personally, I am inclined to favor the latter view. Mr. O'Flaherty has sounded like the budding parliamentary candidate he is when he protests against the waste of taxpayers' money on behalf of Canadian authors struggling to make ends meet. (Unfortunately, I have never had any

grants. All my books have been published abroad, except one, which won a Governor-General's Award.) Perhaps the professor might tell us where the subsidy came from to publish his somewhat obscure anthology of Newfoundland and Labrador writing, which he co-edited some years back.

If Patrick O'Flaherty remains as severe as he is, "untroubled," as Browning said, "by the spark," and if he is allowed to indecently expose himself in book review columns, then one can begin to understand his concern about Canadian prose. One only has to read what the professor writes.

Heaps is owed the last word... but I can't quite bring myself to let him have it.

In January 2009, at a dinner celebrating the sixtieth birthday of the aforementioned senior writer, I was introduced to the second critic of my first book. On learning my name he paused—here it comes, I thought—and then said: "You wouldn't be any relation to Reverend David Busby? I was one of his altar boys."

"Yes," I replied. "My late uncle."

"Nice man," said the critic.

"Yes, very nice," I said.

And then we parted.

ROMANCE

Bizarre Love Triangle

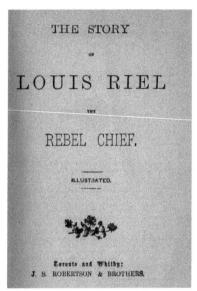

THE STORY

OF

LOUIS RIEL

THE

REBEL CHIEF,

ILLUSTRATED.

Toronto and Whitby:
J. S. ROBERTSON & BROTHERS.

The Story of Louis Riel, the Rebel Chief
[J. E. Collins]
Toronto: Rose, 1885
176 pages

Instant books, those slapdash things designed to capitalize on death and doom, nearly always raise a sneer, and yet I can't help but be impressed by the industry involved. To go from standing start to published volume in nineteen days, as did the team behind *9/11 8:48 AM: Documenting America's Greatest Tragedy* (2001) demonstrates such energy and determination. Of course, the *9/11 8:48 AM* folks, whose book was spewed forth by POD publisher BookSurge, had the advantage of twenty-first-century technology. Not so this relic from the days of stereotypes, electrotypes, and composing rooms.

Transplanted Newfoundlander Joseph Edmund Collins wrote *The Story of Louis Riel, the Rebel Chief* in the spring of 1885, as the North-West Rebellion was being fought. The finished product was available for purchase well before the start of Riel's trial in late July.

How did they do it?

Collins does his part through overwrought prose, evident in the first sentence: "'Along the banks of the Red River, over those fruitful plains brightened with wild flowers in summer, and swept with fierce storms in winter-time, is written the life story of Louis Riel."

Indeed, look to the banks of the Red River because you'll find little of the Métis leader's life in this book. Collins fabricates events, characters, and dialogue, creating a world that will strike students of Canadian history like something from an alternate universe. Key is the relationship between Riel and Thomas Scott, the Orangeman executed during the Red River Rebellion. Collins portrays this unstable, violent eristic as a likable fellow, a whistler, with "a very merry twinkle in his eye." In this account, the true nature of the conflict between the two men has less to do with the future Red River Colony than it does with a beautiful Métis maiden named Marie, whose preference for the good-natured adventurer over the uncouth Riel seals Scott's fate.

While historians consider *The Story of Louis Riel, the Rebel Chief* as fiction, it wasn't always accepted as such. Blame falls squarely on the author, who pads the book with footnotes, including Riel's "Proclamation to the People of the North-West" and lengthy excerpts from Alexander Begg's *The Creation of Manitoba* (1871)—identified incorrectly as "History of the North-West Rebellion"—and a comprehensive list of the non-Métis who lost their lives or were wounded in the conflict.

The Rose Publishing Company padded things out further with a dozen or so etchings. Only a handful have any relevance to the text—in fact, Riel appears in only one. Though captioned "REBELS [sic] ATTACKING MAJOR BOULTON'S SCOUTS," a reference to the shared fate of men under the command of Major Charles A. Boulton, the image has nothing to do with the Rebellion and everything to do with trouble in the republic to the south.

Collins later wrote that *The Story of Louis Riel, the Rebel Chief* held "no historic truth," and that he chose to leave his name off the book because he was "unwilling to take responsibility for the literary slovenliness." Yet, the author demonstrated no hesitation in appending his moniker to his next book, *Annette, the Metis Spy: A Heroine of the N. W. Rebellion* (1886). Here, Collins not only repeats the plot device that has Riel and Scott as romantic rivals, but lifts whole sections from his previous work. Of this second kick at the can, Collins writes, "I present some fiction in my story, and a large array of fact. I do not feel bound, however, to state which is the fact, and which is the fiction."

Collins' died from drink at age thirty-six. It is said that he maintained contact with his mentor, Sir Charles G.D. Roberts, through the aid of mediums.

Portrait of a Former Mistress

Barbara Ladd
Charles G.D. Roberts
Boston: Page, 1902
377 pages

Sir Charles G.D. Roberts died at the age of eighty-three, outliving nearly all of his contempories. Right to the end, he demonstrated an enviable degree of energy and stamina marrying his second wife—thirty years his junior—the month before his death.

This latter Mrs Roberts—Lady Roberts, if you prefer—most certainly had an easier time of it than her predecessor. The author had a habit of cheating on his first wife. For two years he carried on with Jean Carré, a Guernsey-born visual artist who came to him by way of Nova Scotia. To Roberts, sweet Jean was "she whose name is writ in music"—at least that's how he referred to her in letters written to his cousin Bliss Carman.

There are lessons to be learned from this correspondence, not the least of which is to pick up the phone when dealing with matters of the heart. In it, Roberts comes off by turns a love-struck adolescent and an excitable fop. In the closing days of 1891, he writes Carman, "I fear that she whose name is writ in music shall henceforth have it writ in mud!" Four months later, Roberts announces his plans to run off with her. Of course, he did nothing of the kind; rather, he replaced "she whose name is writ in music" with "the Queen of Bohemia," a tall and slender slip of a woman by the name of Maude Clarke, who just happened to be governess to the Roberts children.

I mention all this because Jean Carré not only designed the cover of *Barbara Ladd*, but served as model for the title character. Roberts did nothing to hide this connection; indeed, he was quite open about it, inscribing in one copy: "The cover of this novel was designed by the lady from whom I drew the heroine of the story."

(This is a good time to add that Roberts' working title, the highly appropriate *Mistress Barbara*, was changed after the 1901 publication of a Halliwell Sutcliffe novel by the same name.)

So, just how does Sir Charles reimagine his ex-lover?

We first encounter Barbara as a nymph-like, sylph-like orphan, newly arrived in pre-Revolutionary Connecticut from the Province of Maryland. Carefree and careless, self-absorbed and intolerant, Barbara is "one of those who colour the moods of others by their own, and are therefore apt to be at fault in their interpretation of another's motives."

Like fellow orphan Anne Shirley, whose story would appear in bookstores six years after *Barbara Ladd*, she's an unusual, unconventional girl.

How unusual? How unconventional?

Here is Sir Charles treating the reader to a description of her sexually charged "mad negro" dance:

> She danced with arms and hands and head and feet, and every slender curve of her young body. She moved like flames. Her eyes and lips and teeth were a radiance through the live, streaming darkness of her hair. Light, swift, unerring, ecstatic, it was like the most impassioned of bird-songs translated into terms of pure motion.

Barbara Ladd has few characters. There's Barbara's Aunt Mehitable, who as a stern, joyless figure won over by her lively charge, bares considerable resemblance to L.M. Montgomery's Marilla Cuthbert. Young, talkative Richard Gault provides interaction with someone Barbara's own age. Finally, there are the doctors Jim and John, two bachelor brothers who together serve as the community's moral compass. The two siblings spend much of the novel vying for the love of Mehitable, as in this exchange, which begins with Doctor John getting down on one knee before her "black-satin-shod small feet":

> "Nothing more utilitarian than silk stockings, most dear and unexpected frivolous lady," he vowed, "shall be my tributes of devotion to you henceforth!"
>
> "And mine shall be garters, fickle Mehitable!" cried Doctor Jim, dropping on his knee beside Doctor John, and swearing with like solemnity. "Silk garters,—and *such* buckles for silk garters!"
>
> "And little silk shoes, and such *big* buckles for little silk shoes!" said Doctor John.

"And silk petticoats!" went on Doctor Jim, antiphonally. "Brocaded silk, flowered silk, watered silk, painted silk, corded silk, tabby silk, paduasoy silk, alamode silk, taffety silk, charry-darry—" till Mistress Mehitable put her hand over his mouth and stopped the stream of eruditions.

"And silk—and silk—" broke in Doctor John, once more, but stammeringly, because his knowledge of the feminine wardrobe was failing him.

Yes, Doctor John, best stick with shoes—*buckled* shoes—your brother is the petticoat expert.

Fun and fetishes are sadly set aside with the advent of the American Revolution. As the mood shifts, Richard declares his love for Barbara, but is rejected for not being a Patriot. When he leaves to fight on the side of the Loyalists, she writes him off, though Roberts never writes him out. We know that it's only a matter of time before headstrong Barbara will accept Richard's love. Will it be when he's injured fighting a duel in defence of her honour? No, the moment comes when he's lying near death in her arms, and only then does Richard give up his fight for George III.

For some, loyalty will always take second place to the love of a beautiful woman, no matter how headstrong she might be.

Chivalry Pays (Eventually)

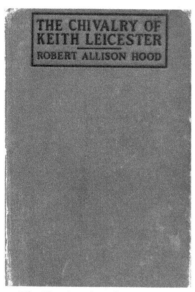

The Chivalry of Keith Leicester: A Romance of British Columbia

Robert Allison Hood

Toronto: McClelland, Goodchild & Stewart, 1918

339 pages

Born in Scotland, raised in England, a son of privilege, Keith Leicester lives on a ranch near the banks of the Fraser River. He is not to be confused with a remittance man; Keith's troubled past is entirely the fault of former fiancée, femme fatale Patricia Devereux, who threw him over a few years earlier. Now a solitary figure, he has taken refuge in our westernmost province with his pipe, paper, and dog. This lonely life is disrupted by the unheralded arrival of the beautiful, mysterious Miss Coon—who, unbeknownst to him, is actually an English heiress named Marjorie Colquhoun. Having run off on a forced engagement, she is herself taking refuge at the homestead of her old Canadian nurse.

To misquote Elvis Costello: Chapter One, they didn't really get along. But then Keith and Marjorie don't get along in chapters two through twenty, either; a surprise this, given the transplanted Scot's many chivalrous acts. Keith, who considers himself a misogynist, has "no desire to play squire to distressed damsels," yet finds himself coming to Marjorie's aid time and time again. True to the genre, each good deed is negated by a silly misunderstanding, leaving the long-suffering reader to speculate as to which act of kindness will stick.

The novel takes its most dramatic turn after Hood moves the action to Vancouver, where Marjorie looks to sell her jewellery in an effort to save her former nurse's farm. She walks through a city entirely unrecognizable to today's reader:

> Down Granville Street she went to the Post Office and then east along Hastings Street as far as the B.C. Electric Station, but although

she saw all kinds of stores and many attractive windows, there was no sign of what she was in search of. There were barbers' poles and electric signs of every description, but the three golden balls were nowhere to be seen. At last she decided that she must ask some one, and she picked out for the purpose a benevolent looking old gentleman with a white beard. For anything else she would have asked a policeman, but she felt instinctively that for this it was best not to consult one of the Force.

"Why bless my soul, what did you say—a pawnbroker?" he spluttered in astonishment, evidently distrusting his ears.

Marjorie repeated her query to reassure him. He looked at her amazed.

"A pawnbroker, miss!" he repeated after her. "No, I'm afraid not; I never heard of one here…"

Marjorie is eventually successful in her quest, but gets mistaken for Slippery Sal, a "female diamond thief that has been operating in the Eastern cities." Once again, Keith comes to the rescue. The next chapter finds the heiress dining in "a gown of pink" as our hero drones on about his adopted home:

"You've never known the charms of English Bay at sundown," he said, waxing eloquent, "the shimmering tints of crimson and violet and yellow and gold; the opalescent splendours as the radiance gradually dies away; the dark blues and purples of the hills outlined against the sky; the flickering lights of the fishing boats sway out near the horizon; and then, landward, the beach full of people and behind, the town all cheery with its street lamps and its countless gleaming windows."

"It is everything you said for it and a hundred times more," Marjorie later tells him.

I've spoiled very little here. Harlequin readers know that matters of the heart are never so simple. Before long, several members of the English aristocracy descend on Vancouver, bringing with them a whole new set of complications.

The Most Depressing Canadian Novel of All Time?

The Wine of Life
Arthur Stringer
New York: Knopf, 1921
389 pages

She was the original Gibson Girl, an Amazonian actress whose career was hindered by her height. He was a tall Adonis from Ontario, just beginning to make a name for himself in the world of letters. Together they were "the handsomest couple in New York."

The romance between Jobyna Howland and Arthur Stringer began in 1900, with a chance encounter at a party on Washington Square. They married seven weeks later at the Little Church Around the Corner on East 29th Street.

Theirs was a shaky relationship, cushioned somewhat by the ever-increasing flow of money brought by Stringer's writing. When it finally ended, in the spring of 1913, beautiful Jobyna returned to the stage then sought publicity through a series of syndicated, tell-all newspaper features. "Peculiar Romance-Tragedy of an Actress and a Poet" ran one headline. The titillation promised by another—"How He Gave Himself Away!"—is tempered somewhat by the subheading:

What was Poor, Beautiful Jobyna Howland to Think When Husband Arthur Stringer Told Her That He Adored Her, and Then Wrote That Women Weren't Necessary to Poets—COULD Any Wife Stand It?

I'd have thought most could.

There was no real scandal in the collapse of the Stringer marriage; the husband was never accused of infidelity, or even flirtatiousness. "It was just that he kept continually saying one thing and writing another," reported one desperate wag.

Here are two examples:

The poet or artist seldom marries a beautiful woman. He marries a woman he imagines to be beautiful.

Woman is mysterious to man because no man can understand her until he abhors her. For the eye, both artists and scientists will tell you, sees more when looking down than when looking up.

Stringer's "The Advantages of Being Ugly" may have been the final straw. The *Toronto World* ran this Swiftian essay shortly before Valentine's Day, 1913, along with a photograph of Jobyna captioned: "Mrs. Arthur Stringer (Jobyna Howland), Who Was Gibson's Original Model, but Who, According to Mr. Stringer's Theory, Would Be Still More Successful If Ugly."

Mrs. Stringer filed for separation shortly thereafter.

Unlike his wife, Mr. Stringer avoided the press during the break-up, expressing himself, instead, in verse:

ULTIMATA

I am desolate,
Desolate because of a woman.
When at midnight waking alone
I look up at the slow-wheeling stars,
I see only the eyes of this woman.

...

I am possessed of a great sickness
And likewise possessed of a great strength,
And the ultimate hour has come.
I will arise and go to this woman,
And with bent head and my arms about her knees
I shall say unto her: "Beloved beyond all words,
Others have sought your side,
And many others have craved your kiss,

But none, O body of flesh and bone,
Has known a hunger like mine!
And though evil befall, or good,
This hunger is given to me,
And is now made known to you,—
For I must die,
Or you must die,
Or Desire must die
This night!

Arthur Stringer fancied himself a poet. Anyone questioning the man's talent should consider Jobyna's declaration that her heart had been won by "The Passing of Aphrodite," verse composed seven years into their marriage.

"Ultimata" wasn't nearly so effective. In the dying days of 1914, they divorced.

Stringer was a remarkably energetic writer. The years immediately following the dissolution of his marriage to Jobyna saw *The Door of Dread* (1915), *The House of Intrigue* (1916), *The Hand of Peril* (1918), and *The Man Who Couldn't Sleep* (1919). It was also during this period that Stringer wrote *The Prairie Wife* (1915), a novel academics cite as influential.

The Prairie Wife has been out of print for over ninety years.

The vast majority of his novels were published by Bobbs-Merrill, a hugely successful publisher located, improbably, in Jobyna's hometown of Indianapolis.

Then came *The Wine of Life*, a novel Bobbs-Merrill wouldn't touch.

Published by Alfred A. Knopf, *The Wine of Life* is an atypical work. It tells the story of Owen Storrow—rhymes with "sorrow"—a young sculptor who arrives in New York after having achieved a certain success in his native Canada. That our hero is not a writer shouldn't distract: *The Wine of Life* is a *roman à clef* born of the author's relationship with Jobyna Howland.

Storrow has been in Manhattan but a short time when he encounters Torrie Thorssel (née Millie Roder), an actress whose milk-white skin reminds him of marble. They share drinks and a bed, after which the sculptor makes himself scarce.

Weeks go by.

Quite by chance, Storrow rents a studio adjacent to the one in which Torrie is staying. Their physical relationship resumes, leading Storrow, good Canadian boy that he is, to propose marriage.

The pair wed, though they keep the union secret from all but a couple of friends. "There's my work to think of," says the actress. "People aren't interested in a married stage star."

As it turns out, they're not much interested in Torrie as an unmarried stage star either, though "Hebrew" Broadway producer Herman Krassler hovers around, determined to put her maiden name in lights.

The bride starts going through the groom's money—"You'll find me a very expensive luxury," she'd warned—as the Canadian sets aside sculpting to work on a novel. The description Storrow provides is of a novel that resembles Stringer's *Empty Hands* (1924):

> "I always wanted to write the story of a man and a woman thrown empty-handed into the wilderness, tossed through some trick of fate into our northern Barren Grounds, for instance, as naked as Adam and Eve turned out of the Garden!"

He's guided in the endeavour by friend Chester Hardy, a practical work-horse of a writer who keeps to a schedule and eschews the Bohemian crowd in which Torrie circulates. When Storrow follows his example, it puts a strain on the marriage.

Stringer himself was a workhorse. One of wealthiest Canadian authors of his day, he treated writing as a business, his office as an office, Hollywood as a cash cow, and pulp magazines as a herd. He recognized opportunity and proved adept at investing his writing riches.

The Wine of Life isn't nearly so commercial. The prose here is elevated; greater care is in evidence, yet somehow the plot rambles. This reader wondered about the scattered, seemingly meaningless appearances by Storrow's cousin Catherine. And what was the point of all that stuff about "Pine-Brae," his fruit farm in Southern Ontario?

Again, *The Wine of Life* is not a commercial novel; no happiness is found in the ending:

- Cousin Catherine is stuck in a passionless marriage, having married after the man she truly loves, Storrow, had chosen another.
- Torrie marries Krassler, but this is only to further her career.
- Storrow marries his perfectly nice housekeeper for the very same reason he wed Torrie: he's sleeping with her and feels it's the right thing to do.

In our world, Arthur Stringer married his cousin—Margaret, not Catherine—shortly after the divorce from Jobyna. The couple spent many of their early years at "Shadow-Lawn"—not "Pine-Brae"—just south of Chatham.

Jobyna became engaged—fleetingly—to Andrew Freedman (né Friedman), a Broadway impresario who is better remembered today for having owned the New York Giants. He died in 1915, leaving her $150,000, which she promptly lost in the stock market.

As with all *romans à clef*, *The Wine of Life* is made more interesting through knowledge of the source material. It's for this reason that I chased Jobyna Howland, a pursuit that led, surprisingly, to her friendship with H.L. Mencken. In *My Life as Editor and Author* (1992), the curmudgeon's posthumously published autobiography, Mencken refers to Jobyna and Ethel Barrymore as "the champion lady boozers of Broadway." His accounts of the actress nearly always mention her height and her drinking. Mencken relates one particularly wet evening in which Jobyna broke down in tears:

> It was simply impossible, she sobbed, for her to forget Stringer. She loved him as she had always loved him, and she would never love another. The quarrel that caused their divorce was a trivial one, and should have been patched up. Unhappily, Stringer married another woman immediately after the decree was issued, leaving poor Jobyna in desolation.

Adds Mencken: "The love agonies of a woman six feet in height are always extra poignant."

The hurt behind the fiction.

As if this novel weren't already depressing enough.

Back to School with Miriam of Queen's

MIRIAM of QUEEN'S

LILIAN VAUX MacKINNON

Miriam of Queen's
Lilian Vaux MacKinnon
Toronto: McClelland & Stewart, 1921
310 pages

Imagine a Canadian college novel published just one year after *This Side of Paradise*. I expected nothing quite so impressive from *Miriam of Queen's*, though what I'd thought would be a light *fin d'été* read turned out to be the year's toughest slog; it took three runs at the first chapter before I found my footing. The opening pages bring Elizabeth Danvers, Aunt Laura, Mrs Roderick Campbell, Pauline, Sedley, John Hielanman, Aunt Hannah, Cora Hotchkiss, and, of course, Miriam. Many more characters follow. Most, though not all, are related in some way to one another—but how? It's much like being thrust into a wedding reception at which one knows no one. Indeed, a wedding is in the offing, as Mrs Roderick Campbell reveals:

"You're getting another son, Ellen. Isn't that the modern form of consolation? And a bookish sort like Sedley, too." She turned suddenly to listen. "That is not his voice now is it? Mr. Rutherford's, I mean. It sounds familiar, though."

"And so it should be, my dear," Mrs. Danvers rejoined, rising and leading the way across the hall. "It should be familiar, since it is your own nephew's—Fyfe Boulding, you know. He is to have a little part in tomorrow's ceremony, just a bit of distraction because of his connection."

I'm of the opinion that there's much to be learned from bad writing. In *Miriam of Queen's*, lessons come on every page, and are of such clarity that I feel no need to do anything but quote. This paragraph comes at the end of Miriam's first year:

And at last came the days of the trial, when Convocation Hall was turned into a vast arena, where the competitors gathered in mortal combat and the witnesses were those bygone seers on the wall who, unmoved, had witnessed many a struggle, from their eventual element of calm, and whose lofty gaze inspired the frantic souls below to fight on. Elbowed by a science man on one hand, by a theologian on the other, Miriam wrote away. All her store of hardy-won knowledge was registered once and for all on paper, before the cares of this work-a-day world should have blotted it out. There was something fitting in the act, and a feeling of triumph visited those well-doers who were enabled to give an account at last of the laborious days they had lived.

Prose like this leaves little room for plot. Miriam, our heroine, attends Queen's and looks on as dramatic events envelop others. Kind-hearted Cousin Sedley makes the mistake of marrying a vicious, vacuous flirt. Cousin Fyfe, a ne'er do well, is arrested, tried, and sent to Kingston Penitentiary. But before this takes place, both fall in the drink whilst playing hockey in the novel's most dramatic scene:

They are coming from all quarters. The ice is blackening with fleet figures. Will it be too late? The girls are lying flat and Elizabeth has caught Sedley's foot and Miriam, Elizabeth, and the living chain moves nearer. Slowly, slowly, and oh, how carefully! Up, up and cautiously, cautiously! Out of the deathly waters, over the treacherous edge, Fyfe Boulding is drawn to safety. Then, just as the cry of thanksgiving rises to their lips, the ice gives way under double strain. There is an ominous crack, the sound of a heavy body splashing down, and as Boulding creeps to safety Sedley Danvers goes down, down, into the icy waters of Lake Ontario.

Stretch out your stick to save him now! If he can come up! Will he strike under the ice? Will the current bear him away? Or is there a chance, one chance in a thousand, that he may be seen again? The crowd presses nearer, strong arms stretch out to aid. Yes, there it is, that dark, struggling, helpless object at the edge of the break. Too late! Down, down it goes, while a cry of anguish breaks from the lips of the onlookers. Once more, once it comes. Now, men, now! They reached him, they drag him out, white and sodden and spent. Miriam, turning in horror from that death-like form, looks into Hugh Stewart's face.

"Oh, Hugh!," she screams. "'Take me home! Take me home! Sedley is drowned! Don't you see? Sedley is drowned!"

But no! It is a collapse, consequent on shock and exhaustion.

As I say, there's much to be learned from prose like this, though the true value in *Miriam of Queen's* lies in what it captures of student life at Queen's University during the earliest years of the last century. Though their respective debuts were published close together, F. Scott Fitzgerald and Lilian Vaux MacKinnon were of different generations. Mrs MacKinnon graduated from Queen's in 1902, a decade before the petting parties of Princeton. Her university experience—and Miriam's—consisted of muscular Christianity, college songs, and fleeting glimpses of the Very Reverend George Munro Grant.

Modest mention in the September 12, 1942 *Regina Leader-Post* has Mrs MacKinnon as the author of two novels: *Miriam of Queen's* and *The Guinea Stamp*. I have found no record of the latter. The Queen's University Archives holds the manuscript of an unpublished romance "set near Brockville" with the rather ribald title *Hard by St. Lawrence*.

Unpublished?

I'm not at all surprised.

Romance Amongst the Racists

The Window-Gazer
Isabel Ecclestone Mackay
Toronto: McClelland and Stewart, 1921
308 pages

Lured by an offer of lodging, Great War veteran Prof Benis Harrison Spence has left his aunt's altogether too busy Ontario home for the quiet of coastal British Columbia.

It seemed like a good idea at the time.

Spence is burdened by several ounces of shrapnel and a nervous disorder, both souvenirs from his time at the Front; rest is just what the doctor—physician friend John Rogers—ordered.

Unfortunately, host Herbert Farr turns out to be an unstable, unlovable charlatan. The man's home is nothing more than a leaky—albeit spacious—cottage shared by daughter Desire and Chinese servant Li Ho. Spence has no sooner arrived than he collapses from the stress placed upon his shrapnel-filled leg. Weeks pass, during which the professor is nursed back to health by young Desire.

Make nothing of her name. Theirs is a platonic relationship with a foundation formed by shared interests and outlook on life. Neither cares much for marriage—"a hideous thing," says Desire. Spence proposes just the same as a means of freeing his newfound friend from her crazy father's clutches. Believing the professor to be the sort who will one day find true love, Desire declines. The quick-thinking Spence comes up with a sad story about losing the love of his life, a blonde named "Mary," to another, which leads her to reconsider. After all, the professor is not a man to "love twice."

The pair run off to Vancouver, are married, and share a chaste working honeymoon in separate tents on fictitious Friendly Bay. They soon settle in Bainbridge, an Ontario town beset by blonde Marys.

Recounting the plot doesn't quite do this novel justice. On the surface, *The Window-Gazer* is a simple romance, without the cocaine addiction, opium addiction, kidnapping, and exploited shopgirls that are key to previous Mackay novels. The unpleasantness lies below, in the twin veins of race and racism that run through the book. The reader will spot this first in Spence, who is studying Indians' "primitive psychology." The professor is sitting with Desire when he encounters his subject for the first time:

"A Jap?" exclaimed Spence in surprise.

"No. He's Indian. Some of the babies are so Japaneesy that it's hard to tell the difference. Father says it's a strain of the same blood."

Spence's aunt allows that she doesn't mind having her luggage handled by Pullman porters, but she does worry that her nephew's new bride might be part Indian. Her concern is shared by the gentile ladies of Bainbridge. "Well, if Indian blood can give one a skin like hers, I could do with an offside ancestor myself!" one writes in a letter.

And then we have Li Ho, who is described by a less-than-honest boatman as "one of the Chinkiest Chinamen I ever seen." For much of the novel, Farr's servant appears as a stereotype out of... well, something published early last century. He speaks in a manner that will make today's reader cringe—"Me much glad Missy get mallied"—and yet he is later revealed to be the most intelligent of Mackay's creations. Indeed, he is the one character to really display character. In the end, Li Ho proves the hero of the novel, a fact ignored by reviewers of the day. I wonder why?

But Why Would You Want Him To?

He Will Return
Helen Dickson Reynolds
Toronto: Ryerson, 1959
256 pages

Newly minted art-school graduate Constance Manning faces the challenge of making a living as a portrait painter in Depression-era Vancouver, as detailed on the second page of Helen Dickson Reynold's twenty-third novel:

"You know, Ivor, this pretty little girl has just been given a diploma by the Vancouver Art School. I'm afraid you're going to find this city a poor market for pictures, Connie, and this Depression doesn't help."

"Don't be such a crape hanger [sic], John," his wife reproved. "Our new Art Gallery will give young artists a place to exhibit and sell their paintings."

"Oh sure," the doctor agreed amiably. "We're a young city, you know, Ivor. It's only forty-six years since this town was completely wiped out by fire."

"Great Scott! It's inconceivable. The houses and gardens look so well established."

Pay no attention to crepe hanger John and wife—this is their only scene. Focus instead on Ivor. He of the title, Ivor Owen-Jones is a thin young Welshman with "jet-black hair brushed back from a good forehead, a well-shaped nose and sensitive, mobile mouth." This is the moment of their meeting... by which I mean the meeting of Constance and Ivor, not nose and mobile mouth.

In the months that follow, they play tennis in Stanley Park, swim at Second Beach, visit the Pauline Johnson Memorial and take in cricket matches at Brockton Point. One afternoon by rustic Lumberman's Arch, Ivor says something about maybe one day visiting Wales together.

For reasons I cannot fathom, Constance interprets this as a marriage proposal. Ivor seems equally dumfounded, but goes with the flow just the same. In the second chapter, the young couple marry and move into a small bungalow in North Vancouver.

This being the Depression, life isn't easy for the Owen-Joneses. Ivor has a nondescript office job with a firm called Western Imports, while Constance gives art lessons and receives the occasional commission for a child's portrait. Things would be a whole lot easier if only the groom would make use of his God-given talents. Ivor has a voice like Devonshire cream and an extensive repertory of traditional Welsh songs. Fussy Shaughnessey matrons look to hire him to perform at their soirées—"a refreshing change from the usual ballads and arias"—but Ivor takes offence at not being permitted to mingle with the guests. "Honestly, it was like the Middle Ages, when musicians ranked with scullions," he tells his bride.

The pair live frugally, giving poor Constance precious few opportunities to don her trousseau dresses. Things go from bad to worse when Ivor is fired on the very day Constance announces that she's pregnant. Her father gets him another job, but the firm goes bust just after the baby is born. Constance becomes pregnant again, and Ivor struggles to make ends meet as a door-to-door washing-machine salesman. (Must've been hell on the back.) When the couple fall behind on their bills, losing their electricity, Ivor decides to apply for public relief:

> He stared at the window curtained with raindrops. "I'll wait till the mail comes. I've made applications to firms with box numbers... there may be something. Anyway, it's a filthy day."
>
> The postman came with letters held under his glistening raincoat. He shoved one legal-looking envelope through the slot in the door. Ivor snatched it up.
>
> "It's from a legal firm in Wales." His fingers shook as he tore the stiff paper of the envelope. "My God, it's a will... Great-aunt Gladys has died... and left me a thousand pounds. I can't believe it."

I could believe it. I'd been waiting for Great-aunt Gladys to kick off from the minute Constance sent the old girl sketches of her babies.

Ivor races to the bank, leaving Constance in the dark with pencil stub and paper figuring out just how to stretch the inheritance. He returns holding the deed to a farm outside Nelson. "I bought it at a tremendous bargain because the owner, quite an old man, has died recently, and the heirs want to wind up the estate."

Oh, dear.

The farm isn't at all as described. The Owen-Joneses manage to stave off poverty just long enough for Constance to give birth to a third child. When Great-aunt Gladys's money runs out, Ivor runs off, leaving behind a note promising he'll return once he's found work. Constance carries on for several seasons, all the while expecting Ivor to walk through the door at any minute. If only he'd write. She eventually sells the farm, moves with her children back to Vancouver, and secures a position as a public school art teacher.

"The war years passed..." They did—and still no word from Ivor. Constance, cautious, manages to clothe and feed three children. No occasions now to dip into her trousseau. Straight-laced next-door neighbour Stephen Cochrane expresses interest, but is shot down: "Stephen, I am sorry, but I firmly believe that Ivor is alive and that in the course of time he will come back to me."

It was at this point I began to think Constance had become unhinged. It had been, after all, more than eight years since Ivor had gone off in search of a job and he hadn't so much as sent a letter. In the face of this, Constance's love and faith remain constant; she looks forward to the day he too will laugh at their children's antics.

Where once time crawled, then passed, it now flies. "Life went on fairly quietly until David's twenty-first birthday," begins the twenty-first chapter. What happens is this: David, her eldest, announces that he is going to marry a mousy pianist named Mona. The news brings on a dizzy spell. A few weeks later, daughter Faith earns a scholarship to study ballet in far off New York City. Another dizzy spell. Constance, who had demonstrated such fortitude in raising three young children alone, is suddenly frail. When number-two son Robert gets a job as pilot up north, Constance suddenly faces long evenings alone in a house that "echoes with emptiness." She fills her leisure time with visits to her elderly parents and taking shut-ins for drives. One particularly lonely night she decides to go to the cinema. There, Constance takes in a bland feature, followed by a cartoon, followed by a travelogue in which she spots Ivor walking in Trafalgar Square.

You caught that, right? Ivor walking in Trafalgar Square? I nearly missed it myself. After all, he disappeared in the first half of the novel and hadn't been heard from since. Oh, there were times I thought he might turn up, like in the odd, overly detailed description of Vancouver's VJ-Day crowd in chapter 18, but with just nine pages to go his reappearance was a real surprise.

On the next page, Constance manages to get a letter to her husband:

Dear Ivor,

A few days ago I saw you in a film of Trafalgar Square. I have never stopped loving you and hoping you would come back. I have a good position teaching art in a high school, and the three children are self-supporting. David teaches and sings at concerts. He married his accompanist. Robert is flying, up north, and Faith is studying to be a ballerina, with a place secured for next winter. I am very lonesome. If you would come back to me, I would send you the price of air transport. You will find it easy to get the sort of job you like, and I can take care of my share of the expenses. Oh, Ivor, come back and take care of me. I need you.

Your loving wife

Come back and take care of me? When did Ivor ever take care of you, Constance? You've been better off without him; that Welshman is a leech! As the good folks at Western Imports will attest, he has absolutely no work ethic! Besides, what kind of husband buys a farm—*sight unseen*—without consulting his wife? For that matter, what kind of idiot buys a farm when he knows nothing about farming? For goodness sake, what kind of father refuses to sing for his baby's supper?

Ivor does indeed return. Before he does, Constance, "happy as a young bride," shops for his favourite foods, a new tie, and socks. She picks him up at the airport. They embrace. All is forgiven. The next day they go off on what Constance describes as their "second honeymoon."

The ending is so very sudden and so very strange that I began to wonder whether it was all in Constance's head. Could it be that the omniscient narrator isn't? Might it be that this story is told by Constance herself? Is it all an abandoned wife's fantasy?

Nothing so interesting, I'm afraid. The sad truth is that *He Will Return* is just a very bad novel.

He will return? Sure, but only if the lady's paying.

Loving the Mayor of Toronto

Firebrand
Rosemary Aubert
Toronto: Harlequin, 1986
309 pages

Breathless, she couldn't say any-thing, and taking her silence as acquiescence, he kissed her again, whispering, "I'll call you tomorrow."

Then he was gone. Before she went in, Jenn took a good look at the spot on her front porch where she'd just been kissed—twice—by His Worship, the mayor of Toronto.

During the few years I lived in Toronto, a clownish, elfin figure named Mel Lastman was its mayor. Come election time I cast my vote for transgender rights advocate Enza Anderson. She came in third. Toronto politics seems to swing wildly between the conventional and unconventional—or maybe that's just my perception. In 1986, the year *Firebrand* was published, the city's mayor was Art Eggleton. Then, in the third of his four terms of office, he went on to Ottawa, where he served as President of the Treasury Board, Minister of Infrastructure, Minister of International Trade, and Minister of National Defence.

When he was through, Lastman returned to his Bad Boy furniture stores.

Michael Massey, the hunk at the centre of this novel, is more like Eggleton than Lastman, though I'm betting John Sewell was the model. Like Sewell, Mike starts out as an activist politician, gets his face smacked by a fellow alderman (Horace Brown, author of *The Penthouse Killings*), and rises to become mayor of our largest city.

We first meet Mike in a police van after he's been picked up for disrupting the demolition of an old house (as did John Sewell). Seated across from him is tearful Jenn MacDonald. Mike got himself arrested on purpose—something to do with bringing attention to the cause, I think—but Jenn is along for the ride only through a misunderstanding. Whatever will husband Bobby think? Fast friends, Mike and Jenn spend the night in neighbouring cells, are freed in the wee hours, and part without a peck on the Gerrard Street Bridge. It's not that Mike isn't attracted to her, it's that Jenn is a married woman.

The second chapter begins fifteen years later. Jenn has split from Bobby, and is now working as a librarian at Toronto City Hall. After all this time, her thoughts drift back to the innocent evening spent with Mike. It isn't that she wasn't attracted to him, it's that she was married.

Mike married, then divorced, a Rosedale ice queen. Now mayor of Toronto, Jenn sees him walking through the lobby from time to time, but he never sees her, until one day, they find themselves standing next to each other watching skaters on Nathan Phillips Square.

Firebrand being my first Harlequin Superromance, I had no idea what to expect. Still, these things surprised me:

- Elizabeth II as a character.
- Ribaldry.
- A debate over whether the Toronto Police Service should be armed with Uzis.
- A rally against arts cutbacks (with an allusion to the cancellation of *The Friendly Giant*).
- A sex scene in the mayor's office.

Yes, a sex scene in the mayor's office. What's more, it takes place in front of expansive windows overlooking the city:

Suddenly the room behind her was plunged into darkness, and the square outside seemed to spring into full vibrant light. The fountain in the middle gleamed beneath its lighted arches. Queen Street and Bay Street glowed from Saturday night traffic. The clock tower of Old City Hall shone the hour with benign dignity, while all around, office buildings, banks, insurance companies and hotels cast glitter from myriad windows into the night. And above it all shone the full moon, golden, warm, familiar, seductive.

Firebrand is as much a novel about Jenn and Mike's love as it is about the author's love for her hometown. This is no brilliant observation on my part. The author's bio begins: "Rosemary Aubert has based her fourth romance novel, *Firebrand*, on her own love affair—with the city of Toronto!"

Jenn and Mike stroll through Chinatown, drive along the Danforth, and sneak out of a ball at the King Edward Hotel. There are times it's all a bit forced, though I'm ready to blame an editor's heavy hand for sentences such as this: "She was in The Room, the most exclusive boutique in Simpsons, a huge department store on Yonge Street not far from City Hall."

"I love you, you big heap of brick and concrete," Jenn cries out one morning as she gazes upon the city. The greatest threat to the budding romance between mayor and librarian is their disagreement over the future of the Leslie Street Spit. That obstacle evaporates unresolved; others, promised by the cover copy, prove no more intrusive than Timothy Eaton's left toe, and things move merrily along toward the usual conclusion. Like City Hall itself, *Firebrand* alternates between the conventional and the unconventional. Or maybe not. It's my first Superromance.

STRANGE SISTERS & LAVENDER MEN

The Jacket, the Dressing Gown and the Closet

Dark Passions Subdue
Douglas Sanderson
New York: Dodd, Mead, 1952
296 pages

This is an unpleasant novel filled with unpleasant characters, but you mustn't complain. As the dust jacket cautions:

> Mr. Sanderson is a terrifying critic of the social scene. His Montreal frauds can be found in big cities everywhere. His hero's crisis is the crisis not of an individual, but of an era.

A hero, a crisis… it's hard to identify either. The *protagonist* of this, Sanderson's debut, is Stephen Hollis, a young McGill student who lives a life of privilege with his wealthy, pious, Protestant parents in post-war Westmount. Stephen is handsome and he's intelligent, but the reader will find that this poor little rich boy has the personality of a cinder block. To the characters in this novel, however, he is very attractive indeed. Everybody, male or female, wants to be Stephen's friend, while he cares for no one.

And then Stephen meets Fabien, a sophisticated Noel Coward type who never leaves his large, luxuriously decorated Montreal house. Young, well-groomed, and impeccably dressed, Fabien is very much the sophisticat, always at the ready with a *bon mot* or catty remark. A contentedly directionless aesthete, he bathes in the delights of fine wine and an intimate entourage of attractive young men. This includes Duncan, a perpetually shirtless dancer, whom Fabien has not only taken into his home, but supports financially.

Here I'm about to spoil things for the potential reader: it's not true that Stephen's "crisis is the crisis not of an individual, but of an era"— quite the opposite, in fact. The moment comes with just pages to go when he professes his love for Fabien. Stephen begs to be held, Stephen is rejected. It is only then, when attempting physical intimacy, that Stephen learns Fabien is not a "queer."

"Whoops! Stevie dear, Whoopsie!" says Crystal, who enters the room, revealing herself as Fabien's girlfriend.

Fabien himself is not nearly as good-natured: "You fool! You bloody fool! You misunderstand me. I am a foreigner." Because, you see, foreigners are often mistaken for homosexuals.

What comes as a surprise to Stephen also came as a surprise to me. Sanderson is guilty of toying with the reader; playing upon stereotype in order to deceive. Here, for example, is our first glimpse of Fabien:

> Up on the landing a shaft of light appeared from an opening door and a figure, smoking a cigarette and wearing a bronze-colored Charvet dressing gown, emerged, advanced, and leaned nonchalantly over the bannister. The voice was as pleasantly languid as the pose.
>
> "Greetings, you infamous cow. You won't mind if I mention that I cooked a perfectly delicious Lobster Newburg and opened a bottle of Chablis?"
>
> Duncan laughed. "I beg your pardon."
>
> "Granted, of course."
>
> "I was out with a woman. She wanted to know if I was an intellectual."
>
> "You are, my dear. Far too. Did you convince her?"
>
> "I don't know. I went home with her and she offered me some wine." He sat down on the bottom stair. "I suppose there is no way of helping anyone. That poor lonely woman. Christ, it was ghastly." He burst into tears.
>
> The figure did not move. The voice softened. "Come upstairs and have a shower and tell me all about it, my pet. And let that great heart bleed for the world if it must, but please, please don't weep on the staircase. It simply isn't done. Come now."

Dear Duncan—in tears again. Earlier in the evening he'd wept while rejecting the advances of beautiful Westmount matron Miriam:

> "I can't," he said, his breath was coming in sobs; "I'm sorry, but I can't." His hands were over his face, muffling his voice so that she could barely understand what he was saying.

"Duncan—"

"No, it's no use. I tried, honestly. When you came into the room I told myself I could do it because I was a man."

Poor Duncan. You see, he's a Scot, thus also a foreigner.

In terms of sales, *Dark Passions Subdue* went nowhere, though Avon did bring it out in paperback, describing it as "a story of the men who don't belong." My first edition was marked down several times with no takers.

The reviews were awful and very unfair. Writing in *Saturday Night*, B.K. Sandwell chose to concentrate on the botched French dialogue. I doubt John Brooks read more than a few pages. Writing in the *New York Times*, he described the work as a "first novel about a young couple living in Montreal."

Frauds.

Bewitched, Bothered, but Not Bewildered

Murder Without Regret
E. Louise Cushing
[New York]: Arcadia House, 1954
221 pages

There are two ways to approach this novel: the first is as a murder mystery, the second is as an account of four pivotal days in the life of a repressed, frustrated, and somewhat unpleasant lesbian. Both lead to intertwining paths, but the latter is much more interesting.

Murder Without Regret was Enid Louise Cushing's second novel, and is one of several to feature Inspector MacKay of the Montreal Police Service. He's the one who solves the crimes, but the roles of protagonist and narrator fall jointly to twenty-something Barbara Hiller. Babs opens the novel by driving through the gates of the Randall mansion on Peel Street. It's been some time since her last visit. She'd once been close to Julie Randall, presumptive heiress of the Randall fortune. The two had "gone around together" for years, but then Julie met Joyce Prescott and Babs was replaced. What Babs refers to as a "bewitchment" came to an abrupt end: "It hurt at first, but I got over it."

So, here we have Babs in her car, steeling herself in anticipation of Julie, whom she hasn't seen in years. Babs is at Randall House because Julie asked her—*now that phone call was unexpected*—saying something about the reading of her grandfather's will. It seems tonight's the night the fortune becomes hers. Just a formality, really, but Julie wants Babs present.

After all that build-up, the meeting between the two comes as an anticlimax. Julie sends Babs upstairs to her bedroom, though it's just to freshen up. Once there, Babs notices a girl slumped over the vanity, places her hand on a cooling left breast, and determines that she's dead.

Who's the dead girl? Why, Joyce Prescott, of course.

Enter Lieutenant Brandy Fernley, Royal Canadian Navy. He'd met Babs once during those years she and Julie had been close. She's forgotten all about him, but not he her: "Funny, I remember you so well... Your red hair, and the way your eyes always followed Julie." Brandy has returned for a reason, though Joyce's dead body serves as a spanner in the works:

> "I was going to announce my engagement to Brandy," Julie sniffed.
> "Your engagement?" I said somewhat flatly. For some unaccountable reason, I had a funny letdown feeling.

Who killed Joyce? Who cares. By this point I wasn't so much interested in the solution to the crime as I was in getting a read on Babs. News of a second murder victim, former acquaintance Paul Hadrill, doesn't distract much, though his name brings further insight. Babs is quick to make clear that they'd "never gone around": "It was true that we'd driven a lot together—he and Julie in the back seat and me alone in front." Babs later reveals that she'd taken in the action through the rearview mirror.

Who killed Paul? As with Joyce, MacKay is on the case. Babs is somewhat helpful—much less than she likes to think—but everyone else moves on. Joyce hasn't been dead twenty-four hours when Julie invites Babs to Malcolm's, an upscale downtown restaurant. Babs, who had anticipated an intimate luncheon, is irritated to discover her old friend surrounded by women she doesn't know: "Even before I'd a chance to declare my neutrality, I was ignored with the successful rudeness cultivated by and perfected by female cats who have decided after one glance that the latest arrival is not One of Them." Babs' own feline glances linger:

> Kitty Buckley was a languid, black-haired would-be beauty, with mascara that thick. I gulped when I saw her dress. It was black and very smart, but it dropped down to here in the front. I was fascinated, and practically had to tear my eyes away to take in Kathleen Haines, beside her.

Cushing's Montrealers are either catty, cold, or insensitive. Even nice Inspector MacKay can't help but joke with Babs at the inquest into Joyce's death. Still, the detective is dedicated, solving her murder within a matter of days. Nothing is spoiled by revealing that the killer turns out to be Julie; she's the only character the reader might have cause to suspect.

You'd be wrong to suppose that her arrest would upset Brandy Fernley. Julie's fiancé reveals that their engagement was meant as a joke played on assembled friends. It doesn't speak well for the mystery writer that what follows comes as the novel's greatest surprise:

> "So you see, even last Tuesday night I had no idea of marrying Julie."
>
> "Oh," I said flatly. He had seemed to expect some noise from me.
>
> "Yes, I decided then and there I'd like to marry you. The party Thursday night rather clinched it. How does that appeal to you?"
>
> "Quite a lot," I admitted honestly.

There's no talk of love, no embrace, no kiss; the two don't so much as touch. And so, navy man Brandy trades an engagement of convenience for a marriage of convenience, and Babs prepares for union to a man who likes nothing more than being at sea in the company of other men.

That's it, really, though an awkward page is tacked to the end in which Babs learns that she, not Julie, will be inheriting the vast Randall estate.

All in all, a strange book… and I do like strange books. I'll be reading more E. Louise Cushing. One of her mysteries is about a Montreal bookseller who finds a body in her shop.

The title is *Blood on My Rug*.

Figuring Out the Queers of New York

The Queers of New York
Leo Orenstein
Markham, ON: Pocket, 1972
272 pages

The late Leo Orenstein was a producer, a director, an educator, an illustrator, a playwright and, with *The Queers of New York*, a novelist. That there aren't other novels in his bibliography comes as a bit of a surprise. As a young man, he played a part with the country's early paperback publishers. Orenstein's art for Fireside Publishing's *Baron Munchausen* is a personal favourite. "ILLUSTRATED BY GUSTAVE DORÉ"… except, of course, for the cover.

The Queers of New York is the product of a much different time. Its appearance owes a great deal to Pocket Books' belated effort to establish a line of Canadian mass-market paperback originals. Orenstein's novel, one of the first, would soon be joined by titles like *The Happy Hairdresser, Daddy's Darling Daughter*, and *The Last Canadian*, which I maintain has the stupidest ending of any novel yet produced in this country.

A much better book, *The Queers of New York* begins with a "panty-pink Cadillac convertible" being chased through Manhattan. At the wheel is our hero and narrator, charismatic go-getter Paul Norman. A Jewish gag writer for *Punch Line*—read: *Laugh In*—Paul is doing his darndest to reinvent himself.

In the past, he sunk money into mining and a suicidal daredevil; this time it's film production. Paul has gambled on an option for *Fruitfly*, "a play about homosexuals," which he's trying to mould into something that will sell in Hollywood. The thing is, he knows nothing about his subject, and the play's author, GT Baker, rightly rejects all his ideas. The gag writer thinks he's onto something when he learns that a blackmail ring has been secretly filming the city's wealthiest gays. Adding the blackmail element, along with actual blackmail footage, will make *Fruitfly* "something every producer in the business would be breaking their neck to get."

What seems too easy a solution becomes complicated when Paul's contact is run down by the crooks as he's walking away from the panty-pink Caddy. And so, the chase. As the novel progresses, Paul is also punched, kicked, drugged, kidnapped, and shot at. A lead pipe is thrown in his general direction. It's pretty exciting stuff, relayed with a fair amount of humour—he is a comedy writer, after all—but the pacing is all off.

Blame lies with GT, who encourages Paul to learn a thing or two about homosexuality. His education begins with a visit to Dr Stanhauser, a professor of Anthropology at "the Forensic Clinic of Columbia University." Paul begins with a question:

"Are there any figures on what percentage of the population is homosexual?"

"I think Kinsey provides the most reliable figures so far, on that. At least judging from my work here at the clinic, I have no reason to doubt them. The picture that shapes up in these studies shows that 4% are exclusively homosexual, and another 33% have been involved in at least one enjoyable homosexual experience in their lives."

"Thirty-seven percent altogether? That's more than one out of *three!*"

"Yes, and that's to the point of orgasm. Mind you, I think Kinsey was a bit too wide on the 33% because he takes it from adolescents on; but altogether it's generally assumed that 37% of the male population has at one time in their lives become involved with a male homosexual."

And on it goes, page after page. The whole thing reads a lot like an interview with a sexologist, circa 1970. Who knows, maybe it was. After the meeting, Paul feels it necessary to detail the life story of every second or third "queer" he encounters. Consider them case studies.

Ultimately, what might have been a fun and funny little novel suffers from want of a good editor. Pocket's Canadian branch plant was hardly known for its high standards; for evidence, one need look no further than the first page—not of the novel itself, but the two-page "GLOSSARY OF YIDDISH WORDS AND PHRASES USED IN THIS BOOK," which would have been useful if Paul's own definitions didn't already pepper the narration. Here's our hero in the midst of an otherwise tense break-and-enter:

> With all my *"potzkehing"* around, (potzkehing means fooling around and making a mess of things), I began to worry about Jinx. Could she hear me down here?

Nearly four decades have passed since publication, but I'm betting that in 1972 "Rosh Hashonah," "kosher," "schmuck," and "shmoose" were familiar to the "Goyim" (a word that also features). An equally useless "GAY GLOSSARY" follows the novel. Here, the reader is filled in on obscurities like "heterosexual," "homosexual," "bisexual," "straight," "gay," "queer," "faggot," "fruit," "pansy," "lesbian," "S&M," "narcissism," "buns," and "hooker."

I doubt Orenstein had anything to do with the glossary; there are differences in spelling between it and the novel proper. What's more, Paul's own definitions—and those of the OED, for that matter—don't match. "Pediaphilia" is "anal enjoyment in sex—homosexual or heterosexual" we're told on the last page of the book.

The Queers of New York received only one printing. There was no opportunity for a correction.

TRUE CRIME

Kelley Pulls a Fast One

Bad Men of Canada
Thomas P. Kelley
Toronto: Arrow, 1950
148 pages

Scott Young, Neil's dad, has a pretty good story about Thomas P. Kelley. It begins with the two men taking a morning stroll on Toronto's Wellington Street. A panicked pulp editor interrupts, offering Kelley good money to deliver a story before noon. Kelley accompanies the man back to the magazine's offices, is given a title—"I Was a Love Slave"—and begins typing. He joins Young for lunch two hundred dollars richer.

No blockhead, Kelley wrote for money and he wrote rapidly; there were no second drafts. With fiction, he'd sprint with an eye on word count, coming up with an ending only as he approached the finish line.

Non-fiction didn't offer quite the same freedom. *Bad Men of Canada* is typical of his approach. Short on names and dates, and filled with imagined dialogue, the stories are excited and repetitive. Reading Kelley's words is not unlike listening to an old-timer down at the local pub. Here, for example, is the writer's description of American serial killer H.H. Holmes:

> Physically, he was a weakling. He had buck teeth, his nose was some-what flattened, and he had a habit of drooling from the corners of his mouth.
>
> In brief, in appearance, H.H. Holmes was an awful mess! And yet, the gals went for him in a big way! Don't ask me why—your guess is as good as mine!

The inclusion of Holmes, subject of the first of the book's ten chapters, is a cheat. True, the man once visited Toronto—he even stayed long enough to murder two children—but Holmes has about as much to do with this country as Charles Ng. Not all the chapters concern bad men of Canada, and the pitch line—"A History of the Ten Most Desperate Men in Canadian Crime"—is used as loosely. Just who is the desperate man in the chapter titled "Four Bad Men"? And what about chapter two, "The Terrible Donnelly Feud"? Is it one of the Donnellys or a member of the mob that killed them?

It's no surprise to see the Donnellys in this book; Kelley mined their sordid story throughout his career. In fact, he included the Donnellys in *Famous Canadian Crimes*, a collection of pieces from *New Liberty Magazine* he'd published with Collins White Circle just one year earlier. There's a good deal more overlap between *Famous Canadian Crimes* and *Bad Men of Canada*—overlap that goes far beyond subject. Whole paragraphs are carried over, unchanged, from one book to the other, while others undergo minor rewrites. In *Famous Canadian Crimes*, the line "It was a spring morning in 1879 when four desperadoes galloped into the small village of Ashcroft, B.C., with guns blazing," becomes: "On a bright summer morning in 1879, four desperadoes galloped into the small village of Ashcroft, B.C., with guns blazing."

Spring, summer… who remembers? Anyway, it was morning.

All this recycling seems a bit disingenuous given Kelley's introduction:

To be sure there are other cases that could have been included in this volume. But a volume allows just so many pages—and just so many cases. If the reader, after perusing this volume would like to read the stories of more *Bad Men of Canada*, a letter to the publisher might encourage a sequel.

That Kelley, already looking to pull another job.

A Friend of the Family

Adopted Derelicts
Bluebell S. Phillips
Toronto: Harlequin, 1957
188 pages

I grew up in a house of books, but not of writers. Not really. My father had just begun work on what might have been his debut, a history of the CBC, when he was struck down by a heart attack at age forty-two. Two decades later, his younger brother, my uncle, co-authored a slim volume on the Anglicans in Mission program.

As a kid, the only writer I knew was Bluebell Phillips. A generation older than my mother, Mrs Phillips was an occasional visitor to our house. I don't think she crossed the threshold more than once a year, but when she did Mrs Phillips always left behind a copy of her latest book. *The Plate Glass Sky, Selected Poems, A Glass Prairie, Windrush, The Alleyne Curse*... these looked for all the world like vanity publications. Still, I was in awe of this elderly lady.

I knew there had been other books in the past; books published by real publishers. Ryerson had put out *Something Always Turned Up* and her novel, *The Fair Promise,* had been published by Robert Hale—*in England!* Though both were hardcovers, the height of accomplishment to my young mind, the book to which I was most attracted was this mass-market paperback. "Murderers, gunmen, prostitutes..." promises the cover. What adolescent could resist?

For more than a decade, Mrs Phillips and her husband, Rev Gordon Phillips, had welcomed newly released prisoners to share their five-room Montreal apartment. I read and reread the crimes these houseguests had committed. Down-and-out lovers Joe and Lillian supported themselves by shoplifting, petty crook Abie Cohen was framed for bank robbery, and a very passable transvestite named Willa ended up in the

Bordeaux prison after fending off an assault by an "aggressive Lesbian." Titillating and exciting, yes, but Mrs Phillips' goal was to show "the WHY as well as the WHAT of their anti-social behavior." Her hope was that the reader would raise a sympathetic voice in support of reform, not punishment.

Revisiting the work after all these decades, I see much that escaped me. I overlooked the larger story, the one of a generous couple who had dedicated themselves to helping these folks become a part of society. That they succeeded even once is so much greater an achievement than having had a book published in hardcover.

Something else I missed: the acknowledgements features thanks to Maurice Busby, my father.

A Bank Swindler Tries to Cash In

The Confessions of a Bank Swindler
Lucius A. Parmelee
Waterloo, QC: Duval, 1968
202 pages

The author begins by boasting that a member of the Canadian Banking Association once suggested he be offered a pension as an inducement to retire, adding: "I achieved fame of a sort and did very well." These modest words set *The Confessions of a Bank Swindler*'s tone.

Born in 1889, Lucius Parmelee was blessed in being from a family of affluence and influence. Newspaper editor and three-term Liberal Member of Parliament Charles Henry Parmelee was an uncle. Another uncle once served as Quebec's Minister of Protestant Education. The latter's good work is reflected in this, nephew Lucius' only book; until Conrad Black, *The Confessions of a Bank Swindler* was likely the best book by a Canadian felon. I provide as evidence this passage, in which the author looks back to his earliest years in Waterloo, Quebec:

> One must remember that in this day there was no auto, radio, TV, and the thousand and one distractions, which are today offered to gratify our jaded appetites. Nor were they distracted by the innumerable incidents of a bizarre, and even sinister nature, which is the record of our daily lives. I do not agree with the French philosopher Rousseau, that the solution to the world's ills consist [sic] of a return to a state of nature. I do feel that there have been times in the past history of mankind, when the clock of destiny could well have been arrested, for a temporary breathing space, at least. Our characteristically North American attitude of service to the Gods of progress, may well mean serving an illusion.

Parmelee was no common criminal.

As a young man, Parmelee set off down the straight and narrow as a bank clerk, only to develop a rooted resentment toward the very industry that employed him. The low pay, which our grand banks expected to be supplemented by clerks' families, led to his resignation. Parmelee tried his hand at a number of occupations, including farmhand and barkeep, but returned to the banks as an unwelcome visitor during the Great War:

> From a moral point of view I had no scruples whatever. They paid their employees atrocious wages. They offered very little in the way of a life career. They obtained subsidy from the general public, due to the fact that their employees must have help from their parents for a few years, and in the case of the institution in which I served they had no pension plan. All in all I considered them bigger, and more cowardly robbers than myself.

Make no mistake, Parmelee's crimes weren't robberies; they were swindles carried out though study, impersonation, and forgery. The author's criminal activity spanned three decades, interrupted by an ill-considered investment in a chicken ranch, work at a wartime munitions plant, and time spent in San Quentin. His final foray into financial fraud, in 1947 Ottawa, was, in his own words, a "disaster." Parmelee hit the Royal Bank, the Bank of Toronto, the Bank of Montreal, and the Dominion Bank, walking away with some $17,000... only to be arrested a few hours later at a railway station in Vars, Ontario. Contemporary crooks will get no tips from *The Confessions of a Bank Swindler;* Parmelee's scams and schemes were dated well before his book was published. The world into which he was ultimately released, on June 15, 1955, was foreign. "Montreal proved a revelation to me," he wrote, unable to reconcile the metropolis with the tranquil city of his youth.

The Confessions of a Bank Swindler owes its existence to the late *Weekend Magazine*, which in 1956 published a rudimentary version of the memoir. I expect the reception wasn't quite what editorial director Craig Ballantyne had anticipated. Readers took considerable offence to Parmelee's unrepentant attitude; the banks, it would seem, were unassailable. The swindler's memoir attracted no interest from McClelland and Stewart, Macmillan, or Ryerson; it ended up being self-published through a little printer in the author's birthplace. No fame followed. Having gone straight, the man was accorded no obituary.

Crime pays.

VERSE

Local Poet!

The 4 Jameses
*Canada's Four Worst-
And Funniest-Poets*
William Arthur Deacon/Introduction by Doug Fetherling

The Four Jameses
William Arthur Deacon
Toronto: Macmillan, 1974
204 pages

The whole thing looks a bit fake, but as George Fetherling (then Doug) notes in his introduction, Deacon's book is "that rare thing in Canadian literature: an underground classic." As is often the fate of titles that fall into this category, *The Four Jameses* has an unusual history. First issued as a hardcover in 1927, its publisher, Graphic, was felled by the Great Depression. After a period in limbo, unbound sheets were bought and issued in paper wraps. In 1953, Ryerson published a revised edition, followed a little over two decades later by this Macmillan paperback. With one publisher done in by hard times, and the others victims of manifest destiny, you'd almost think *The Four Jameses* was cursed. Still, I keep it on my shelves.

Deacon's book centres on James Gay, James McIntyre, James D. Gillis, and James MacRae, four poets of the late nineteenth and early twentieth centuries. They are, as Fetherling points out, united by Christian name, nationality, and sheer lack of talent. That said, I'm quick to express my doubts that they are "Canada's Four Worst—And Funniest—Poets," as is claimed on the cover. True, their work can raise a smile or two, but I've read much worse.

Of the four, I much prefer James MacRae (né John James MacDonald), who published his first book of verse, *Poems written by J. J. MacDonald, a Native of Glengarry*, in or about 1877. Deacon is good enough to provide several lines from this extremely rare volume, including these from "The Ultra-fashionable Maids":

How oft thus lay the secret way
In which the game is played:—

A shapely mass, by name a lass,
Is artfully arrayed.
Is neatly bound with metal round
And trimmings wisely made,
And padded o'er with worthless store
To cover unbetrayed
The sad defects, which one detects
When nature is displayed.

Forty-seven years elapsed between the poet's debut and his second book, *An Ideal Courtship*. Published in 1923 under the *nom de plume* James MacRae, it's held aloft by Deacon as the poet's magnum opus. *An Ideal Courtship* is a long narrative poem telling of the company kept between chaste Mary Campbell, "a model for the public to admire," and William Chisholm, a stick-in-the-mud farmer from the Maritimes. There's neither *amour* nor ardour in this poem; for MacRae, an ideal courtship ends not at the altar, and most certainly not the marital bed, but in the grave:

> Mary suddenly took sick, and human skill could find no relief
> Render her in her distress, which made the tragic struggle brief.

Days later, grief-stricken William is found dead, lying across his fiancée's final resting place:

> Though so often disappointed by events beyond their power.
> They were finally reunited at their own appointed hour.
> But so well their lives were ended, and so holy was their love,
> We may hope that they were married at the altar steps above.

MacRae didn't let another forty-seven years pass before publishing his next book. As a septuagenarian, he didn't have the luxury. His *Poems and Essays*, the final tome, was published in 1930.

Sadly, *The Four Jameses* provides little biographical information about MacRae. Deacon tells us that the poet was born in 1849 in what was then Alexandria, roughly forty kilometres north of Cornwall. In 1875, he arrived in St Marys, Ontario, where he was living when his first volume was published. It seems MacRae stayed in the town for about a decade before settling out to farm in nearby Downie Township.

According to Deacon, in 1918 the poet returned to St Marys, "where he spent a pleasant old age, and where the Public Library was an unfailing source of enjoyment... Among the townspeople he was reported to be mildly eccentric, which probably means nothing more than a strongly marked personality intensified by a touch of the artistic temperament, without which no poet is properly equipped."

The poet died on June 23, 1937, just short of his eighty-eighth birthday. This sad news was reported the following day on the front page of the *St Marys Journal-Argus*, under the headlines:

JOHN J. MACDONALD PASSES TO REWARD
AGED CITIZEN HAD SCHOLARLY
MIND AND CONTRIBUTED TO
CURRENT LITERATURE—
WAS NATIVE OF GLENGARRY

Here I admit that my preference for MacRae is influenced by my move to this pretty little town. I too have found the library to be an unfailing source of enjoyment, though I regret to report it contains not a single volume of MacRae's verse.

It doesn't have a copy of *The Four Jameses* either.

Hurray for the Crippled Children's Bus!

Everyday Children
Edith Lelean Groves
Toronto: The Committee in Charge
of the Edith L. Groves Memorial Fund
for Underprivileged Children, 1932
155 pages

Unearthed during a book buying trip to Cambridge, title, publisher, and the promise of a biographical sketch by eugenics advocate Helen Macmurchy, CBE, conspired to remove five dollars from my wallet.

Of Edith Lelean Groves I knew nothing, but was soon set straight by Dr Macmurchy's sketch. It provides plenty of detail, beginning with an account of her subject's great-grandfather and his imprisonment during the Napoleonic Wars. I daresay Mrs Groves is a much more admirable figure. She devoted most of her sixty-one years to the education of children, particularly those we describe today as having "special needs." Nearly a century ago, Mrs Groves fought for their integration into Toronto's public school system. After she succeeded, she turned her attention to providing wheelchair ramps and transportation.

Sadly, Mrs Graves wasn't nearly so remarkable as a poet. *Everyday Children* is everyday poetry. Typical of what was foisted on young readers in the first half of the last century, the collection stresses the importance of good manners, study, respect for authority, and healthy living:

A HEALTHY RECIPE

Take an ounce of sunshine,
Of fresh air many a dram,
Hold your head up, stand erect,
And breathe through your diaphragm.

Still, the reader who sticks with it will find interest in "My Upstairs Brother," about a young girl's relationship with her bedridden older sibling: "His name is Welcome Jack and he's got a twisted back,/ His arms and legs don't seem to want to go." This is followed by "Mended," in which a girl's "queer little mis-shaped limb" is straightened through surgery. These poems and others dealing with "crippled" everyday children are no better, but they do provide uncommon glimpses of past attitude towards disability.

THE CRIPPLED CHILDREN'S BUS

I'm waiting on the sidewalk in my rubber-tired wheelchair,
My mummy says it's good to get the crisp, keen morning air,
And soon, hurray! Around the bend will swing the big gray bus,
That's going to take us off to school, and only carries us.

S'posing 'at a great big man with millions in his pocket,
Was to hold his finger up and do his best to stop it,
The driver he would say, "Oh, no that is against the rule,
This is the Crippled Children's Bus, and I'm taking them to school."

S'posing 'at a prince or king along the road should scurry,
And say, "Oh Mister, pick me up, I'm in a dreadful hurry!"
The driver he would shake his head, "I'm sorry as can be,
I mustn't crowd these children, 'cause they're crippled, don't you see!"

And don't forget the mostest fun a-riding in the bus,
Forgetting 'bout our braces, 'bout our crutches we don't fuss,
We tell each other all the news, and don't care if we're late,
'Twill be the bus man's fault, not ours, if the bus man has to wait.

It's not at all surprising that *Everyday Children* is forgotten, but what of Mrs Groves? She has no entry in *The Canadian Encyclopedia*. There was once a school named in her honour, but no more—it's since been renamed Heydon Park Secondary School. Seems no one remembers why.

Chasing Down a Thriller
Writer's Hidden Verse

Poems of Arthur Henry Ward Jr.
Arthur Henry Ward
[pseud. Richard Rohmer]
Don Mills, ON: Musson, 1980
60 pages

It all began when I noticed *Poems of Arthur Henry Ward Jr.* sandwiched between *Periscope Red* and *Separation Two* in Wikipedia's Richard Rohmer entry.

Poems of Arthur Henry Ward Jr.? Rohmer as anthologist? Of poetry? A joke, right? And who the hell is Arthur Henry Ward Jr?

Turns out Arthur Henry Ward was Sax Rohmer's real name. I didn't know this because my knowledge of early twentieth-century English mystery writers is next to non-existent. I understand that his novels aren't half bad.

I could be wrong.

In any case, the discovery gave rise to a question: If Ward is Rohmer, could it be that Rohmer is Ward?

Further investigation revealed that *Poems* was added to the entry by someone using the name "General Richard Rohmer." To date, the Wikipedian has made just one other edit—this to the very same entry. More have been made under the username "Richard rohmer [sic]." IP addresses traced to the general's adopted hometown of Collingwood, Ontario (pop. 19,241), have also been used.

Richard Rohmer, right?

So convinced am I that *Poems* is the work of the man who gave us *Ultimatum, Exxoneration, Exodus/UK,* and *Separation* that I purchased the lone copy listed for sale online. The investment paid off in that what I received is now the most unusual volume of verse in my personal library.

The slim tome's first poem, "Critic," begins:

I am a Critic!
As such I render competent artists incoherent, impotent
through my unfeeling castration of
talented painters, sculptors, authors, actors and
the beautiful disorderly horde of intuitive creators of
intellectual art

Ninety-four lines follow, but I'll stop here because I was lost on first reading. Still am. I don't quite get why the castration of the talented renders the competent impotent. Were they standing too close? Did the castrator's knife catch? Is psychological trauma to blame? More than anything, I'm left wondering whether castration is ever performed with feeling.

That first stanza is the easy one. This, the fourth, is more typical:

but of course, if you are a critic and therefore a
perverted, certified insanist with no relationship
to the real world, it is agreed by all who are
not mercenary critics and therefore by the whole
of those humanly afoot / abroad that critics are as
above described —

Rohmer was never the critics' darling. Before John Gellner's incompetent reviews of *Massacre 747* and *Starmageddon* I'm not sure he'd ever received positive notice. Rohmer once sued Larry Zolf and various higher-ups at the Montreal *Gazette* over a review of *Balls!* I'm not sure even Erwin Rommel was so great an enemy as William French, whom Rohmer once described—unjustly—as "the most skilled literary critic (so-called) in Canada when it comes to putting down Canadian authors."

Ah, but then a lot of authors hate critics. It wasn't until the first eight lines of the second poem, "Smoker," that I knew for certain Ward was really Rohmer:

Polluters
contaminators who foul the already grit-crud filled
atmosphere of a crowded world, chemical waste

pouring into steams, rivers, lakes, oceans upward
into the moving air masses that insidiously fly
parasitical minute particles of man-generated
poisons to be lowered imperceptibly, secretly
enveloping the unsuspecting body

You see, smokers, who crowd Rohmer's novels, invariably fall into one of two camps: the weak and the villainous.

Some will take exception to me and "General Richard Rohmer," pointing to words like "already grit-crud filled / atmosphere," "chemical waste / pouring into steams, rivers, lakes, oceans," and the "parasitical minute particles of man-generated / poisons." They will ask how these could come from Rohmer, a man who has spent decades arguing for aggressive expansion of the oil and gas industry in our far north. To these doubters I say there have always been contradictions within Rohmer's writing.

Consider his 1979 best-selling fifth novel, *Balls!* In it, a natural gas monopoly shuts off supply to the City of Buffalo without warning. Twenty thousand people die as a result—the President of the United States included—and everyone agrees that Congress is at fault for not imposing stringent industry regulations. The new president sets things right, spending billions to purchase and retrofit several dozen oil tankers. These in turn are handed over to the very same corporations that caused the crisis. As the Vice President explains, the government is a great believer in private enterprise. So is Richard Rohmer.

I dwell on *Balls!* because it was the first Rohmer from General Publishing. In 1979, the company paid $35,000 for the privilege. A year later, it gave Rohmer $75,000 ($230,000 today) as an advance on *Periscope Red*, *Patton's Gap*, and *Triad*.

I doubt one of those books earned out.

Poems was set loose by Musson, the General imprint that forty years earlier had published John Buchan's *Memory Hold-the-Door*. I suggest that its existence has at least something to do with the company's desire to please its best-selling author.

Rohmer the poet isn't the same writer as Rohmer the best-seller. The language is different. A man who typically dictates his books while driving, I suspect he actually wrote *Poems*; hence "thence" and a hundred or so other words not found in his prose. His style is best described by my old pal Chris Kelly, a more accomplished certified insanist than I and to whom I sent scans of this rare book:

What's the difference between a poem and an angry diary entry? A poem has arbitrary line breaks. Also, in a poem, whenever you get to something you know two other words for, use all three.

That way people know you won't be silenced, censored, cowed.

I haven't encountered a more angry book than Rohmer's. Only once, in "Flyer," does one detect another emotion:

> I fly
> airborne!
> free, up
> a bird machine
> strapped to my ass
> in my hands, under
> the coordinates of my
> concentrating brain

Poems cannot easily be dismissed. Months after its purchase, I still hadn't made my way through the twenty poems contained within its stiff cardboard covers. It's not possible to read one after another; it's not even possible to read one stanza after another. My reading for today comes from the eighteenth poem, "Woman," stanza six (of twelve):

> womankind, whose exclusive role of potential/actual
> re-creation brings usually therewith a
> lesser strength, physical, emotion but superior
> determined doggedness peppered with erect, stiff,
> bitchiness not overpowering for the mate but oftentimes
> precipice teetering as equality syndrome
> balloons prickly proofing deflatable on the edge-push
> of the drive of woman to be her own person,
> but just only/merely/something more than a semen
> receptacle

Again, I'm lost.

WAR

Getting to the Fenian Raids

In the Midst of Alarms
Robert Barr
New York: Stokes, 1894
275 pages

Each St Patrick's Day, thoughts turn to the Fenians. And why not? Their ill-considered incursions helped induce the birth of my country. Tragicomic, the Fenian Raids seem well-suited for satire, so how is it that after nearly fifteen decades this forgotten novel stands alone in using those troublous times as a backdrop?

Never having read Barr, I had more than modest expectations for this book. After all, the writer was very much respected in his day. It's true he was "popular," but so were his friends Joseph Conrad, Henry James, and Arthur Conan Doyle. And consider this: as a volunteer soldier, Barr helped defend the Niagara frontier during the raids.

Sadly, nothing of his experience seems much in evidence here.

The novel begins well, with a strong chapter focused on the reunion of old school chums Stillson Renwick and Richard Yates in a Fenian-infested Buffalo hotel. Fifteen years have passed since their last meeting, during which Renwick has become a proper, polite professor at the University of Toronto. Yates, in stark contrast, has quit Canada for the fast-paced life of a New York journalist. He is a drinker, gambler, womanizer, and overall *bon vivant*; in short, a man whose drive very nearly put him behind asylum gates. A change of pace is required, so he's been advised, and the journalist has decided a week or two of camping with his passive pal Renwick is just the thing to cure his ills.

The next day, the pair cross the Niagara into Canada, leaving behind all intrigue and excitement for woodland pleasures. "The Odd Couple Go Camping" isn't much of an idea; Barr seems to recognize as much by introducing Kitty Bartlett and Margaret Howard, two beautiful farmers' daughters for the men to pursue. Further pages—chapters, in some instances—are devoted to topics such as soap making, bread baking, and the duelling roles of the rural blacksmith and village grocer in the years preceding Confederation. All quite accurate observations, I'm sure, but it does become a bit tiresome. The chapter devoted to Canada West's mid-nineteenth-century public library policies bores even a bookish fellow like myself.

But where are the Fenians in all this? They're rarely mentioned, and no one takes the threat of invasion seriously. "They won't venture over," predicts journalist Yates, the man with his ear closest to the ground. "They fight with their mouths. It's the safest way."

When the Fenians finally invade, well over halfway through the novel, encounters are fleeting. Renwick and Yates are captured and marched to the Fenian camp, where they have a brief exchange with "General" John O'Neill before being released. The professor and the journalist are far away when the actual fighting begins. Barr's description of the absurd comedy of errors that was the Battle of Ridgeway is limited to a dispassionate, two-page factual account that reads like something ripped from an old high-school textbook.

"The farce is known as the Battle of Ridgeway, and would have been comical had it not been that death hovered over it," Barr concludes.

Too soon?

Dreaming of the Hun

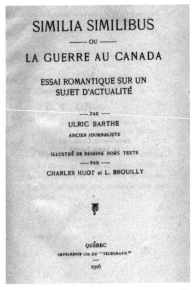

SIMILIA SIMILIBUS
—— OU ——
LA GUERRE AU CANADA

ESSAI ROMANTIQUE SUR UN
SUJET D'ACTUALITÉ

—— PAR ——
ULRIC BARTHE
ANCIEN JOURNALISTE

ILLUSTRÉ DE DESSINS HORS TEXTE
—— PAR ——
CHARLES HUOT et L. BROUILLY

QUÉBEC
IMPRIMERIE Cie DU "TELEGRAPH"
1916

Similia Similibus; ou, la guerre au Canada
Ulric Barthe
Quebec: Telegraph, 1916
254 pages

Ulric Barthe was a well-connected political animal. His most common title is *Wilfrid Laurier à la tribune*, a collection of speeches by the great man, after which we find *Regional Guidebook for Settlers: Colonization District of Abitibi*, issued by Quebec's Ministère des terres et forêts, and *L'épouvantail des milliards*, a publication of the Banque Provinciale du Canada.

Similia Similibus, Barthe's only novel, is a work of propaganda. Written and published during the Great War, it takes the form of a *cauchemar*. The dreamer is journalist Paul Belmont, who after a bout of insomnia, lapses into a twenty-four-hour sleep in which he imagines a German invasion of Quebec City. Under this *"grande tragédie,"* influenced greatly by alleged atrocities during the Rape of Belgium, communications are cut, property is confiscated, and resistance fighters executed in the street.

As a novelist, Barthe was more than competent, but his imagery pales next to Charles Huot's rich illustrations. A graduate of the École des Beaux-Arts, Huot provided three paintings for the book, including one depicting the German assault on the Legislative Assembly, a building he'd helped decorate.

Greatly respected and admired in his time, if sadly neglected in ours, it seems odd that Huot shares pages with Louis Brouilly, a lesser talent.

Leur dernier soupir serait un cri de miséricorde—*Parce, Domine!* . . . (Page 196).

I expect this curious pairing may have something to do with Huot's style, which doesn't lend itself well to propaganda. Brouilly seems better suited to Barthe's effort to scare Canadiens into volunteering for *"la cause sacrée pour laquelle tous les amis des libertés britanniques sont appelés à faire des sacrifices."* Despite his limitations, the violence Brouilly depicts is more horrific than traffic congestion and the Legislative Assembly's overturned wastepaper basket.

And I do so hate a mess.

Sex, Betrayal, and the Scars
of the Great War

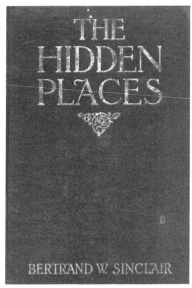

The Hidden Places
Bertrand W. Sinclair
Toronto: Ryerson, 1922
318 pages

Along with H. Bedford-Jones and Thomas P. Kelley, Bertrand W. Sinclair must surely rank as one of the most prolific Canadian pulp writers. I know of 246 magazine appearances, and am betting there are many more. Whether or not his short stories are worth reading I can't say, but I think *The Hidden Places* is the best Canadian novel published on the heels of the Great War.

This is not a war novel, but a post-war novel; for its tortured hero, the conflict changed everything. Born, raised and educated in Eastern Canada, Robert Hollister was once a man of more-than-modest means. Before the war, he shared his life with wife Myra, whom he "loved with a lover's passion." But war creates the very worst of long-distance relationships, and two years into the fighting, Robert receives a "Dear John letter." Days later, he becomes one of the 24,029 Canadian casualties at the Battle of the Somme, "lying just outside the lip of a shell-crater, blind, helpless, his face a shredded smear." He's saved by German surgeons, and spends the remainder of the war in a prison camp. Upon his release, Robert learns that he'd been reported killed in action; Myra, meanwhile, has remarried, taking his money with her.

We catch up with Robert in the winter of 1919, just after his arrival in Vancouver as "a single speck of human wreckage cast on a far beach by the receding tides of war." Though Robert is intelligent, educated, and healthy, his disfigured face limits opportunity; rebuilding one's life is a challenge when others won't so much as look at you. Walking city streets, he's "a disagreeable spectacle" from which people turn in annoyance. Robert retreats to Toba Inlet, one hundred and fifty miles up the coast. There, on his lone remaining property, he attempts to make a modest living through logging.

Chance features big in pulp fiction, but I found it difficult to pass off the fact that Myra and her new Englishman husband live on the neighbouring land as mere chance. Something sinister must be afoot, I thought; after all, Myra is supposed to have known nothing of the Toba Inlet property. But no, it turns out to be a great coincidence. Much more believable is Robert's meeting with Doris, a pretty woman who had years earlier lost her sight after being struck by a falling tree on, yes, his very own Toba Inlet property. Following a whirlwind courtship, the disfigured man and blind woman marry and move into a new house overlooking Myra's modest cabin.

The Hidden Places is frank about marriage and sexuality in a manner foreign to Canadian literature of the time. Never having divorced, Robert is tormented by the secret knowledge that he's a bigamist. He suspects that he has an "overstimulated sexuality" and wonders whether Myra suffers from the same. She left him for another, but this was not the man she married. Now, Robert watches from afar as other men visit in her new husband's absence. Sinclair never paints Myra in anything but a sympathetic light. A woman who's coming to terms with, as she puts it, "the nature I was born with," Myra struggles to remain faithful to her second husband, while nearly running off with another man. Ultimately, she offers herself to Robert.

Titillating, to be sure, but what I find more interesting about *The Hidden Place* is its detailed condemnation of the British War Office as an impersonal machine that "would neither know nor care nor tell." Greater still is the indictment of Canadian society, as represented by the men and women who seek to avoid Robert on Vancouver's streets:

> A great many men had been killed. A great number had lost their legs, their arms, their sight. They had suffered indescribable mutilations and disabilities in the national defense. These people were the nation. Those who passed him with a shocked glance at his face must be aware that fighting involves suffering and scars. It appeared as if they wished to ignore that. The inevitable consequences of war annoyed them, disturbed them, when they came face to face with those consequences.

What makes this all the more remarkable is that *The Hidden Place* first appeared in an October 1921 issue of *The Popular Magazine*: less than three years after the armistice and already comes the damning accusation that Canada has turned away from its veterans.

Plus ça change.

Betrayal by a woman is one thing; betrayal by one's county is quite another.

Ralph Connor's Beautiful War of 1812

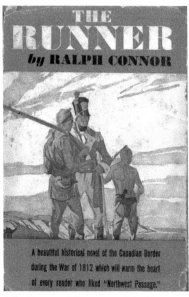

THE
RUNNER
by RALPH CONNOR

A beautiful historical novel of the Canadian Border during the War of 1812 which will warm the heart of every reader who liked "Northwest Passage."

The Runner: A Romance of the Niagaras
Ralph Connor [pseud. Rev Charles
W. Gordon]
New York: Triangle, 1939
481 pages

The Runner is the first Ralph Connor novel I've ever read, which says more about him than it does me. One hundred years ago, Connor stood with Sir Gilbert Parker as our best-selling novelist; today, like Parker, he's pretty much forgotten. My father had a nice collection encompassing most, if not all, of Connor's twenty-six novels. They might have been handed down from my grandfather or maybe they'd been a gift from his neighbour; I wouldn't know, I never opened a single volume. At some point in the seventies the whole thing was donated to our church's annual rummage sale.

This novel reminded me of *In the Midst of Alarms* (1894), Robert Barr's tale of the Fenian Raids. Such lovely descriptions of the Niagara Peninsula, so much fascinating stuff about things cultural and political in nineteenth-century Upper Canada, but after a couple of dozen chapters one does begin to wonder just when the fighting will start. Not soon enough. It's off to Boston next, where the reader is treated to a fancy ball followed by a number of debates between Federalists and Republicans. I learned to be patient.

The Runner moves at a slow pace, even at moments of high drama and emotion, such as when bull-headed Colonel Brookes' hot-headed son, Hubert, challenges thick-headed Lieutenant-Governor Francis Gore:

"Hubert, you have insulted His Excellency in my house. You must apologize or leave this house at once." (p. 154)

"Hubert, will you withdraw your words?" (p. 155)

"How can I? They are true." (p. 156)

"But to-night, Hubert? Must you go to-night?"
"Yes, Mother, it is better to-night." (p. 157)

"Good-bye! Good-bye, my son! My first-born son!"
"Go, Mother! Go! Go! You will break me up." (p. 158)

"Have you said good-bye to Hope, Hubert?"
"To Hope? Why, yes Mother, we have said—good-bye." (p. 160)

"Good-bye! Ha-ha! Good-bye! Why, certainly! Good-bye!" (p. 161)

Hubert, his mother, the colonel, and Lieutenant-Governor Gore all have parts to play in *The Runner*, but the starring role belongs to young René LaFlamme. He of the title, René is—forgive me—a dashing figure. We see him first at fifteen, diving into the mighty Niagara to retrieve a ship's line that has eluded some clumsy wharfmen. Onlookers applaud. During the lengthy journey to conflict, René will save one girl's honour and another's life. He will demonstrate superior skills in shooting, fencing, fisticuffs, and will master ballroom dancing in six easy lessons. René will serve as scout and spy for Isaac Brock, help forge the alliance with Tecumseh and—on page 297 of this 481-page book—bring news to York that the Americans have declared war... At long last, those who purchased *The Runner* as a "beautiful historical novel of the Canadian border during the War of 1812" are rewarded.

For this reader, it was too little, too late and, most of all, far too fanciful. René helps capture Detroit, is a hero at Queenston Heights, kills the man who killed Brock, rescues Laura Secord, and plans James FitzGibbon's attack at the Battle of Beaver Dams. This novel has so very many faults, but the greatest lies in positioning René as a key figure in the war. No mere observer, no simple soldier, he's on par with Brock and Tecumseh.

We couldn't have done it without him.

A Fabulous Bachelor's Final Novel

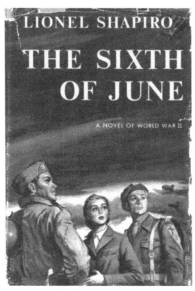

The Sixth of June
Lionel Shapiro
New York: Doubleday, 1955
351 pages

Time was that copies of *The Sixth of June* were pretty thick on the ground. I saw them at thrift stores, garage sales, church bazaars; I even scooped one up once while shovelling the walk. This was in Montreal, Shapiro's hometown and mine, and yet I've never heard anyone mention the man or his novel. For a decade, Shapiro was amongst Canada's highest-earning writers—he probably led the pack—so why was his not a household name? A 1955 Canadian Press story, published just as *The Sixth of June* landed in bookstores, reports:

This fabulous bachelor, who at 47 has produced three novels without a rejection, is known to few Canadians outside the newspaper field or show business. In Hollywood, which has bought two of his books and accounted for most of his earnings, he is a personal friend of stars and many producers.

The same article tells that his three novels, all published within the ten years that followed the end of the Second World War, grossed $350,000. *The Sixth of June*, the last of the three, was a Book-of-the-Month Club main selection—which explains all those copies I tripped over walking home from the Peel Pub.

A competent commercial novel, *The Sixth of June* was crafted from the author's experiences as a war correspondent. Its hero is Brad Parker, an energetic newspaperman from fictional Malton, Connecticut. Three years married to Jane when his country enters the war, Brad enlists and soon finds himself in London. Within days, the Nutmegger falls in love with crisp and prim Valerie Russell, who, in turn, is being politely pursued by Lt Col John Wynter. All resembles something of a soap opera, as amongst the suds there's little of substance. Social historians might find something to discuss in Shapiro's depiction of promiscuity in blitz-ravaged London. A few Canadian readers will be interested in the chapters dealing with Dieppe. "Strictly experimental, just to find out if the Jerry is on his toes in the port areas," says Brad's commanding officer before the raid. "Between ourselves, Brad, I think it's murder."

The climax, as the title hints, takes place on the sands of Normandy, and not between the sheets of Brad Parker's bed. Shapiro, who was on Juno Beach that bloody day, describes the action with a journalist's keen eye, then muddies things up with Brad's thoughts and speech. "The greatest story of love and war since Hemingway's *A Farewell to Arms*," pitches the 1956 Bantam paperback. But Hemingway never wrote like this:

> He thought, how wrong the English are about us. We Americans are the most disciplined people on earth. Especially this American. We got where we are because we're dumbly dedicated to home and career, to a routine that would drive us nuts unless, once in a lifetime, a war comes along and we can get up on our hind legs and holler and wear a holster low on the hip the way our grandfathers did and test whether we've still got the toughness they had. You, Val, were part of the process for Brad Parker, American, dumbly dedicated to wife, mother, and career, but it didn't turn out that way, not by a long shot. I'm in love with you and can't go on without you.
>
> That is what he thought.

Worse still is the dialogue, much of which reads like something out of a bad movie. In this early snippet, Brad is accosted by a buddy at a New York night club:

> "As I live and laugh," he whooped as he came up to their table, "it's the printer and his doll! H'ya doll!" He grabbed at Brad's hand and at the same time planted a kiss on Jane's cheek. "H'ya Brad! What the hell you doin' here? I figured you over with the Limeys helpin'

Whoosenhauer or Ossenpoofer or whatever his name runs our show—and here you are livin' it up—"

Sure enough, the novel was made into a bad movie. Titled *D-Day: The Sixth of June*, it's remarkably faithful to the novel, and includes much of Shapiro's dialogue (though not the above). Screenwriters Ivan Mowat (*Giant, Tender Is the Night*) and Harry Brown (*Ocean's Eleven*) deserve some credit in managing to cram 351 dense pages into 106 minutes.

The Sixth of June brought Shapiro a certain level of recognition. It followed *The Fall of the Titan* by former Soviet cipher clerk Igor Gouzenko in receiving a Governor General's Award. Shapiro later made the news with a speech in which he credited Lester Pearson for having averted a third World War. But by this time, things were coming to a close for the writer. The author's bibliography ends with this book. A victim of cancer, he died at the Montreal General Hospital on May 27, 1958, mere months after his fiftieth birthday. His death was covered in the city's English-language dailies.

THE WRITING LIFE

Our Strangest Novel?

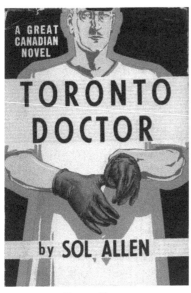

Toronto Doctor
Sol Allen
Toronto: Rock, 1949
390 pages

This could be the only Canadian novel to open with a description of a gynecological examination. If I appear unsure, it's because I haven't read the author's other titles: *They Have Bodies*, *The Woman's Doctor* and, lastly, *The Gynecologist*.

There are a good many Toronto doctors in *Toronto Doctor*—most, but not all, are gynecologists; most, but not all, exist only in the author's imagination. Anyone starting in on this novel is advised to keep pen and paper at the ready so as to record the names, relationships, and occupations of the many dozens of characters, real and imagined, that populate its three hundred and ninety pages. Note the title: *Toronto Doctor*, not *The Toronto Doctor*. The novel's greatest weakness is that it has no central figure; the second greatest is that it lacks a narrative arc. As in the old CTV series *Doctor's Diary*, patients come and go, never to be seen again. The same can be said of most of the gynecologists, but a few have real staying power:

- Roger T. Walsh, the most respected gynecologist in Toronto. A cautious and honest individual, he's haunted by the realization that his wife is nearing "the unlovely age of hot flashes and cold perspiration."
- Guy Fowley, Roger's best friend. An arrogant go-getter, he "knows everything about his profession except when not to operate."
- Paul Hutchison, a closet misogynist with a weak professional reputation. His industrialist father-in-law, A.J. Hollis, is

working behind the scenes to place Paul as head of Obstetrics and Gynecology at Toronto's Metropolitan Hospital.

Doctor/patient relations are professional; talk of sterility, marital relations, and female problems is couched in clinical terms. The atmosphere outside the office is charged with sex. Heavily made-up married women gaze upon each other's husbands at dinner parties, their thoughts drifting toward the bedroom. Sitting alone before their vanity mirrors, these same matrons fret over their fading youth and desirability.

Mrs A.J. Hollis will flirt with any man at her dinner table, but given that it's gynecologist Guy Fowley who holds the greatest attraction, I found it curious she'd choose to consult him, when confronted with her own female problem.

Meanwhile, Roger Walsh's wife fantasizes about both Guy and pit-faced lawyer Sam Logan:

> Unlike Roger, they both possessed reserves of character that made them exciting and hard to fathom. Poor Roger, on the other hand— she had often taken to thinking of him with the adjectival prefix— poor Roger was like an open book. When you read a few pages or chapter you knew exactly what was coming. Lying in bed with Roger, you knew exactly how things were going to begin and end, but with Guy she didn't know how she would react—or whether things would end at all. Once more she had a crawling sensation all the length of her spine.

The ladies of *Toronto Doctor* have much stronger libidos than the men, though it should be noted that, when dining with Roger's wife, Sam experiences the sensation of nettles in his nether regions. I should also mention that Paul makes out with Roger's daughter at an otherwise genteel gathering. The real focus of Paul's lust, however, is his mother-in-law. While this has much to do with Mrs Hollis' looks—she's as beautiful as her daughter is plain—his sexual role-playing hints at an Oedipus Complex. It's all quite vague... intentionally so, I think.

Allen was no stranger to censorship. His 1928 debut, *They Have Bodies*, was seized by Toronto police for its depiction of depravity amongst the city's privileged. At first blush, he appears to have shown no greater caution with *Toronto Doctor*. While there are no affairs, and nothing more titillating than a few kisses, Allen dares include several prominent figures as characters:

> Since this is a story about Toronto, it cannot help being also a story about Torontonians. Rather than employ devious means in alluding to certain well known persons who, because of their importance to the Canadian scene, are important also to the plot of this realistic novel, the author has chosen instead to name names and describe such figures in accordance with his own impression of them. These include Ontario ex-premiers Hepburn and Drew, Ontario Opposition Leader, E.B. Jolliffe. Ontario Supreme Court Judges Barlow, Hogg and Aylesworth, Canada Supreme Court Judges Kerwin, Taschereau, Rand, Kellock and Locke; Edson L. Haines K.C., F.A.A. Campbell, K.C., Mrs. G. Howard Ferguson and Dr. Mark Zimmerman.
>
> It is stressed that all other characters, including the various doctors, are purely fictional and are not meant to reflect in any way on any persons, living or dead.

Former premiers Hepburn and Drew, justices of the Supreme Court and others move through imagined situations, carrying on conversations with people who never existed. I expect Allen's ability to dodge lawsuits had much to do with advice received from novelist Philip Child, politician Alex Ross, and lawyers Fred Catzman and John R. Cartwright (himself a future Supreme Court justice). I'm thinking that it was Messrs Catzman and Cartwright who had something to do with footnotes like this:

> There is no intention of belittling Mr. Joliffe in the succeeding pages any more than there is Mr. Drew or Mr. Hepburn in the foregoing or in what follows. These gentlemen, the author feels, are an important part of the Toronto scene and not to have included them would have resulted in a distortion of the contemporary social picture this book is intended to convey.

E.B. Joliffe's comment on the dust jacket's back cover shows that Allen displayed further caution in sending out proofs for comment:

Unlike Desmond F. MacAuliffe—*who he?*—this reader never once thought of Flaubert and Huysmans. What's more, I just can't agree that Allen's phrases are unforgettable, or that they "sear the mind like a knife being drawn across the hesitating and reluctant flesh." I will say, however, that weeks after I finished the novel, disturbing images lingered. The colourful, graphic descriptions of operations were no doubt provided by Doctor "X," who is thanked for placing his thirty-one years' experience as an obstetrician and gynecologist at the author's disposal.

I've written elsewhere that Ted Allan's original *Love Is a Long Shot* features one of the darkest, most horrific scenes in any Canadian novel. I stand by those words, adding that there's something in *Toronto Doctor* that made my hesitating, reluctant flesh crawl a far greater distance. The most disturbing is a graphic six-page scene in which Roger and Guy remove ovaries through the vagina of a cooling corpse.

Throughout the remaining two-thirds of the novel, I expected to see the gruesome, clandestine operation, so vividly described in great detail, come back to haunt the two gynecologists; I truly believed that the law would appear at some point. But no—minor deviations aside—things proceed just as before: patients come and go, dinner parties take place and businessmen pull strings. The novel's ending is a surprise in that it comes at the beginning of a scene. Walking into a consultation room, Mrs Hollis is just about to accuse Guy of misdiagnosis when:

"THE END"

The abrupt conclusion is followed by a note that had me wondering whether I hadn't been wrong in thinking that there was no central character:

> This is the first of a
> trilogy of books by Mr. Allen
> depicting Toronto from the days of Munich
> to the present time through the eyes and heart-
> beats of the same set of characters. The
> second book, which picks up the
> thread of the story in Guy's
> office where this one leaves
> off will be entitled
> TORONTO SURGEON

There was no *Toronto Surgeon*. Whether the story of Guy and the others in the "set of characters" continues in *The Gynecologist*, Allen's next and last novel, I can't say.

I'm no more certain as to whether *Toronto Doctor* is our strangest novel. Perhaps, but then I haven't read any other Sol Allen titles.

OUR STRANGEST NOVELIST?

Was Sol Allen a gynecologist?

You'd think so, but no; the author of *They Have Bodies*, *The Woman's Doctor*, *Toronto Doctor*, and *The Gynecologist* was in fact a lawyer.

Police Ponder Ban on Book

TORONTO, March 24 (CP). —Police officers and officials of the crown attorney's department said Wednesday they will investigate whether "Toronto Doctor," a new book by Toronto theatre executive Sol Allen, is immoral, indecent or obscene. The book, published by the Rock Publishing Company, went on sale here Wednesday.

The book, with a gynaecologist as the central character, goes into medical details of examination and treatment of ailing and pregnant women, refers to living political figures and mentions law cases in which Mr. Allen has been involved.

The book purports to describe life in Toronto in 1938 but several incidents are taken from court proceedings of a year or so ago, Mr. Allen's footnotes say. One of the case was his own. He sued Maple Leaf Gardens for evicting him during a hockey game but lost the case.

Living political figures — George Drew, national Progressive Conservative leader; E. B. Jolliffe, leader of the C.C.F. opposition in the Ontario legislature; and former Ontario Premier Mitchell Hepburn— turn up in the book as minor characters, since one of the central figures is supposed to be a C.C.F. supporter.

In addition to the medical and legal complications, the plot involves a big industrialist whose lust for power and domination brings him to meddle in the running of a large hospital.

Mr. Allen said in an interview that the book is "an honest attempt to portray life."

Saskatoon Star-Phoenix,
March 24, 1949

The first hint I had of Allen's chosen profession came on page 164 of *Toronto Doctor,* in which the spotlight shifts abruptly from operating rooms and physicians' offices to unhappy men arguing before the Supreme Court of Ontario.

The case in question concerns the City of Toronto and its claim that a Jewish private school is operating contrary to bylaws. The eyes fairly glaze over... until they land upon this footnote:

The counsel in this case, which was tried before Mr. Justice Barlow without a jury on February 5th, 1947, was not Mr. Haines, but Mr. F.A.A. Campbell. The author has taken the liberty of shifting the date in accordance with the well-known tradition of author's license. He has perhaps strained the tradition ever so slightly in substituting Mr. Haines for Mr. Campbell, who actually appeared for the City. This was done in the interest of foreshortening the picture of Mr. Haines in action at the bar, the more salient features of which are not derived in any way from this case but from one in which Mr. Haines did in fact act as counsel. It is stressed that all description of real persons in this trial scene are made, not as they would have appeared in 1938, but as they actually looked to the author in February 1957 or in November 1948.

A little digging reveals that the lawsuit featured in the novel, *City of Toronto v. Central Jewish Institute*, is based on a real case that ended up being argued by the author and John R. Cartwright before the Supreme Court of Canada.

Mr Allen would like to remind us of "the well-known tradition of artistic license," and hopes that certain readers will consider the flurry of footnotes that follow.

In this footnote, the author dispassionately refers to his own participation in the proceedings:

> This case, which is reported in [1948] S.C.R. 101, was tried before Kerwin, Taschereau, Rand, Kellock and Lock, J.J. in the Supreme Court of Canada on December 4th, 1947. The author has once more taken liberties with the calendar for the purpose of integrating his story.
>
> Logan is, of course, purely a fictional character. The real case was argued, for the appellant by John R. Cartwright K.C. [sic] and Sol Allen respectively, and for the respondent by F.A.A. Campbell, K.C. Again, the author stresses that physical descriptions of the judges are not as they would have appeared in 1939 but as they looked to him on December 4th, 1947.

Sadly, Allen's efforts weren't nearly enough to mollify those in power.

Allen was spared prosecution by Crown Attorney J.W. McFadden. In a Canadian Press story published the following day, he recognizes what censors do not: "I think the best policy is just to leave it alone. Any action we would take would probably have no other effect than to publicize it for the publishers."

Frankly, considering the time, I'd have thought that the two, four, six pages that Allen devotes to his gruesome, graphic, and grotesque description of Ralph and Guy's illegal autopsy would've been enough to justify a ban on the book.

The matter of *City of Toronto v. Central Jewish Institute* is jarringly out of place; any editor worthy of the title would've insisted it be cut. However, *Toronto Doctor* was self-published and—and here I'll allow this advert to interrupt, just as it interrupts the novel, bound between pages 222 and 223.

I won't go into the author's "Psycho-Analytic Holiday Camp *for adults* [emphasis his]," a subject of further research, other than to say the retreat yields not a single Google hit.

And, um, Psycho-Analytic Holiday Camp? Shouldn't that be PAHC, not PACH?

I suppose I might as well add that the Albion Building, in which PACH had its offices, still stands as a gay bar called Zippers. Ladies welcome.

Returning to Sol Allen, I'm going to hazard a guess that his appearance before the Supreme Court on behalf of the Central Jewish Institute marked the pinnacle of his legal career. He spent nearly all his adult life working for the Premier Operating Corp Ltd. A family firm founded by Allen's father, at its height Premier Operating owned more than forty movie theatres in Canada and the United States.

On January 7, 1968, Allen died at his lovely Toronto Forest Lawn Road home, and the screens of Premier Operating Corp Ltd went black out of respect. The next year saw the second, and last, reissue of *The Gynecologist*, his final novel. The edition's author bio has Allen very much alive as "a barrister who writes in his spare time and dabbles in psycho-analysis." It goes on to state that he is the author of *The Black Sheep,* of which there is no record, and that he is preparing a non-fiction book titled *Sex and the H Bomb.*

The Messy World of Ronald J. Cooke

The House on Craig Street
Ronald J. Cooke
Toronto: News Stand Library, 1949
158 pages

Ronald J. Cooke's house was on Madsen Avenue in the Montreal suburb of Beaconsfield; I used to pass walking to and from after-school art class as a kid. A bland bungalow, I knew it was his because of a sign nailed to the carport:

RONALD J COOKE
PUBLISHER PRINTER

Black letters on small plates of cheap metal, glued to a piece of plywood, Cooke's name stayed with me. From time to time I would come across one of his sad-dle-stapled, self-published book-lets at the local library:

Everyday is Pay Day: More than 19 Ways You Can Make Money from Home Including Details on the Mail-Order Business (1979)
Re-writing News for Big Cheques! (1979)
How to Write & Sell Travel Articles (1979)
Tips for the Beginner in Self-Publishing & Mail Order! (1980)
20 Ways to Make Big Money with Your Camera (1980)
How to Clip Newspaper Articles for Big Profits (1981)
How to Write & Sell Short Articles (1981)
Canadian Publications Listings: A Listing of Daily Newspapers, Trade Journals, and Consumer Magazines (1982)
Tips on Writing and Selling Romance Novels (1985)
How to Publish & Promote Your Own Writing (1986)
Here's How to Write and Sell Features & Fillers to Newspapers and Syndicate Your Own Work, Too (1986)
Self-Publishing and Mail Order Made Easy (1988)

Cooke was also the publisher and editor of something called *Canadian Writers Journal*. I once made the mistake of purchasing a copy. Cheap and nasty, the cover cartoon, depicting a cheery postman delivering rejection letters, seemed designed to discourage. By this point I was a university student living in Montreal proper. As the years went by I thought little of Mr Cooke, and most certainly never considered turning to his publications for career advice. I don't imagine my twenty-two-year-old self would have anticipated reading a Cooke book—but then my twenty-two-year-old self had no idea that Ronald J. Cooke had written pulp novels.

Published thirty years before *Re-writing News for Big Cheques!, The House on Craig Street* was the first. It's the story of Clive Winston, a brooding, yet cocky, young man who lives with his family in the Craig Street house of the title. To Clive, life is "a bloody mess." Who can blame him? This is Montreal of the thirties. Clive's sister is in danger of becoming a "dime a dance girl," Ma Winston has been forced to turn the family home into a rooming house, and Pa does nothing but sit around all day working on get-rich-quick schemes. *How to Clip Newspaper Articles for Big Profits* would have appealed to the old man. Clive, on the other hand, has smarts, ambition, and drive. He's spent the last four years teaching himself about advertising and making daily visits to every agency in town. An aspiring copywriter, Clive knows that all he needs is a break. Sure enough, within weeks of being hired by the firm Stevens and Smith, Clive is known as the most promising ad man in Montreal. This new-found status doesn't escape notice of virginal Marian Anderson, the obedient daughter of a moneyed Westmount couple. It's less important to Rena Marlen, a fun, good-natured model who bedded Clive the night they met. Of the two, our hero can envision only Marian as his future bride. Why? Well, you don't marry a girl who sleeps around. Besides, well-connected, refined Marian better suits Clive's desire to make something of himself.

The cover copy for *The House on Craig Street* promises a "gaudy, wicked, wide-open city which was Montreal in the roaring days." It's an interesting example of—*ahem*—false advertising, but not nearly as fascinating as the unlikely reference it follows: "For [Clive] the choice was typified by two women; seemingly far apart in their wants and desires, he came to realize that Kipling was right when he said that 'the Colonel's Lady and [sic] Judy O'Grady are [sic] sisters under the [sic] skin [sic].'"

The novel itself never references Rudyard Kipling's "The Ladies" or any other literary work. Indeed, there's no indication, least of all from Clive, that any character cares about such things. So, it comes as a great surprise when our ad man announces that he wants to become a novelist. The decision, abrupt and jarring, is prompted by Clive's fear that he's being exhausted by the biz. How long has he been at it? A few months? A year and a bit? Cooke's timeline is vague and contradictory. And how old is Clive, anyway? Twenty-two? Twenty-three? As he tells a disapproving Marian, writing novels is a young man's job:

> "In many respects it's just like explorers, most of them do a better job when they are under 45. By the same reasoning a young man can write a novel and put that missionary zeal and force into it that batters itself in the people's consciousness. It lives because by its very strength it can't be killed. I want to write sociological novels that will make people happier, and better able to continue their task because of having something to read I wrote."

Our hero takes seven of the twenty thousand Depression Era dollars he's banked, puts them down on a place in the Laurentians, and escapes the city. There's no writing, but he does go fishing:

> Suddenly Clive saw a long, lean brown form dart toward the fly. Then the fly and fish disappeared in a spray of blue water and Clive's rod was pumping wildly in his hands, and the reel was singing like a clothesline in a wind storm.
> "I got a fish!" cried Clive. "I got a fish!" He began winding the reel, then he felt the tautness leave the line. Now there was full slack and the line went limp. He held up the empty rod in disgust.

The sexual imagery is unintentional. Sure, it might all be a joke, but nothing remotely similar occurs at any other point in the novel. Or am I wrong? Rena stumbles upon the above scene, catching Clive off-guard. "I should be ashamed of myself," says our hero. "You certainly should," replies Rena.

And let's not forget that her surname is Marlen.

With just thirteen pages to go, Rena's reappearance marks the beginning of a rush to the end. There's plenty of action, most of it involving cars being driven through a rainstorm. Exciting stuff, but in the midst of it all I found myself wondering about the title. The house on Craig Street is so seldom used as a setting, and plays no role in the plot. The mystery is solved in the last couple of paragraphs. By this time Clive has realized his love for Rena, who, it turns out, isn't a tramp after all.

The couple decide to remain in the mountains, where Clive will work on a great novel:

"I'll write about all the frustrated little people who are searching for the answer to life. And I'll center them around our little house—the house I knew so well," cried Clive.

"Wonderful," cried Rena triumphantly. "Why not call it 'The House on Craig Street'?"

FIN

Oh, my battered consciousness.

Mordecai's Mom's Memoirs

The Errand Runner: Reflections of a
Rabbi's Daughter
Leah Rosenberg
Toronto: Wiley, 1981
149 pages

It would be wrong to suggest, as some have, that this book would never have been published had the author not been Mordecai Richler's mother. Leah Rosenberg was also the daughter of Jehudah Yudel Rosenberg, one of the foremost Talmudist, kabbalistic rabbis of the nineteenth and twentieth centuries. Would this subject normally have attracted the attention of a publisher like Wiley? Maybe not, but such a memoir would likely have found a home somewhere—that is, if it were any good.

The Errand Runner is an awkward, clumsy thing. One need only look at the dust jacket to realize that blame lies as much with Wiley as it does with the author. An image of Rabbi Rosenberg graces the front, but there's no mention of his name. The back cover informs: "When people say, 'I've read about your famous son,' Leah Rosenberg's retort is invariably, 'Which one?' In fact, Leah Rosenberg is the mother of Mordecai Richler." Discard the dust jacket, however, and Mordecai Richler's name disappears. It is not to be found in the text—nor is that of Rabbi Rosenberg.

The author explains this peculiarity in the prologue: "To protect the reticent members of my family, I have given them all new names. But they are all here. I could not tell my story without them."

Thus, Mordecai Richler, from whom she was famously estranged, becomes "Moshe Willensky." A ghostly figure, save for two brief paragraphs, each devoted to a childhood anecdote, he receives only passing mention.

The Errand Runner doesn't concern the son, but the father. If the book has a strength, it's in Rosenberg's ability to convey her limitless love and devotion to the rabbi. He all but consumes the author's story; a mere sixth of the book's 149 pages (glossary and blanks included) is devoted to the four-and-a-half decades that follow his death.

Life with father envelops the happiest years of the memoirist's life. It's an idyllic time that comes to an jarring end with her marriage to "Aron Willensky"—Moses Richler—whose weak will stands very much in contrast with the "lion of a man" who is her father. Rosenberg's depiction of her husband's family as a band of crooks is likely another reason why she chose to hide the Richler name. Her new father-in-law, "Pinchus," repeatedly preys on Rabbi Rosenberg, amassing thousands of dollars through fraud and outright theft. Mordecai Richler wrote about his paternal grandfather's dishonesty in his 1982 essay "My Father's Life," but here it beggars belief. When Rosenberg's sister Riva, a "very financially shrewd" woman—who had witnessed Pinchus' previous thefts—is also taken in, one begins to question the author's own honesty.

The Errand Runner is anything but a reliable memoir. The most obvious fabrication concerns the dissolution of the memoirist's marriage. In The Errand Runner, this tortured, unhappy union ends with the arrival of Reuben, a man of culture who Rosenberg says she met while taking courses on the Talmud at the Jewish library. Of their affair, she writes, "I find it unbelievable, but if I encountered him now I would not recognize him. I sometimes wonder if I invented him." In fact, Reuben is an invention. Readers of the recent Richler biographies will recognize him as a character, a stand-in for Julius Frankel, with whom Rosenberg had an extra-marital affair. Their trysts did not take place amongst library shelves, but in the Richler home, where Frankel was a roomer.

Rosenberg writes that the affair "was like a storm that came and quickly passed. It did not leave a wreck."

Well, aside from divorce.

"I received a get, and my marriage was annulled." True enough, an annulment was granted, but this was only made possible by claiming that she'd wed against the wishes of her father at the age of seventeen. In fact, the author had been nineteen-year-old bride in a marriage arranged by the rabbi.

The reader is left wondering just how Rosenberg, who describes herself as a willing slave to Judaism, was able to justify such a deception. There's little introspection in The Errand Runner; the words on its pages aren't so much "reflections" as disjointed recollections that form a selective, self-serving history.

Mordecai Richler, who had seen an early draft, was right in judging his mother's work unpublishable, and it's clear that Wiley had a struggle in moulding the manuscript. What were described in the press as "production problems" pushed publication from the spring to well into the summer of 1981. One wonders what improvements were made. There's a good deal of repetition in *The Errand Runner*, information that the reader comes across again and again. Two consecutive pages are repeated verbatim, providing much needed bulk to what is, in the end, a very slim volume.

There was no opportunity to correct the error; *The Errand Runner* enjoyed one lone printing. The announced follow-up, a book of short stories set in a rooming house, never materialized. It would appear that Wiley just wasn't interested.

I Lost My Lunch in Montreal

I Lost It All in Montreal
Donna Steinberg
New York: Avon, 1983
259 pages

Mordecai Richler. Philip Roth. Move over.

—Thomas Schnurmacher, Montreal Gazette, July 31, 1982

The hype began many months before this novel's release; there were radio spots and a number of pieces in the *Gazette*. It was through the latter that I learned of an *I Lost It All in Montreal* t-shirt. I never saw one, nor did any of my friends. We were all entering Concordia, which Donna Steinberg had also attended. *I Lost It All in Montreal*, then titled *Don't Pack Me a Sandwich*, had been her master's thesis. This was seven years before alumnus Nino Ricci earned a GG for *Lives of the Saints*, the novel derived from his own thesis.

Steinberg was admirably open. In interviews, she revealed that the reception to her thesis had been lukewarm. McClelland & Stewart had rejected it outright. Avon had been receptive, but had wanted a new title.

We teens rolled our eyes, all the while envying her success. A cocky lot, we felt no need to read it. We were sure we had this novel pegged. As it turns out, we were very nearly right.

I Lost It All in Montreal is another story of a sheltered, spoiled young woman who falls for fantasy, encounters reality, and emerges a strong, independent person. The young woman here is Shayna Pearl Fine, a self-described Jewish Princess who lives with her parents in their fourteen-room Hampstead house. At twenty-three, Shayna is still a virgin, though she does have a boyfriend in Stanley Drabkin, "B. Comm. (Bachelor of Commerce), B.C.L. (Bachelor of Common Law), C.M. (Certified *Mensch*)." We open on a scene in which Stanley appears at the Fine home, having made no small secret of his intent to propose. Shayna's mother is pleased, but the prospective bride is horrified:

> "Propose as in m-m-marriage?"
> "I'm willing to bet my life on it."
> "M-m-marriage as in 'Till Death Us Do Part'?"
> "Knock wood," she banged the cupboard door.

Shayna has much she wants to accomplish before marriage. Besides, balding, loafer-wearing Stanley is far, far from her ideal man: Kris Kristofferson.

On the way to the restaurant where he plans to pop the question, Stanley takes Shayna to see Peter Simon Freeman and the Extinct Species Band at the Cock 'n' Bull. And why not? They're "Canada's answer to the Eagles." Sure, it's not exactly Stanley's scene, but Peter Simon Freeman is a client.

> It was love at first sight.
> The moment Peter Simon Freeman walked out onto the stage in his faded jean shirt and skin-tight beige Levis, I fell head over heels in love with him.

So begins "Knight Rider," the second of the novel's five parts. Shayna treats Stanley like crap and flirts with Peter. Early the next morning, the musician shocks the Fine parents by picking up their daughter on his Norton Commando. That same morning, Shayna loses her virginity to Peter in his McGill Ghetto flat.

Then it's off to L.A.!

No, not Shayna, but Peter and his band. They fly west and south to record their debut album while she returns to her job writing filler for the *Cote Saint Luc Weekly Register* (read: *The Suburban*). Given that Shayna and Peter shared little more than a one-morning stand, I didn't expect she'd ever hear from him again.

I was wrong. A telegram is quick to follow:

SHAY: TAKE A CHANCE. COME LIVE WITH ME. I'LL BE IN MONTREAL SAT. TO CLOSE UP MY APARTMENT. THEN I WANT TO TAKE YOU BACK TO L.A. WITH ME IN 10 DAYS OR

SO. THINK YOU COULD WRITE SCREENPLAYS IN A BEACH
HOUSE OVERLOOKING THE PACIFIC? SO WHAT DO YOU
SAY, BABE? I NEED YOU. LOVE, PETER. P.S. ARRIVE DORVAL
10 A.M. AIR CAN. FL. 124 FROM L.A. SEE YOU THEN.

A telegram? In the eighties? The *nineteen*-eighties? Oh, why not—telegrams are easier to share with others, like Jo Ann Pecker: Shayna's best friend and personal blow-job instructress, she suggests things might be moving just a little too fast.

Who am I to disagree with Jo Ann Pecker?

A twenty-something loses her virginity to a man she just met, while that man looks to shack up with a woman with whom he hasn't yet spent a day. And then they do. No novel has moved at such a lightning pace since *Sugar-Puss on Dorchester Street*.

Five months before the novel's release, Thomas Schnurmacher wrote: "*I Lost It All in Montreal* is as inspired and controversial a reflection of Jewish life in Montreal in the 1980s as *The Apprenticeship of Duddy Kravitz* was in 1959."

I can't say this is an inspired work. I remember no controversy, though *I Lost It All in Montreal* does feature several sex scenes, beginning with one in which Shayna masturbates in the Fine family's sunken marble bathtub.

Had it existed at the time, the five-page scene in which Shayna loses her virginity might have been a contender for the *Literary Review's* Bad Sex in Fiction Award, but it fairly pales beside the one in which Shayna pleasures Peter whilst his five-year-old son, Nicky, and much older drummer, Bozo, watch television in the adjoining room:

I slid down to the floor and knelt between his legs, running my hands over the bulge in his pants.

"Take me inside your mouth," he groaned, "before I come right inside my pants!" Without further ado, he arched up, unzipped his jeans and whipped them down in a flash. His position was such that his erection sprang right into my face and landed just about lip level. My tongue snaked out to caress it.

All of a sudden there was a loud thump. Then another. And another.

"Nicky," I cried, jerking away. "Or Bozo!" I had forgotten all about them.

We both stopped to listen. We could hear nothing except peels [sic] of laughter coming from the den. Nicky and Bozo's.

"They're glued to the TV," Peter reassured me, "don't worry. They won't come in."

"You're sure?" I said. "I'll die if either of them walks in and…"

He pressed his penis to my lips and cut me off in mid-sentence. "I'm sure," he rasped as he poked and prodded my lips apart. "I know my own kid."

On that reassuring note, I opened wide and took him inside, my mouth and tongue sliding up and down, up and down. Fast and furious. Probing and sucking. Licking and slurping. Bobbing and weaving.

Peter was pretty close to coming when there was another thump. I started to jerk away, but he put his head on top of my head and held me down.

"You can't leave me hanging like this," he pleaded in a hoarse whisper. "Nothing can tear them away from 'Mork and Mindy'! Nothing!"

Without wasting another precious second, he rammed himself down my throat and started pumping away like there was no tomorrow.

"Nothing…" he grunted.

"Nothing…" he groaned.

Noth…" he gasped.

"…ing…"

"…ng…"

"…ggg."

"…g"

"…"

Famous last words if ever I heard any.

Just as Peter's semen came spurting into my mouth, "Mork and Mindy" paused for station identification and little Nicky came charging into the bedroom, full speed ahead.

"Make way for Mork from the Planet Ork!" he yelled as he took a flying leap onto the bed and proceeded to jump up and down, up and down. "Nannoo-Nannoo!"

As Peter jackknifed to his feet, he jacked-off all over me. What I didn't swallow got sprayed all over my face and hair.

I wanted to fold up and die.

There you have it, the worst sex scene I've encountered in any work of fiction. Decades ago, not even the most cynical amongst us would've anticipated such a thing, which isn't to say that we still wouldn't have been jealous.

Given the author's sales, I expect we all remain so today.

Acknowledgements

Any journey of this nature is made easier through the aid of book-sellers. Nelson Ball, Vanessa Brown, Jason Dickson, and Adrian King-Edwards kept eyes out for things that might interest. Nelson has been patient in answering numerous queries over the years, as have Jason Byars, George Fetherling, Jim Fitzpatrick, Thad McIlroy, Mary Smith, and Glenn Wildenmann. It was through William Weintraub that I learned of *The Canada Doctor*; he was most generous in giving me his copy.

Editor Emily Donaldson set me right, as she so often does.

About the Author

Brian Busby is a writer, anthologist, *écrivain public*, and literary historian. He is the author of ten books, including *Character Parts: Who's Really Who in CanLit* and *A Gentleman of Pleasure: One Life of John Glassco, Poet, Translator, Memoirist and Pornographer* (short-listed for the Gabrielle Roy Prize). He is the editor of *In Flanders Fields and Other Poems of the First World War*, *The Heart Accepts It All: Selected Letters of John Glassco*, and *George Fetherling's The Writing Life: Journals 1975–2005*. Busby serves as series editor for Ricochet Books and is a contributing editor at *Canadian Notes & Queries*. His writing has appeared in *The Literary Review of Canada*, *The Walrus*, and many other Canadian, British, and American periodicals.

A Montrealer, Brian Busby lives with his wife and daughter in St. Marys, Ontario. He is currently working on a book about the Maria Monk hoax.